Bottom Line's

MIND BOOSTING SECRETS

Natural Supplements That Enhance Your

MIND, MEMORY AND MOOD

Ray Sahelian, MD

Bottom Line
Books
www.BottomLineSecrets.com

Bottom Line's Mind Boosting Secrets
Natural Supplements That Enhance Your Mind, Memory and Mood

Figures 3.2, 3.4 and 3.5 reprinted with permission from M.A. Schmidt, *Smart Fats: How Dietary Fats and Oils Affect Mental, Physical, and Emotional Intelligence,* (Berkeley, Calif.: Frog Ltd., 1997).

ISBN 0-88723-464-X

10 9 8 7 6 5 4 3 2

Bottom Line Books® is a registered trademark of Boardroom® Inc.
281 Tresser Boulevard, Stamford, CT 06901

CONTENTS

ABOUT THE AUTHOR

A popular and respected physician and medical writer, Ray Sahelian, M.D., is internationally recognized as a moderate voice in the evaluation of natural supplements.

Dr. Sahelian received his degrees from Drexel University and Thomas Jefferson Medical School, both in Philadelphia, and is certified by the American Board of Family Practice. He has appeared on many television programs including Today and the *NBC Nightly News with Tom Brokaw* and has been quoted in major magazines such as *Newsweek,* *Modern Maturity and Health,* and in newspapers including *USA Today* and the *Los Angeles Times*. His books have been translated into several languages, including Japanese, Korean, Italian, German, Russian and Chinese.

Dr. Sahelian is in private practice in Marina del Rey, California. He is on the board of *Today's Health and Wellness,* and writes regular columns for *New Living, Yogitimes and Whole Life Times*. He also consults and formulates products for vitamin companies. Dr. Sahelian's Web site is *www.raysahelian.com.*

ACKNOWLEDGEMENTS

Lise Alschuler, N.D., is Chair of the Botanical Medicine Department at Bastyr University in Seattle, Washington.

David Benton, Ph.D., is Professor of Psychology at the University of Wales in Swansea. He researches the influence of B vitamins on mood and cognition.

Robert Clarke, Ph.D., from the Clinical Trial Service Unit at Radcliffe Infirmary in Oxford, England, researches the influence of homocysteine on the brain.

Craig Cooney, Ph.D., Research Assistant Professor at University of Arkansas for Medical Sciences, Little Rock, Arkansas, is an expert on methyl donors.

Tom Hamazaki, M.D., Ph.D., is at the Department of Internal Medicine, Toyama Medical and Pharmaceutical University, in Toyama, Japan. He studies the effect of fish oils on stress and hostility.

Joseph R. Hibbeln, M.D., is Chief of the Outpatient Clinic, Laboratory of Membrane Biochemistry and Biophysics, National Institute on Alcohol Abuse and Alcoholism, in Rockville, Maryland. Dr. Hibbeln is an expert in omega-3 fatty acids.

Lloyd Horrocks, Ph.D., is professor emeritus of medical biochemistry at Ohio State University, Columbus, Ohio, and an expert in fatty acids.

Burton J. Litman, Ph.D., at the Laboratory of Membrane Biochemistry and Biophysics, at the National Institutes of Health in Rockville, Maryland, is an expert in the biochemistry of vision.

Mark Mattson, Ph.D., is Professor of Anatomy and Neurobiology at the University of Kentucky Sanders-Brown Center on Aging in Lexington, Kentucky. He studies the effect of caloric restriction on the course of neurodegenerative conditions.

Kilmer S. McCully, M.D., from Pathological Services at Veterans Affairs Medical Center, in Providence, Rhode Island, is a pioneer in homocysteine research.

Lucilla Parnetti, M.D., Ph.D., at the Institute of Nervous and Mental Diseases, Perugia University in Perugia, Italy, is an expert on Alzheimer's disease.

Malcolm Peet, M.D., is at the Department of Psychiatry, Northern General Hospital, in Sheffield, England. He studies the influence of fish oils on schizophrenia.

Vittorio Porciatti, Ph.D., at the Institute of Neurophysiology in Pisa, Italy, has studied the effects of CDP-choline on vision.

Helga Refsum, M.D., from Bergen University in Norway, researches the role of homocysteine in Alzheimer's disease.

Norman Salem Jr., Ph.D., is Acting Scientific Director at the National Institute on Alcohol Abuse and Alcoholism in Rockville, Maryland, and Chief, Laboratory of Membrane Biochemistry and Biophysics, at the National Institutes of Health. Dr. Salem is an expert in omega-3 fatty acids.

Artemis P. Simopoulos, M.D., President for the Center for Genetics, Nutrition and Health in Washington, D.C., is an expert on fatty acids.

Andrew L. Stoll, M.D., is at the Psychopharmacology Unit, Brigham and Women's School, Department of Psychiatry, Harvard Medical School. He studies the effects of fish oils on bipolar disorders.

Owen Wolkowitz, M.D., from the Department of Psychiatry at the University of San Francisco, studies the influence of hormones on mood and memory.

Shlomo Yehuda, Ph.D., from the Department of Psychology, Bar Ilan University, Ramat Gan, in Israel, studies the influence of polyunsaturated fatty acids on brain cells.

Steven H. Zeisel, M.D., Ph.D., is Professor and Chairman, Department of Nutrition, University of North Carolina at Chapel Hill, North Carolina, and one of the world's leading experts on choline and phospholipids.

My thanks also to the following individuals for the information they provided: Steven Bock, M.D.; David P. Crass, M.D.; Thomas Crook, Ph.D.; Subhuti Dharmananda, Ph.D.; Barry Elson, M.D.; Paul Frankl, Ph.D.; Terry Grossman, M.D.; Abram Hoffer, Ph.D., M.D.; Joseph P. Horrigan, M.D.; David Horrobin, DPhil (Stirling, UK); Dharma Singh Khalsa, M.D.; David Kyle, Ph.D.; Danise Lehrer, O.M.D.; Jay L. Lombard, D.O.; Fred Madsen, Ph.D.; Lester Packer, Ph.D.; Mason Panetti; Ascanio Polimeni, M.D. (Rome, Italy); Jo Robinson, Michael Schmidt, Shailinder Sodhi, N.D.; Karlis Ullis, M.D.; Roy Upton, Benita von Klingspor, and Byron Weston, M.D. 🍎

INTRODUCTION

Over the past few years, dozens of new natural supplements have been introduced that promise to enhance mental function. It may be quite daunting for you to walk into a vitamin store and see shelves and shelves of products that claim to improve memory, intelligence, mood, sex drive, vision and mental performance. Many of these products are also promoted as playing a positive role in preventing or treating certain psychiatric and neurological disorders.

How do you determine which of these supplements is appropriate for you? And how do you decide how much to take, in what combinations, how often, and for how long? The process is admittedly complicated. Even health-care practitioners experienced in nutritional therapy can't make complete sense of it all.

I have always been fascinated by how nutrition affects the mind. This interest motivated me to seek an undergraduate degree in nutrition science. Then I attended Thomas Jefferson Medical School in Philadelphia and later completed a three-year residency in family practice. Over the past two decades I have reviewed thousands of published articles on nutrients that have an influence on brain health. I have also supervised patients

interested in improving their mental performance and have discovered that the benefits of nutrients are often quick and remarkable, and in many cases equivalent or superior to those obtained by pharmaceutical drugs. There is no doubt that many of these brain supplements enhance quality of life.

My goal in writing this book has been to gather the published and clinical information regarding the role of dietary supplements on the mind, properly categorize it and present it in a straightforward and practical way that can help consumers and health-care practitioners alike.

The medical community has not adequately investigated the use of natural supplements for the purposes of mental enhancement or for the therapy of neurological and psychiatric disorders. My hope is that the information presented here will help patients improve their mental capacities in a safe and natural way. I also wish that more physicians would become aware of these supplements and prescribe them to their patients, and thus lessen reliance on pharmaceutical drugs. If your health-care practitioner is not familiar with any of these supplements, recommend that he or she review this book.

An amazing aspect of the brain is its ability to improve its own performance. A computer certainly can't improve its hardware or software on its own. By using our intellect to make the right choices, we can make ourselves even smarter. By cautiously and intelligently taking advantage of the variety of natural supplements at our disposal, we can help our brains function better, faster and more efficiently—as well as treat many brain disorders in a more natural way. It is now also possible to take advantage of the growing scientific knowledge regarding brain nutrition to help keep our brains young as long as possible.

In the following chapters, you will find a discussion not only of the benefits of these nutrients, but also their shortcomings. I will also inform you on how not to waste your hard-earned dollars on nutrients that either don't work well, or could easily be obtained from your diet.

The premise of this book is that you already have tried, or are currently trying, many of the non-pill approaches to improving your memory and mind. A brief discussion on simple non-pill steps to a better brain is presented in Part III. But perhaps you are now searching for additional avenues to enhance your mental performance. The comprehensive and practical information presented in *Mind Boosting Secrets* will help you attain your goal.

PART I

USING YOUR BRAIN TO BOOST YOUR MIND

THE BORN-AGAIN BRAIN

We live in an age when we are constantly barraged by information from dozens of television channels, daily newspapers, weekly and monthly magazines, faxes, e-mails, and the endless data posted on the Internet. Even the young and healthy are overwhelmed trying to keep up with this accelerated rate of information overload. The modern world seems to be requiring too much effort from our mental abilities.

Fortunately, science continues to discover ways to enhance the mind's performance. Enough research evidence has now been accumulated to give scientists a detailed picture of how the brain's intricate machinery works. This understanding makes it easier for us to use the variety of supplements currently available to provide the nutritional, neurochemical, and hormonal substances necessary for the brain's optimal functioning. Enhancing one's mind no longer depends on guesswork. Doctors now can manipulate the brain with a good deal of certainty in order to increase intelligence and mental productivity, and to help treat several mental disorders that previously required the exclusive use of pharmaceutical drugs. I propose that the intelligent use of natural supplements can improve our mind, memory, and mood, and help us better adapt to this information onslaught.

Supplements are also beneficial in additional situations. Many individuals report of fear of losing their mental abilities as they get older. Some are afraid of getting Alzheimer's disease or Parkinson's disease, especially if they have parents or relatives with these conditions. But these diseases affect only a small portion of the population compared to those who have a "normal" loss of brain function with aging. In fact, there's even a term coined for "normal" brain aging: it's called ARCD.

Age-Related Cognitive Decline (ARCD)

Also known as "age-associated memory impairment," ARCD is a term applied to individuals who experience age-related loss in cognition. The word *cognition* refers to mental activities such as thinking, memory, learning, and perception. Cognitive loss occurs to some degree in almost everybody. We lose our ability to easily remember telephone numbers and names, do mathematical calculations, and learn new concepts. However, some individuals experience a faster cognitive decline than

most. This decline can be very frustrating, especially if a person wishes to continue working in an intellectually demanding career that requires fast thinking and a full memory capacity.

Is this decline in mental functioning inevitable, or are there steps we can take to slow down, stop, or even reverse this process? New scientific research indicates that there are nutritional therapies that can have a positive influence in improving mental function in middle and old age. These nutritional therapies are readily available over the counter. The research is accumulating so quickly that the difficulty lies in knowing how to best take practical advantage of this information.

Several medical conditions can also play a role in the decline of cognitive functioning. The most common include hypertension, atherosclerosis and stroke. We must also recognize that, in older age groups, there are medicines prescribed for a variety of conditions that could have negative effects on brain health. Of course, cognitive decline also occurs as a consequence of neurological disorders such as Alzheimer's disease and Parkinson's disease.

Although the causes of ARCD are not fully understood, we know that it involves multiple changes in the brain. Thus, in order to treat ARCD effectively, several aspects of brain-cell health have to be addressed simultaneously.

What Can Natural Supplements Do For You?

Through many years of delving into the deep secrets of the brain, scientists have started to recognize that natural nutrients can improve…

- Learning and memory

- Alertness and mental arousal
- Mood, energy, and vitality
- Speed of thinking and reaction time
- Verbal fluency and capacity to be humorous
- Concentration and focus
- Creativity and development of novel concepts
- Complex problem-solving abilities
- Sex drive and sexual enjoyment
- Vision, hearing, awareness and sensory perception

Yes, it's true. Some of these supplements can even improve vision and hearing, senses that are intricately associated with awareness.

Many doctors are now beginning to recommend natural methods as therapies for cognitive impairment. Although natural substances can't yet completely replace the benefits of some pharmaceutical medicines in treating certain chronic neurological conditions, they can provide a number of advantages with a lower risk of side effects. The proper use of certain nutrients could potentially lessen the required dosage of pharmaceutical drugs.

There are skeptics, including doctors, who claim, "There's no such thing as a natural supplement that can improve brain function. It's all hype." Whenever I hear someone saying this, I immediately suspect that this person has little or no personal or professional experience with these supplements. Many studies have been published reporting the positive effects of nutrients, herbs and hormones as they relate to improving brain function. Many of these natural supplements can even act as powerful antioxidants that

may prevent or slow the degeneration of brain cells that almost invariably occurs with time.

However promising and persuasive the results of published studies, many people are not entirely convinced that mind "boosters" work until they take them themselves. Once you personally notice the enhancement in mood, memory, energy, thinking ability and visual perception, you won't need the results of a double-blind study to be swayed that these natural pills really do work.

Having said this, I do wish to emphasize that the brain is an extremely complicated organ, and much remains unknown about its functions and nutritional requirements. In this volume I present to you, the intelligent reader, the latest information on natural supplements and how they affect the brain. It will then be up to you, in consultation with your health-care provider, to decide whether these supplements are appropriate for your unique circumstance.

There are at least two types of individuals (including both patients and physicians)—conservatives who want to wait until more information is published before taking a particular course of action, and optimists who don't mind taking supplements based on preliminary information. Where do you fit in?

Personalizing Your Mind-Boosting Regimen

In this book I discuss and evaluate many nutrients, herbs, amino acids and hormones. Then I take it a step further by providing you with an individualized regimen. This is based on your age group and your preference for nutrients, herbs or hormones. In addition, I have provided step-by-step recommendations for which supplements to try first, and how

you can combine them to achieve the best possible response. Keep in mind that these are just guidelines. Your requirements and responses may vary depending on your biochemical makeup.

It may take trial and error to find out which of the supplements discussed in this book are appropriate for you. Everyone is different, and you may not respond to a particular supplement that others find very helpful. Or, you could find one supplement that gives you a wonderful cognitive enhancement, while another person experiences a side effect and thinks it's a terrible pill. The dosage requirements could also vary significantly. Some individuals may require a large amount of a particular nutrient due to their body's lack of the proper enzymes to make this nutrient on its own. Another person could notice a positive effect from a tiny dosage.

The Importance of Medical Supervision

The natural supplements discussed in this book are readily available over-the-counter, either in health-food stores, retail outlets, pharmacies or through mail-order vitamin companies. I recommend that you consult with your health-care practitioner before you take any of these supplements. Many of these pills are very potent and could interact with medicines you may take, or they could influence the course of a previously existing medical condition. Some of them have significant side effects if misused. One can't assume that just because a supplement is available over-the-counter, that it is completely safe at any dose.

The Experience of Patients and Users

This book includes the latest published studies regarding a wide range of supplements that influence the mind. Since research on some of these supplements is extremely limited, we have little practical information on how they affect the average person who takes them. In fact, some of these supplements have been introduced to the public with few actual human trials. Moreover, little is known regarding the combination of two or more nutrients, hormones, or herbs.

In order to provide you with additional insights on what people really notice when they take these supplements, I have included brief case reports from actual users. Many of these are from my patients, and some are from interviews I conducted with individuals who regularly use natural brain boosters. Over the years, I have met many individuals who take brain supplements, and I regularly keep in touch with them to discuss their experiences. I have included anecdotes in this book only when a number of users have reported similar experiences. For instance, I have reports from dozens of patients and individuals who notice visual enhancement from the hormone pregnenolone. Therefore, even though human trials regarding pregnenolone's effect on vision have not been published, I am convinced that this occurs.

I understand that including anecdotes may provoke criticism from the medical community. Science generally frowns upon anecdotal evidence, and for good reason: This type of information can sometimes be incomplete or even misleading. Nevertheless, until additional formal studies are available, anecdotes are a primary source of knowledge and can sometimes provide information not otherwise available.

The Experience of Clinicians and Experts

I strongly believe that a physician with good observation skills can sometimes observe effects from nutrients or drugs that have been missed or overlooked in published studies. Thus, I have sometimes included reports from clinicians and experts who use nutrients and herbs in their practice. Scientific studies often lag years, decades or sometimes hundreds of years behind clinical observations. For instance, St. John's wort has been recognized to improve mood by European doctors since the Middle Ages. Polynesians knew for centuries that kava reduces anxiety. Yet it wasn't until the 1990s that scientists finally acknowledged the clinical effects of these herbs.

The Author's Experience

Before I write about supplements, or recommend them to patients, I try to find out for myself what effects they have on me. I often encounter positive and negative effects that have not been previously reported in the medical literature. For instance, I have observed that melatonin makes my dreams more vivid. This effect had not been previously reported in the medical literature. I have also observed that a large intake of fish or flaxseed oils improves visual perception. Again, these observations have not been reported in the medical literature. In these two particular cases, I believe that my observations are accurate. Scientists often miss very obvious findings even in placebo-controlled, double-blind studies. This could be due to several reasons—researchers' inexperience, not asking

the right questions, not performing the right laboratory tests, misinterpreting the findings, the bias of the researchers, or poor statistical analyses. Furthermore, research methods are sometimes not able to recognize subtle changes or effects from medicines.

Over the past few years, I have experimented with almost all of the supplements discussed in this book, and have included accounts of some of my experiences. I believe these accounts will help you better understand the effects you may notice immediately if you take these supplements. Having experimented with several dozen natural supplements in varying dosages for extended periods, I have become an expert at noticing subtle changes in mood, alertness, vision and other senses. My personal experience helps me understand how a supplement works, and gives me additional insights into its potential clinical role. This experience, combined with interviews with patients and doctors and results from clinical studies, provides me with a more comprehensive understanding than relying exclusively on research findings.

I do wish to mention that my personal experience is obviously quite subjective, and your personal reaction could be different. Many factors could influence an individual's experience, including dosage, timing, existing medical conditions, age, gender and interactions with other nutrients and medicines. Not all supplement brands are the same, either. There could be different amounts of ingredients in different products sold over the counter, due to the particular method of laboratory synthesis and the source of the material or plant.

A Word About the Book's Outline

In Part II of this book you will find a straightforward explanation of how brain cells work and the function of several brain chemicals. Part III provides practical suggestions on how to improve one's mind through diet, exercise and other lifestyle factors. Part IV gives a detailed explanation of how each supplement works and the research supporting its benefits. Once you take a supplement and notice positive results, you may be interested in learning more about it. Part V provides guidelines on which nutrients to take for your particular age group. Finally, Part VI discusses natural therapies for depression, Alzheimer's disease and Parkinson's disease. There's even a chapter on how to sharpen vision.

I have divided the different supplements in Part IV into several categories, such as brain fats, phospholipids, vitamins, antioxidants, mind energizers, amino acids, hormones, and herbs. Please note that there's an overlap in functions between some of the groups. For instance, CoQ10 is listed under "mind energizers," but it can also act as an antioxidant. Many of the B vitamins are involved in dozens of important chemical reactions in the brain and body. Some of the herbs, like ginkgo, can certainly act both as brain energizers and antioxidants.

But before you jump right into finding out what supplements are recommended for your particular age group, I suggest you learn the top ten important principles of a mind-boosting program.

2

THE TOP TEN
MIND-BOOSTING PRINCIPLES

With the availability of dozens of mind-enhancing supplements, it is tempting for consumers to rush out and buy a variety for a self-prescribed regimen. However, this type of trial is best done cautiously. You should be in touch with your health-care provider to make sure these supplements will not interfere with any of your existing medical conditions or interact with prescription medicines.

There are ten important concepts that I propose in this book regarding supplementation with natural nutrients. It's very important that you review these concepts before you start your mind-boosting program.

1. An Engine Alone Does Not Run a Car.

"If you had to take only one pill, which one would be your choice?" This is a question I am frequently asked. I often reply that a multivitamin and mineral complex would be my first choice. Due to the brain's complexities, it is too simple to believe that one supplement or drug is the answer to improving brain function or treating a psychiatric illness. That

would be tantamount to believing that an engine is all that is necessary to run a car. As we know, a car needs tires, a steering wheel, a carburetor, oil and hundreds of parts to work at all, let alone work efficiently. A car might have the best engine in the world, but if one of the tires is flat, it's not going to travel too far. Likewise, the approach to improving brain function does not rest on supplying one nutrient in a large dose, but rather depends on our ability to combine positive lifestyle habits with the proper mix of nutrients, and in their right dosages.

Your brain needs a variety of nutrients in small dosages rather than one nutrient in a high dose. In Western medicine, doctors often prescribe one or two medicines in the treatment of medical and psychiatric conditions, whereas in Eastern medicine—Chinese and Indian—most of their formulations include a combination of small amounts of different herbs and nutrients. Eastern doctors learned centuries ago that some medical conditions respond better to the combination of several substances, rather than to just one. Providing a high dose of a single nutrient may upset the balance of the complex biochemical interactions of the brain. Doctors and patients are often looking for the magic pill that, alone, will cure all ills. The human body is too complicated, and there are too many biochemical reactions for one pill to be the answer to all problems. The answer lies in intelligently combining a variety of solutions.

2. Sometimes Less Is More.

Each nutrient has its ideal dosage. If you take more than your brain needs, it might actually lead to a negative reaction. You may not think as clearly or you may feel distracted, restless, overstimulated, anxious and irritable. Caution is also advised when combining two or more nutrients since their effects may be cumulative. Hence, when you add a second nutrient, you may need to reduce the dosage of the first one. Keep in mind that caffeine (in coffee, tea, sodas or chocolate) can have a cumulative effect when combined with nutrients that are stimulants. This could lead to excessive alertness, irritability or anxiety.

3. Start Low.

You can't always predict how your brain and body will react to a supplement. Start with a small dose and gradually increase it over the next few days. Keep in mind that many researchers doing studies with brain boosters give a high dose in order to elicit a measurable response. These studies are often of brief duration. If you plan to take these nutrients for prolonged periods, you may need a fraction of the dosage used by the researchers. There is a very wide range of individual response to nutrients.

By starting low and gradually increasing the dosage, potential side effects can be avoided or minimized. You will find that some of the dosages for nutrients listed in this book

are much lower than those recommended in certain other health publications or by some doctors. Since the basic premise of this book is that we all need a variety of nutrients for optimal brain function, the required dosage of each should remain low in order to avoid untoward interactions. This is true in regard to antioxidant combination because many of them help protect each other from being destroyed. Therefore, you need less of each one when you combine supplements. Excessively high dosages of antioxidants can be counterproductive and can lead to a condition called pro-oxidation, in which more disease-causing "free radical" cells are produced. Dosages also need to be kept low when combining stimulants since their effects are additive. Too many stimulants can cause irritability, insomnia, elevated body temperature and even heart palpitations.

Over my many years of practicing medicine, I have become much more cautious about dosages. As physicians and individuals, we often blindly follow the package recommendations provided by drug or vitamin companies, not appreciating the fact that each person is unique. Some people are very sensitive to even a minute dose of a medicine or nutrient. In some cases the dosage contained in pills you purchase may be excessive. You may need to break a pill in small pieces or open a capsule and take a small portion. For instance, in Chapter 14, I recommend the use of 1 to 5 mg of pregnenolone as replacement therapy, even though some pregnenolone pills sold in vitamin stores come in 50 mg doses.

4. Tolerance Is Possible.

Your brain can build a tolerance to some nutrients when they are used regularly. For instance, I have observed clinically that melatonin does not work well as a sleep aid when it is used every night. Perhaps there's a reduction in the number of receptors for melatonin on brain cells if they are exposed to high dosages on a regular basis. Hence you will often come across a recommendation to use a particular nutrient only once or twice a week. Occasionally, take a break ("nutrient, herb or hormone holiday") from a particular supplement for a few weeks. You may also alternate between similar-functioning supplements on a daily, weekly or monthly basis. Regular, high-dosage use of a nutrient or hormone could cause feedback inhibition—this means that the body could shut off its own production of the nutrient or hormone if too high of a dose is given on a daily basis for prolonged periods. Note, however, that this is not a common occurrence.

5. Timing Is Crucial.

A supplement can help boost brain power when you take it at the right time of day, or it can interfere with brain health if taken at an inappropriate time. Most of the supplements discussed in this book cause alertness and are best taken early in the day. Either take the whole dose in the morning, or take most of the dose in the morning and the rest midday. If you take a pill that has a stimulant effect in the afternoon or evening, your sleep may be interrupted and you will be worse off for it. Keep in mind that caffeine—in coffee, tea or chocolate—adds to alertness and stimulation. For obvious reasons, supplements that cause drowsiness, such as melatonin, should be taken at night.

6. Choose the Right Supplement for the Right Setting.

You could have a pleasant or unpleasant experience taking a supplement, depending on your setting. For instance, if you take a high dose of a nutrient that acts as a stimulant and you need to be indoors at your desk the whole day, you may feel restless and irritable. By contrast, if you happen to take this energizer on a weekend when you have the opportunity to walk on a trail by a river, or stroll in a museum, antique store or gallery, you may have a wonderful time appreciating beauty while feeling vigorous. The importance of setting and timing also applies to some of the herbs. For instance, Asian ginseng increases body temperature and is best suited for cold days, while American ginseng has more of a cooling effect and is best suited for warm days. Therefore, it's not only important that you choose the right supplement, or combination of nutrients, but also that you choose the right circumstance, day, time and setting.

Some of the nutrients discussed in this book that act as stimulants include tyrosine, phenylalanine, St. John's wort, DHEA, pregnenolone, androstenedione, choline, ginseng, ginkgo, coenzyme Q10, SAMe, TMG, DMG, ALC, DMAE, lipoic acid and high doses of B vitamins. When combined, their effects can be cumulative and lead to overstimulation or insomnia.

7. Some Nutrients Can Accumulate in the Brain and Body.

Some supplements can, over time, accumulate in brain cells, organs and tissues. This means that with time you may need less of these supplements, not more. Evaluate your supplements regularly and reduce the dosages if you find that you are becoming overstimulated or have unwanted side effects.

8. Brain Supplements Influence the Whole Body.

When you take the nutrients which I describe for cognitive enhancement purposes, they will not only have an effect on the brain, but on numerous bodily organs and tissues. Most of the nutrients and herbs I have included in this book have positive effects on physical and mental health. However, high dosages of certain supplements, when used carelessly and indiscriminately, could have undesirable physical effects. You can find detailed information on particular nutrient side effects in Part IV.

9. Some Natural Supplements Have Not Been Thoroughly Tested.

In 1994, the Congress of the United States passed a dietary supplement law that allowed the entry of new supplements to the market without needing approval from the FDA. (The Health and Human Services Secretary at the time urged Congress to rewrite the law in the aftermath of more than 100 deaths caused by herbal supplements such as ephedra.) Ever since the easing of dietary-supplement laws, the health industry has had virtual carte blanche to introduce a wide variety of nutrients and herbal extracts. Many vitamin companies are in a quandary when a new supplement becomes available. Should

they wait until more studies are published on the product's safety, or should they introduce the product right away? If they wait too long, other companies might begin to distribute the product and gain a large market share. Therefore, in the frenzy to market products as soon as possible in order to beat the competition, many supplements become available to the public when little is known about their long-term effects. Do not assume that just because a nutrient bottle is within easy reach on a store shelf that many studies have been done to support its efficacy or safety. Some of these supplements have powerful, druglike effects—both positive and negative.

10. Train Your Neurons.

You could take the most powerful mind boosters ever invented, but if you don't engage in mental activities such as reading, learning, thinking and creating, you will get only a fraction of the potential benefits from these supplements. Part III will provide you with some practical tips on how to exercise your brain, along with a discussion of a few lifestyle habits regarding diet, positive mental attitude, deep sleep and stress reduction. Supplements can have dramatic benefits, but are only the icing on the cake (except in older individuals who are often deficient in nutrients, or in the treatment of a medical or neurological disorder). Even though I'm very excited about the benefits of the nutrients discussed in this book, I still feel that the most important steps you can take for optimal brain health are to cultivate positive lifestyle habits, get regular sleep and engage in continuous mental stimulation.

PART II

YOUR BRAIN— AN OWNER'S GUIDE

THE ABCS OF THE BRAIN

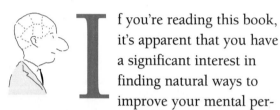 **I**f you're reading this book, it's apparent that you have a significant interest in finding natural ways to improve your mental performance or to treat a particular neurological condition. In order to achieve these goals more reliably, it helps to have a basic knowledge of the structure of the brain and how this incredibly complex organ works. The chapter explains the function of brain cells and discusses changes that occur in these cells during normal aging. The more we learn about how the brain works, the better we can improve its potential.

The Neuron

Everything in our bodies—muscles, organs, skin and bones—is made of tiny cells. This is also true of the brain. The cells in the brain are called *neurons*. An average brain has about one hundred billion neurons (fifteen times the population of the world). In addition to neurons, about nine hundred billion glial cells are present in the brain. These *glial cells* surround and nutritionally support neurons.

Neuron-to-Neuron Communication

Neurons communicate with each other through electrical impulses and chemicals. These chemicals are called *neurotransmitters*. A typical neuron has thousands of connections, called *synapses,* with neighboring neurons.

Every single external stimulation that enters through our five senses (sight, hearing,

Figure 3.1—Neuron-to-Neuron Communication

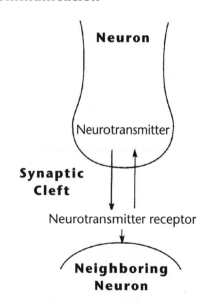

Brain cells communicate with each other through thousands of connections at sites called synapses.

COMMON TERMS USED IN THIS CHAPTER

cell—the smallest organized unit of living structure in the body.

cell membrane—a thin layer, consisting mostly of phospholipids, that surrounds and encloses each cell.

central nervous system—the brain, along with the nerves of the spinal cord. The peripheral nervous system refers to the nerves outside of the central nervous system, such as the nerves in the arms and legs.

cerebrum—the top, main part of the brain, consisting of left and right sides. It controls voluntary thoughts and movements.

cerebral cortex—the outer part of the cerebrum, the main thinking area of the brain.

cognition—mental activities such as thinking, memory, perception, judgment and learning.

dendrite—the treelike branching arms of a neuron.

neuron—a cell in the brain. There are billions of neurons in the brain that communicate with each other with neurotransmitters through connections called synapses.

neurotransmitter—a biochemical substance, such as serotonin, dopamine or acetylcholine, that relays messages from one neuron to another.

phospholipids—fatty acids combined with the mineral phosphorus and other compounds. Phospholipids are the primary constituents of a cell membrane.

synapse—the point of contact between two neurons, where nerve impulses are transmitted from one to the other.

Figure 3.2—Synaptic Cleft

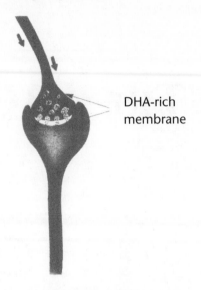

DHA-rich membrane

A single nerve may make up to 20,000 connections with other cells. The place where these cells connect is called the synapse. The portion of the nerve making the connection is called the synaptic membrane. This part of the nerve has a higher concentration of the brain-fat DHA than almost any tissue in the body.

smell, touch and taste) causes tiny electrical nerve impulses and the release of minute amounts of neurotransmitters. At present, about a hundred or so different neurotransmitters have been identified. Some of these include serotonin, dopamine, norepinephrine and acetylcholine.

Neurotransmitters, such as serotonin, produce their effects by interacting with appropriate receptors located on "next-door neighbor" neurons (see Figures 3.1 and 3.2). As is the case with some of the neurotransmitters, serotonin is made in brain cells and stored in small enclosures within the cells called *vesicles*. When a neuron is stimulated, the vesicles open at the edge of the neuron, and serotonin is released outside of the neuron into a tiny space near an adjoining neuron. This space is called a *synaptic cleft*. Thereafter, serotonin will interact with various serotonin receptors located on these adjoining brain cells and influence their function.

After serotonin is released into the synaptic cleft, it can either be taken back into the neuron that originally released it (a process called "reuptake"), or it can be broken down by enzymes located within the synaptic cleft. In general, the most common way that ends serotonin action in the synaptic cleft is its reuptake. Selective serotonin reuptake inhibitors (SSRIs), such as Prozac, increase the amount of serotonin in the synaptic cleft by preventing this reuptake.

Composition of the Cell Membrane

It has been well established that changing levels of neurotransmitters in the brain influence mood, memory, and mental function. The fact that altering the composition of brain-cell membranes can also influence many aspects of brain function is not as clearly recognized.

Discussing cell membranes is important because many of the nutrients described in this book, such as fish oils and phospholipids, have an effect by altering the *cell membrane* of brain cells.

Each neuron is enclosed within a cell membrane, which separates the inside of the cell from the outside (see Figure 3.3). The cell membrane serves as a barrier, allowing certain necessary compounds in and restricting the entry of undesirable substances. Receptors for many brain chemicals are also found on the membrane. The composition of this membrane consists mostly of different types of lipids (or fats), which include phosphatidylcholine (PC), phosphatidylserine (PS) and other lipids. Therefore, as you can guess, manipulation of the composition of the lipids of cell membranes can influence the function of neurons. The composition of a cell membrane is in a constant state of flux, influenced by diet, stress and the immune system.

Figure 3.3—Cell Membrane

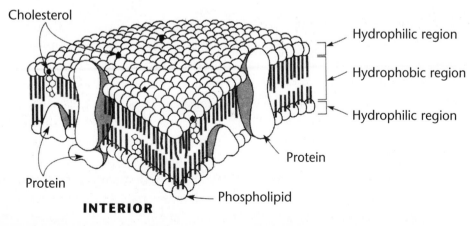

The lining of a cell membrane is composed mostly of fatty acids. The types of fatty acids present are partially influenced by diet.

Figure 3.4—Receptor on Cell Membrane

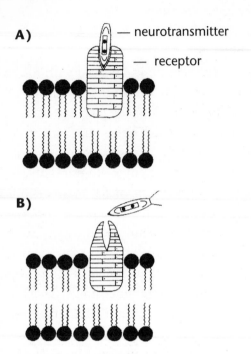

Nerve cells communicate by releasing neurotransmitters into the synaptic space. While in this space, the neurotransmitter molecules seek a "port," or receptor, into which they neatly fit. The ability to "dock" depends upon the shape of both the neurotransmitter and the receptor. Fatty-acid balance affects the shape of the dock (receptor), which may make it difficult for the neurotransmitter (ship) to fit. This may slow nerve communication and affect many aspects of brain function. Part *a)* shows the proper "fit" of the ship in the dock. Part *b)* illustrates how changing the dock's shape prevents the ship from docking.

The cell membrane has two layers, an inner one that faces the inside of the cell, and an outer one that faces the outside. The composition of the membrane includes several types of compounds. The two most common groups include phospholipids and sterols (Aloia 1988). Phospholipids are lipids made up mostly by fatty acids, amino acids and the mineral phosphorus. The major types of phospholipids include phosphatidylcholine (PC,

or lecithin), comprising about 30 percent of the lipid content of the brain; phosphatidylethanolamine (PE), comprising about 27 percent of the lipid content of the brain; and phosphatidylserine (PS), comprising less than 10 percent of the lipid content of the brain (Suzuki 1981). Sterols include cholesterol, comprising about 20 percent of the lipid content of the brain. Cholesterol forms an important part of brain structure and is the precursor from which the steroid hormones, such as DHEA, progesterone, estrogen and testosterone, are formed.

As you can see in Figure 3.4, the composition of the cell membrane influences the structure of neurotransmitter receptors. Figure 3.5 provides an overall perspective, from the brain down to the neuron, the cell membrane, phospholipids and fatty acids.

Training Neurons

Every single thought or emotion you experience is associated with tiny electrical nerve impulses and the release of minute amounts of neurotransmitters between neurons. Reading this sentence is causing electrical nerve impulses and the release of neurotransmitters in certain parts of your brain. Your eyes sense the shapes of the letters, and the information is then relayed to your cerebral cortex. These letters and words are interpreted in the brain, and then converted into thoughts. These thoughts are in turn stored as memory. The nature of your thoughts is dependent on your genetic makeup, prior learning experience, and memory. Everyone has a different brain and no two individuals reading this paragraph will have the same exact thoughts. Memory is mostly due to the strengthening of connections between neurons, and the formation of protein molecules

Figure 3.5—From Brain to Phospholipid

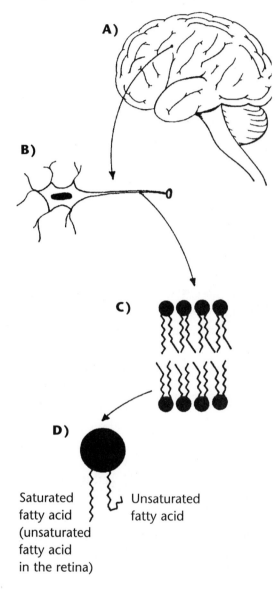

A)

B)

C)

D)

Saturated fatty acid (unsaturated fatty acid in the retina)

Unsaturated fatty acid

The brain is reduced here into simpler and simpler components eventually revealing the location of the fatty acids. This system is highly organized: *a)* the brain; *b)* the nerve cell with a cutaway of the cell membrane, or covering; *c)* the membrane's two layers, in which the fatty acid "tails" face the interior of the membrane; *d)* a single phospholipid molecule containing one saturated fat (straight) and one unsaturated fatty acid (curved). In the brain, the unsaturated fatty acid is usually DHA or AA. In the retina, both positions typically contain the unsaturated fatty acid DHA.

within neurons. A newly formed memory often involves interactions between hundreds and thousands of neurons. If this new encoding doesn't get used, it will soon fade. But if you continue to reactivate the information that you have stored—for instance, by rereading this sentence—the connections become reinforced. There are microscopic anatomical (physical) changes going on in your brain at this moment as a result of your reading this paragraph.

Many parts of the brain are involved in the process of memory acquisition and storage, particularly the *cerebral cortex* (which is the outer part of the brain) and the *hippocampus* (a structure located deep in the brain). The hippocampus is involved mostly in short-term memory processing and is often one of the first areas damaged in Alzheimer's disease.

A fascinating experiment studied two groups of mice (Gispen 1993). The first group was placed in a cage and had no mental stimulation; they lounged all day. The second group was trained to run through mazes. After a few weeks, the neurons of the trained mice were compared to those of the untrained group with an electron microscope. There was a noticeable difference. The group that had been trained had wider and longer *dendrites* (the treelike communicating arms between neurons) and more synapses. The trained group was later taken out of the stimulating environment and placed in cages without stimulation. At the end of a few weeks, their brains were examined. The dendrites and synapses appeared similar to the group that had not been trained. Their neurons had shrunk back to their original size.

Other studies have confirmed that when toys are placed in cages of laboratory animals, dendrites branch out and synaptic connections increase in as little as four days (Black 1991). The brain is living tissue, similar to a muscle that grows and becomes more efficient the more it is used. This "mind exercise" may help prevent Alzheimer's disease and other brain-affecting conditions. A June 2003 study in the *New England Journal of Medicine* (Verghese 2003) indicates that regularly engaging in mentally stimulating activities such as reading, playing cards, board games and crossword puzzles not only reduces the risk of Alzheimer's—the fourth finding in recent years through a major study—but does it better than physical exercise.

The brain grows and changes depending on its stimulation. It can become smarter, improve its capacity for memory and creativity and generally improve in any direction in which it is stimulated. A mind can be channeled in any of several directions, talents, or occupations. Anyone can become smarter and more creative with effort. Fortunately, we can help our brains perform better with the intelligent use of nutritional supplements, especially as we get older.

What Happens When the Brain Gets Old?

A number of changes occur in the brain as we age. *The most obvious include…*

- Deterioration and loss of brain cells, dendrites, synapses and receptors
- Deterioration of cell membranes
- A decline or alterations in hormone levels
- A decline or alterations in levels of brain chemicals
- Malfunction of the energy-production system in cells
- A decrease in blood flow to the brain and within the brain, often as a consequence of atherosclerosis (hardening of the arteries), or small and large strokes
- Accumulation of waste products such as lipofuscin within brain cells

What Can You Do to Keep Your Mind Young?

In order to restore mental performance, many of these age-related changes need to be slowed and even reversed. Fortunately, this is possible. Part III of this book gives practical advice on how to train your mind in order to maintain healthy neurons, dendrites and synapses. Many of the mind boosters that have been introduced in the past few years are able to help the brain stay young and sharp. For instance, cell membranes may be restored by the fatty acids and phospholipids discussed in Chapters 7 and 8, respectively. Accumulation of waste products can be reduced by the antioxidants mentioned in Chapter 11. The energy-production system can be improved by providing some of the mind energizers discussed in Chapter 12. Hormone levels can be restored, as reviewed in Chapter 14. Ginkgo and vinpocetine, two herbal extracts discussed in Chapter 15, can improve blood flow to the brain. As you can see, there are many steps we can take to keep our mind as young as possible. ￼

BRAIN CHEMISTRY
MADE SIMPLE

4

The information you gather when you look, hear, taste, touch and smell is processed in your brain through electrical and chemical messengers. The chemical messengers that help brain cells communicate with each other are called *neurotransmitters*. Dozens of substances or chemicals in the brain—amines, amino acids, minerals, hormones and peptides—act as neurotransmitters, influencing memory, mood, alertness, and thinking. A review of all of these neurotransmitters is not necessary for the purposes of this book. However, a brief explanation of some of the important neurotransmitters will make it easier for you to understand how the natural supplements discussed in this book affect the mind. It will also help you choose the right supplements for your particular needs.

Unless you are already familiar with some of these neurotransmitters, you may find the information in this chapter to be very detailed. In that case, I recommend you use this chapter as a reference. Whenever you take a nutrient that you find helpful, your interest in learning more about its chemistry and function will motivate you

A BRIEF SUMMARY OF BRAIN CHEMICALS AND THEIR MAJOR FUNCTIONS

- Acetylcholine helps with memory and learning.
- Dopamine is primarily responsible for sex drive, mood, alertness and movement.
- Norepinephrine and epinephrine influence alertness, arousal and mood.
- Serotonin is involved in mood, appetite control, emotional balance and impulse control.
- GABA helps with relaxation and sedation.

Please keep in mind that these are simplifications. The functions of these neurotransmitters often overlap and they may have different effects in different parts of the brain.

to return to this chapter and delve into its biochemistry in more detail.

Acetylcholine

Acetylcholine was the very first neurotransmitter to be identified, back in the early 1900s. It is made simply from choline and a two-carbon molecule called acetyl. Acetylcholine plays numerous roles in the nervous system. In the brain, acetylcholine is involved in learning and memory. Chapter 8 discusses how supplements such as choline and CDP-choline influence levels of acetylcholine.

Once produced, acetylcholine is stored in brain cells and released into the synaptic cleft upon stimulation. When released into the synaptic cleft, the enzyme acetylcholinesterase breaks acetylcholine back down into choline and acetyl. In Alzheimer's disease, there is a shortage of acetylcholine, and one of the ways doctors have tried to increase the levels of this neurotransmitter is by prescribing drugs, such as tacrine, that inhibit the enzyme acetylcholinesterase. In Chapter 15, I discuss an alternative to these drugs, a Chinese herbal extract called huperzine A, that also inhibits this enzyme.

Dopamine

Parkinson's disease and a number of psychiatric disorders, particularly schizophrenia, and mood disorders are attributed to imbalances in dopamine levels. Elevation of dopamine levels often leads to an improvement in mood, alertness and sex drive and perhaps even an enhancement in verbal fluency and creativity. Dopamine is made from the amino acid tyrosine (see Figure 4.1). Once produced, dopamine can in turn convert into the brain chemicals norepinephrine and epinephrine.

When released into the synaptic cleft, dopamine is broken down by the enzyme monoamine oxidase (MAO). This is an important point to keep in mind since many pharmaceutical drugs take advantage of this reaction. In fact, there are drugs that block the activity of MAO, and hence are known as "MAO inhibitors." There are two types of MAO inhibitors—type A and type B. They can both act as antidepressants, and the type-B inhibitors are also used to treat Parkinson's disease. Selegiline (or deprenyl) is a well-known pharmaceutical MAO type-B inhibitor. Ingestion of selegiline leads to arousal, alertness, and an increase in sexual drive.

A decline in dopamine activity in the brain is linked to cognitive (learning and memory) and movement problems in those with Parkinson's disease. In upcoming chapters, I will discuss how the amino acids

Figure 4.1—The Making of Dopamine and Norepinephrine From Amino Acids

Phenylalanine

↓ Nicotinamide adenosine dinucleotide (NADH)

Tyrosine

↓ Vitamin C

L-Dopa

↓ Vitamin B-6

Dopamine

↓ Vitamin C

Norepinephrine

↓ methyl donors

Epinephrine

phenylalanine and tyrosine, along with the nutrient nicotinamide adenosine dinucleotide (NADH) and some of the B vitamins, influence the production of dopamine.

Norepinephrine and Epinephrine

As you can see in Figure 4.1, the amino acids phenylalanine and tyrosine are converted into dopamine. Dopamine, in turn, is converted into norepinephrine and then epinephrine. As apparent from this sequence, the ingestion of tyrosine elevates dopamine and norepinephrine levels and hence will lead to alertness and mood elevation. Excess amounts of these neurotransmitters raise blood pressure, increase heart rate and cause anxiety, irritability and insomnia. Certain pharmaceutical antidepressants elevate mood and enhance arousal by increasing levels of norepinephrine and epinephrine.

Both phenylalanine and tyrosine are available over-the-counter, and they are discussed in Chapter 13. Several enzymes are required to make the conversion from phenylalanine to epinephrine, and these enzymes require helpers, such as vitamins and nutrients. Figure 4.1 shows several of these nutrients. For instance, vitamin B-6 helps convert L-dopa to dopamine, while vitamin C helps convert dopamine to norepinephrine.

Serotonin

Serotonin is the most widely studied neurotransmitter since it helps regulate a vast range of psychological and biological functions. Serotonin (5-hydroxytryptamine or 5-HT) was first identified in 1948. The wide extent of psychological functions regulated by serotonin involves mood, anxiety, arousal, aggression and thinking abilities. You may recall

Figure 4.2—The Making of Serotonin

Tryptophan

↓

5-Hydroxytryptophan

↓　　　Vitamin B-6

Serotonin

↓　　　methyl donors

Melatonin

that other brain chemicals, such as dopamine and norepinephrine, also influence mood and arousal. However, serotonin generally has different effects. For instance, excess amounts of serotonin cause relaxation, sedation and a decrease in sexual drive.

Prozac, a common antidepressant, elevates serotonin levels and perhaps influences the levels of other brain chemicals. There is an over-the-counter nutrient called 5-hydroxytryptophan (5-HTP) that is the immediate precursor to serotonin and can in some cases, temporarily substitute for serotonin-influencing drugs (see Chapter 13). Some research suggests that perhaps the herbal antidepressant St. John's wort also works by elevating levels of serotonin in the brain.

Disruption of the normal functioning of the serotonergic system leads to a number of psychiatric conditions, which include anxiety disorders, depression, improper social behavior and sexual aberrations. Common medical conditions associated with disruption of the serotonergic system include disturbance in the sleep-wake cycle, obesity or eating disorders and chronic pain.

Figure 4.2 shows that the starting point in the production of serotonin is tryptophan, one of the amino acids we ingest through food, particularly meat, fish and other protein foods. If enough tryptophan is not supplied to the brain, serotonin levels drop. Furthermore, in order for tryptophan to enter the brain, it has to be transported across the blood-brain barrier by a carrier protein. This carrier protein is also used by other amino acids, including phenylalanine and tyrosine, two amino acids that convert in the brain to dopamine and norepinephrine. Imagine this carrier as a small canoe that can carry only one person across a lake at a time. There's always competition between the different amino acids to jump on the canoe. Therefore, brain levels of tryptophan are not only determined by the concentration of tryptophan in the bloodstream, but also by the concentration of competing amino acids.

Once tryptophan enters the brain, it can go into brain cells and be converted into 5-HTP and then converted into serotonin. After serotonin is made, the pineal gland is able to convert it at night into the sleep hormone melatonin. Other areas of the brain don't have the necessary enzymes to make this conversion.

GABA

Gamma-aminobutyric acid, discovered in 1950, is the most important and widespread inhibitory neurotransmitter in the brain. Excitation in the brain must be balanced with inhibition. Too much excitation can lead to restlessness, irritability, insomnia and even seizures. GABA is able to induce relaxation, analgesia and sleep. Barbiturates and benzodiazepines are known to stimulate GABA receptors, and hence induce relaxation. Several neurological disorders, such as epilepsy, sleep disorders and Parkinson's disease, are affected by this neurotransmitter.

GABA is made in the brain from the amino acid glutamate with the aid of vitamin B-6. GABA is available as a supplement in vitamin stores, but taking it in pill form is not an effective way to raise brain levels of this neurotransmitter because GABA cannot easily cross the blood-brain barrier. Companies are searching for ways to place GABA in an oil base in order to ease its entry across this barrier.

Additional Neurotransmitters

There are dozens of other chemicals—amino acids, peptides and hormones—found in the brain that influence mood and cognition. These include glutamate, histamine, endorphins, enkephalins, growth hormone, vasopressin, prolactin, oxytocin, nitric oxide, prostaglandins and others. It's very likely that many of the supplements discussed in this book affect these chemicals, and further research will certainly identify these biochemical processes.

The Connection Between the Brain and the Immune System

As if all of the chemicals discussed above weren't enough, there are many messengers —such as cytokines—that are released by the immune system and influence brain cells and levels of neurotransmitters; some of these cytokines are interleukins, interferons and tumor necrosis factor. Hence, a healthy immune system is necessary for a well-functioning brain. The brain can, in turn, release chemicals and hormones that influence the immune system. For instance, there are serotonin receptors on white blood cells. The brain-immune connection is a two-way affair. If you've ever had a bad case of the flu and felt fatigued and depressed for a few days afterward, you experienced the immediate negative effects of certain cytokines on your brain cells and neurotransmitters. If you've ever been stressed and then developed a cold, you may have realized the immune-suppressing effect of certain brain chemicals and hormones released by the brain as a consequence of stress.

Summary

I find brain chemistry fascinating, particularly since we now have access to a number of natural supplements that can help us manipulate our neurotransmitters. By understanding brain chemistry and how supplements work, we can more effectively improve our mental capacities and performance.

PART III

LIFESTYLE HABITS FOR A LONG-LASTING BRAIN

5

How to Cultivate a Naturally Healthy Mind

In this book I focus on natural mind-boosting supplements, but every book that discusses mental health must address the significant influence of diet and lifestyle. We may use the most powerful mind boosters available, but if we don't exercise the brain and body, eat the right foods, continue on a path of emotional growth, cultivate healthy relationships and have good sleeping patterns, we will not reap the full benefits of the supplements.

We live in a world that places enormous demands on our mental abilities. Continually expanding mind and memory capacity is crucial to successful adaptation to this ever-changing, information-oriented society. Enhancing mental capacity helps us advance in our careers, and may lead to more work satisfaction, higher income, greater travel and leisure opportunities, less stress and more autonomy.

An increase in intelligence and a large fund of knowledge give individuals an improved sense of self-confidence. As our topics of interest and discussion increase, so can the number and variety of social contacts. Knowledge also improves our ability to foresee future political, economic and historical trends.

The more we learn, the more we wish to continue learning. Understanding the world is like assembling a jigsaw puzzle. The more pieces we fit, the clearer the image and the greater the urge to learn and fill in even more pieces. Increasing one's knowledge can be compared to an avalanche: once the process starts, it gathers a momentum of its own. Perseverance and some initial prompting are required, but the rewards soon pay off. Minds are kept young by continual use, and mentally active people live longer. I consider mind-enhancement to be a lifelong process. Centuries ago René Descartes said, "It is not enough to have a good mind. The main thing is to use it well." The march of intellect need not halt soon after framing the high school or college diploma.

Emotional Connections

During this process of intellectual enhancement, keep in mind that we also need to grow emotionally. Although supplements can help provide the basic ingredients for proper mental functioning, they cannot help us develop healthy relationships. In order to feel truly fulfilled, most people need to cultivate healthy connections on multiple levels.

The need for connection may be fulfilled in several ways. On a personal level, we can connect with fellow human beings through friendship, physical intimacy, romance, marriage and family. We can also satisfy our need for connection with cats, dogs, other animals and nature as a whole. We satisfy the urge to belong to something larger than ourselves by joining religious, humanistic, philosophic or a variety of community groups. As a rule, the more ways we connect, the happier we become.

Supplements can sometimes help in this regard by lifting our mood and improving our motivation to become social and interact with others.

Exercise

If you've reached middle age—or passed it— and have never exercised regularly, it's not too late to start. Maintaining the exercise habit or taking up light-to-moderate physical activity later in life helps us live longer. Physical activity improves mental function by inducing the growth of capillaries (tiny blood vessels) in the brain, which helps many nutrients reach neurons. This is important because the aging process leads to a decrease in blood supply to the brain.

Physical exercise also leads to deep sleep. During deep sleep, the brain gets a chance to consolidate memory and rebalance hormones and brain chemicals to get us ready for a new day.

Learn How to Learn

Learning is an art that improves with time. There are several practical steps you can take to acquire more knowledge.

The more words we learn, the more aware we become of our surroundings. Look up unfamiliar words in the dictionary. Jot a reminder by the word to indicate where you encountered it, whether in a book, a magazine, a newspaper or in conversation. For example, if you come across a new word while reading *The New York Times*, write *NYT* by the word in the dictionary. If you come across the word in a book, write the title of the book by the word. Next time you look up the same word, the previous annotation will help you form an association, and you will have an easier time remembering the word.

I often look up a word in my dictionary and realize I have noted it before. I make a special effort to remember this word to learn it once and for all. The odds are high that I will encounter this word again. Almost every page of my *Webster's Dictionary* has some notation on it. Another great way to stimulate the mind and learn new words is to do crossword puzzles.

Once we start learning new words, it is a pleasant surprise when we encounter the same words again because each new word reinforces a memory. Consider the dictionary or encyclopedia one of your most interesting friends. "Words form the thread on which we string our experiences," according to Aldous Huxley, the British philosopher.

If you have time, read a brief history of the world. Improve your geographical knowledge—buy an atlas and look up the major countries and their capitals. Whenever you encounter the name of a city you have not heard before, look for it in the atlas.

Reviewing the important figures in literature, art, and music will be very helpful. The television game show *Jeopardy!* is a great mental exercise for improving memory and recall. You can learn an incredible amount of information that you will likely come across again in your daily life. I often tape the show, and when I have time, review the episodes. If I can't think of the answer, I put the tape on pause for a few seconds to think hard and to try to remember. Watching shows like *Jeopardy!* or playing games involving trivia or recall can significantly enhance your memory and intelligence. Mind-boosting supplements make a great synergistic combination with games that stimulate thinking and recall.

You may also find that your ability to be funny improves as you learn more words and increase your mental capacity. Your mind will start thinking faster. Making a joke or saying something witty becomes easier, since you mind has access to words, ideas and trivial details.

Cultivate Your Creativity

"The barriers are not erected," wrote Ludwig van Beethoven, "which shall say to aspiring talent, 'thus far and no farther.' "

Creativity, an expression of one's individuality, demands self-discipline—that is, motivation, effort and perseverance. You don't know where your talents will lead if you don't make the initial effort to start. Writing and English were two of my weakest subjects in high school and college. I always excelled in mathematics and science. The last thing on my mind in medical school and residency was to be a medical writer. I would never have guessed when I published my first book that I had the potential to be a prolific writer.

There is a strong drive in humans to create, construct or invent. The end product might be a piece of art, a musical score, a poem, a house or simply a better-tasting salad dressing. We can find original ways to approach daily problems. An office worker can write a better memo; a gardener can sculpt new shapes of bushes; a laboratory worker can find a new solution to a project; and a homemaker can find creative ways to shop and balance the family budget. There are countless opportunities in our daily life to be creative.

Sample! Explore! Expand!

As we age, many people have a tendency to gradually shun novelty and surround themselves with the familiar. This can lead to feeling stuck.

Our Earth provides a bounty of sensual and pleasurable potentials, yet we nibble from the edges. We cloister ourselves from new experiences. Our senses are repeatedly reexposed to the same stimuli. We lose touch with our novelty-seeking drive and may lean toward the ordinary, the routine and the unconscious. We wonder why we're not obtaining pleasure and satisfaction from things we used to enjoy. One week becomes no different from the week before, or the week after. Eventually, familiarity metamorphoses into a master demanding the same television shows, the same meals, the same vacation spots, the same everything. The pendulum arcs to and fro, seasons come and go and we continue our downward slump.

It can happen to any of us. Familiarity can subtly numb our senses and sap our initiative. But there is a way out of this rut. Once we are aware of this feeling, we can take steps to turn the tide. A little effort expands our comfort zone. Having made this effort, we realize how easy it is to continue expanding. The first step is the hardest.

In order to keep your mind at its best, add variety to your life. Make the effort to

31

meet new people, engage in good conversation, attend concerts and take adult classes in art, literature, poetry, music or painting. What about an acting, dance or improvisation class? Engage in a new sport. Travel to destinations you don't normally visit. Have you visited all the museums in or near your town or city? Taking handfuls of brain-boosting supplements while being a couch potato is not the answer.

But if you are stuck in a familiar routine, some of the nutrients discussed in this book can motivate you to break out of your mental decline and boredom. By improving mood, increasing energy levels, enhancing visual perception and increasing motivation, these supplements can be the catalysts that get you back to enjoying our beautiful world. While in the process of expanding, we need to remind ourselves to reappreciate and love the familiar, being grateful for everything we already have and are able to do.

Smart Eating

Mental health is, in many ways, linked to physical health. The cardiovascular system supplies blood and oxygen to the brain. When the arteries to the brain are clogged, the blood supply to important neural centers decreases. Cardiovascular disease can often foretell cognitive decline—those who have poor blood flow suffer mental decline faster than those with good vascular health.

Just about every step you take to improve your physical well-being will influence your brain health—especially the right diet. Since the topic of healthy eating has been covered thoroughly in many books and articles, I just wish to make a few important points.

Breakfast is essential for good thinking. Mom was right, after all, when she urged you to eat before going out to school. Dr. David Benton and colleagues from the University of Wales-Swansea, in the United Kingdom, studied the effects of skipping breakfast versus eating breakfast (Benton 1998). Morning fasting was found to adversely affect the ability to recall a list of words and stories read aloud, and other items. However, failing to eat breakfast did not affect performance on an intelligence test. So the researchers concluded that breakfast influences tasks requiring aspects of memory, partly through increasing blood-sugar levels. Even a small breakfast snack is enough. In November 2001, Canadian researchers reported in the *American Journal of Clinical Nutrition* that breakfast eaters constantly scored better on memory and learning tests than people who skip the morning meal (Kaplan 2001).

For optimum alertness and brain function, I recommend eating small, frequent meals throughout the day and include a balanced amount of protein, fat and carbohydrates. Protein helps us stay alert. If you have trouble falling asleep, toward evening you can switch to having more carbohydrates, which help to induce slumber. Good choices of carbohydrates may include unprocessed grains, barley, lentils, legumes, vegetables and fruits. A small amount of pasta is another option.

Here are some other suggestions for a smart diet…

• Reduce your intake of sugar and simple carbohydrates. Most people don't realize that sugars can convert into fats, particularly saturated fatty acids such as palmitic acid. When appropriate, use the natural, no-calorie sweetener stevia as a substitute for sugar.

- Reduce your intake of saturated fats if you have been eating a large amount. However, don't go to the extreme of trying to cut out all saturated fats. Moderation is the key.

- Decrease your intake of fried foods, margarine and baked goods. These foods contain trans-fatty acids and hydrogenated oils that interfere with the function of good fats.

- Use more olive, canola and flaxseed oils and less safflower, sunflower and corn oils. Include more omega-3 fatty acids in the diet, particularly through consumption of fish. If you don't like fish, or don't eat enough marine products, take fish-oil supplements. When buying canned tuna or sardines, avoid the ones soaked in soybean oil or other omega-6 oils. For example, you can eat sardines packed in mustard or tomato sauce, or olive oil.

- Vary your fruit and vegetable intake by trying new kinds of produce. Each fruit or vegetable has a unique set of carotenoids and flavonoids. On a regular basis, consume citrus fruits, berries, apricots, grapes and other fruits. Your vegetable intake should include garlic, onions, green leafy vegetables, yellow- or orange-colored vegetables, tomatoes and beets.

- Drink a variety of herbal teas instead of just regular tea or coffee. Each morning, have a different type of tea, such as ginger, bilberry, green tea, licorice, peppermint, lemon grass and others.

- Drink one or two large glasses of water when you wake up in the morning to help empty the colon.

Unfortunately, we are also influenced by the dietary choices of our family, friends and community. For instance, the types of meals served at local restaurants certainly influence our choices. Many of the dishes may be deep-fried. In some areas of the country, fish is very expensive or rarely part of the menu. People who live in small towns or rural areas may be limited in their access to a variety of fruits and vegetables.

A Note to Vegetarians

I have many patients who are vegetarians. Some are able to function very well and are able to ingest the right nutrients for optimal health. Others suffer from fatigue and low mood since they may be missing certain nutrients found exclusively in eggs, milk, meat and fish.

If you're a vegetarian, you may not be getting enough CoQ10, creatine, carnitine, and omega-3 oils. Supplement your diet with flaxseed oil for omega-3s, and take about 10 mg of CoQ10; 100 to 250 mg of carnitine, and about 1 g of creatine on a daily basis. Make sure your intake of protein is adequate. Many vegetarians have a tendency to overconsume carbohydrates at the expense of protein.

The Deep Sleep

Nothing seems to improve memory, mood, and overall cognition like a good night's sleep. If you need help sleeping, you can occasionally use a sleep-inducing supplement such as 5-HTP or melatonin, or the herbs valerian and hops. *Here are eight suggestions for a good night's rest…*

1. Expose yourself to morning light for at least ten to twenty minutes. Morning light exposure shortens the sleep cycle so that when you go to bed at night it will be easier to fall asleep.

2. Exercise will definitely give you a deeper sleep. The best times to work out are in the late afternoon or early evening.

Exercise may delay sleep when you do it within three or so hours before bedtime, due to arousal and increase in body heat. If you take some of the stimulants discussed in this book, you will definitely need to do some physical activity in order to use up the excess energy, otherwise you will still be stimulated at bedtime, and your sleep will be shallow.

3. Caffeine in any form (sodas, chocolate, coffee or certain teas, including green tea) is best avoided after dinner. Some individuals may be so sensitive to caffeine's stimulant effects that even afternoon coffee can interfere with sleep. Be careful taking high doses of energizing supplements since some of them, like tyrosine, can cause a restless sleep even if taken in the morning. Their effect can also be additive when combined with caffeine.

4. Eating a small or moderate, late-night snack about one or two hours before bedtime may actually promote sleep, especially if the meal includes carbohydrates (such as bread, whole grains, legumes, fruits, potatoes, pasta or rice).

5. Stop mental activity at least one hour before bed and allow your mind to switch to fun reading, or watching a comedy film or TV show. You could tape your favorite prime-time sitcom and then watch it before bed. Horror movies or violent TV shows are not a good idea before bedtime because some of the violent scenes could be incorporated into your dreams.

6. Use earplugs to muffle noises that may disturb your sleep, like a dog barking, traffic, airplanes overhead, birds chirping or a noisy bed partner. Using earplugs has had a significant influence on my ability to get deep, uninterrupted sleep and has enormously influenced my daytime productivity.

7. Wear eyeshades to block the early-morning light. There is no reason to wake up earlier than you have to and you may be unsuccessful in getting more rest.

8. Try one or more relaxation techniques when you get to bed. While lying on your back, shake and loosen a leg and foot. Take a few, slow, deep breaths by expanding your belly. Proceed to shake and loosen the other leg and foot and then take a few more relaxed breaths. Proceed with this relaxation to your arms, shoulders and neck. Now relax your facial muscles—especially the muscles around the eyes and mouth. Remember to return to your breath after relaxing each muscle group. Before you know it, you'll be drifting into a deep slumber.

Now that we've looked at the positive steps you can take to improve your mind naturally, in the next chapter we'll examine habits that interfere with optimal brain function.

6

BEWARE OF BRAIN BUSTERS

Marty is a fifty-four-year-old accountant who went through a difficult divorce after a twenty-two-year marriage. This chronic stress interfered with his performance at work. "I used to have a photographic memory, but now I have trouble remembering the names of some of my clients," he laments.

Denise, a forty-eight-year-old lawyer, was diagnosed with high blood pressure by her internist. She was prescribed propranolol, a medicine that slows heart rate and lowers blood pressure. However, about a month after starting this medicine, Denise noticed that she was not thinking as sharply and had difficulty recalling phone numbers.

Stress and certain medicines can interfere with optimal mental function. In this chapter, I will discuss several conditions that impede mental health and provide suggestions on how to best deal with them.

Stress, Anger, and Anxiety

There's an intricate connection between the brain and the body. They communicate with each other through hormones, neurotransmitters, and many other types of chemical messengers. For instance, the hypothalamus and pituitary, two regions in the brain that control various hormone systems, respond immediately to stress by releasing hormones that stimulate the adrenal glands to release cortisol. Excess cortisol can wreak havoc with brain cells, interfering with mental functioning and memory. In turn, the immune system and some of the organs in the body release chemicals that pass into the brain and influence the function of brain cells.

Whether physical (e.g., intense athletic competition, illness) or psychological (e.g., emotional difficulties, financial worries), stress has definite harmful biological effects. Our immune system responds quickly to our thoughts and emotions. On the surface of white blood cells, there are receptors to which hormones and neurotransmitters attach. When we are under stress, substances released by the brain attach to the cells of the immune system and disturb their proper functioning. Positive thoughts and emotions are believed to enhance the immune system. The immune system can in turn send substances back to the brain, altering the release of neurotransmitters, thus influencing mood and cognition.

35

Consequences of excess stress include...

• Immune system malfunction, which makes us more susceptible to colds and various infections. Certain germs or immune cells fighting these germs can potentially cross the blood-brain barrier and damage brain cells. Lack of sleep significantly interferes with proper immune function.

• Increased risk for heart disease, high blood pressure and stroke. Chronic damage to arteries leading to the brain can decrease blood flow to vital systems. There is a type of brain deterioration called "multi-infarct dementia" that occurs when frequent small clots travel to the brain and limit the blood supply to brain cells. Tiny strokes that go unnoticed can, over the long run, damage a number of areas in the brain. When enough damage occurs, noticeable signs of mental malfunction become apparent. A large blood clot can cause a blockage of a major artery, incapacitating a wide segment of the brain, thus causing a major stroke.

• A higher likelihood for chronic fatigue and various musculoskeletal aches and pains. These chronic conditions can lead to low mood and can necessitate the use of painkillers that can have detrimental effects on brain function.

Luckily we can do something about stress by attempting to channel our thoughts to a more positive direction. Some of the stress we encounter is not necessarily due to external circumstances. Rather, it is due to our underdeveloped coping skills. While stuck in traffic, we can boil with frustration or we can turn on the radio and hum along with the songs. How we handle stress is often more important than the nature of the stress. Do you get upset throughout the day when small things don't go according to your plans, or do you calmly adapt to unplanned situations?

The first step in dealing with stress is to identify its source. Then take specific action to relieve or eliminate the source. Take a moment now or later to list all sources of stress in your life in a personal/private journal. Beside each entry write down how you plan to deal with that stressor. There are times when life is cruel, and we just want to sit and cry. That's perfectly okay. Crying helps to wash away toxic chemicals and hormones built up during stress, which in turn improves mood. It's healthy to cry once in a while.

There are many ways to relieve stress: vacations, playing with pets, improving sleep and physical health, finding satisfying work, consulting with an understanding friend or family member, establishing financial security and participating in exercise, sports, yoga, prayer or meditation.

If these suggestions are not enough to relieve your stress, you can temporarily use certain natural supplements available over-the-counter to help you ease your tension. The two most effective ones are the herb kava and the nutrient 5-HTP, which converts into serotonin. The B vitamins are also very good in helping us build resistance to stress. Many other nutrients, such as methyl donors (Chapter 10), mind energizers (Chapter 12), and certain herbs such as ginseng can improve energy levels and well-being and hence make it easier to deal with everyday stress.

Smoking

Elderly smokers experience a greater loss in the ability to think, perceive and remember than people who have never smoked or who have quit smoking. The mental decline of elderly smokers may be tied to "silent strokes" —very small strokes that go unnoticed. Smoking is known to cause atherosclerosis, not just of the heart vessels, but also the vessels that supply blood and oxygen to the brain. And this decline in memory and thinking ability begins in middle-age in smokers, according to a study by British researchers in the June 2003 issue of the *American Journal of Public Health* (Richards 2003). In addition to damaging blood vessels, smoking causes constriction of arteries, clot formation, oxidation and raised blood pressure. Smoking or exposure to cigarette smoke may also be linked to an increased risk of hearing loss.

Alcohol

Excess alcohol has a direct neurotoxic effect, meaning that it kills neurons. Excessive alcohol consumption also reduces the availability of certain B vitamins. One or two glasses of alcohol per day should not interfere with memory to any significant extent.

Be Kind to Your Mind

Everything discussed in this book deals with improving mental health. In this section, I wish to explain further how we can make our minds even healthier by replacing negative input with positive input. As you know, whatever enters our stomach affects our body. We need to be as careful about what enters our mind. For instance, unhealthy relationships with parents, a spouse, a lover, relatives, an employer or roommates can give the ego a regular beating. Constant exposure to an emotional insult inevitably has a detrimental influence on the psyche, and will eventually affect physical and mental health. If improving the lines of communication and restoring healthy interactions are not possible, it may be appropriate to temporarily withdraw from unhealthy relationships and give time to heal.

Reduce your exposure to movies, books, and television programs that portray violence, horror or negativity. Viewing violence may make some people, especially children and teenagers, more aggressive. Even if the violence does not manifest externally, violent programs can affect dreams. Radio and television shows that criticize and disparage individuals or groups due to ethnic, racial and sexual orientation are an additional source of negativity. Be conscious of what you feed your mind. Watching excessively violent movies, or reading similar books, is for the mind what consuming junk food is for the body.

If you're a "news junkie," take breaks once in a while for at least a weekend and don't read a newspaper or watch the news on television.

Common Medical Conditions Associated with Cognitive Decline

There are a number of medical conditions that can interfere with proper brain function.

Cardiovascular diseases, such as hypertension and coronary artery disease, are closely associated with brain function. The common pathway that leads to damage to the arteries in the rest of the body most likely also damages the arteries that supply the brain. Therefore, any lifestyle and dietary changes that you make to improve your cardiovascular health—such as exercise, relaxation, increasing whole-foods intake, and so on—will help circulation to the brain.

Common hormonal conditions that can influence brain function include diabetes and thyroid disease, particularly hypothyroidism. Make every effort to keep your blood sugar under control and see your physician regularly for exams to rule out any major problems with your thyroid gland and other organs.

The immune system is intricately involved in keeping the brain healthy. A number of immune compounds released by the body, such as interleukins, are able to cross the blood-brain barrier and influence neurons. Hence the healthier your immune system is, the healthier your brain.

Significant nutritional deficiencies are uncommon in this country, but there are large numbers of individuals, especially the elderly, who have marginal intakes of many nutrients. Hence, B-vitamin supplements and other nutrients can sometimes have a dramatic influence on brain health.

Brain-Busting Medicines

One of the most common causes of rapid cognitive decline is the use of certain prescription drugs.

Sedatives and sleeping pills often have immediate and dramatic effects on memory and clarity of thinking. Regular use of some of these drugs can sometimes cause irreversible memory impairment. The occasional use of melatonin is an alternative to sleeping pills, while kava and 5-HTP can substitute for antianxiety agents in the therapy of mild-to-moderate anxiety. Do not be concerned about the infrequent use of a pharmaceutical sedative—this should not interfere with memory.

Cholesterol-lowering drugs have become mainstays over the past five years, after several studies hinted they reduce the risk of dying from heart attacks. Millions of Americans now take a type of drug called statins. Although these drugs may reduce the risk of coronary artery disease in the short term, they may also have negative effects on mental cognition. Some studies have shown that those who lower their cholesterol levels excessively seem to have reduced mood, attention, and concentration and are more likely to die by car accidents and suicide.

Cholesterol is one of the important components of brain lipids. It plays a crucial role in the cell membrane, helps in the transmission of nerve signals and serves as the precursor to the manufacture of pregnenolone, DHEA, estrogen and the other steroid hormones. By blocking the formation of cholesterol, or excessively lowering its concentration through drugs, are we also decreasing levels of steroid hormones in the brain? Could the shortage of these hormones in the brain lead to depression, memory loss and cognitive decline? The answers are not yet available, but this possibility must be considered. Cholesterol-lowering drugs may be appropriate to use if your cholesterol levels are very high. Keep in mind the negative influence these drugs may have on cognition. Make an attempt to lower your cholesterol through diet or natural supplements.

There are many other types of drugs that may interfere with cognition. These include certain beta-blockers, painkillers, calcium channel blockers, anticonvulsants, chemotherapeutic agents and muscle relaxants. Ask your physician whether any of the medicines you are taking has a negative influence on the brain, and whether there may be better pharmaceutical or nutritional alternatives. ◆

PART IV

A Practical Guide to Mind-Boosting Supplements

7

MIND YOUR FATS

**D**octors generally believe that the best way to treat mood, thought and memory disorders is with pharmaceutical medicines that directly influence levels of brain chemicals such as serotonin, dopamine and acetylcholine.

Although such drugs have very important clinical uses, in my view, they are only part of the solution. A comprehensive approach to treating cognitive disorders should include eating healthy foods and taking supplements that benefit the overall health of brain cells.

One way to influence brain health through your diet is to consume the right fats and oils. About 60 percent of the brain consists of lipids (fats) that make up the lining, or cell membrane, of every brain cell. The types of fats present in the brain influence its structure and function. How well your mind works depends, in the long run, on what you eat.

This chapter will focus on fatty acids, particularly the omega-3s. Omega-3 oils are found mostly in fish and flaxseed, as well as in supplements sold over-the-counter.

Dietary Fats and the Brain

Carolyn, a writer from Marina del Rey, California, speaks for many when she says, "Fish oils make me more focused and serene.

WHAT COGNITIVE BENEFITS DO OMEGA-3 OILS HAVE?

If your intake of omega-3s is currently low and you begin to consume more fish, or take fish-oil or flaxseed-oil supplements, you may begin to notice some of these improvements:

- Improved mood

- Enhanced clarity of thinking

- More serenity and mental stability

- Better concentration and focus

- Better vision

WHICH CLINICAL CONDITIONS CAN OMEGA-3s BENEFIT?

The clinical application of omega-3s is not yet well-researched, but scientists have begun to explore the role of these important fats in the following conditions:

It's quite possible some of these conditions will eventually be found to respond partially or significantly to supplementation with omega-3s.

- Age-related cognitive decline

- Depression and bipolar disorders (manic depression)

- Post-partum depression

- Anxiety disorders

- Addiction disorders

- Schizophrenia

In addition, I get far less brain fatigue in the late afternoon." Marvin, a forty-three-year-old musician from New York, says, "I don't notice the effects from fish oils if I take a low dose. When I take more than 3 grams, I find that I have a sense of well-being and feel more aware." And Kevin, a twenty-eight-year-old actor from Los Angeles, adds, "Within a few hours of taking fish-oil capsules, I notice my vision to be improved. Colors are more vivid and everything is in better focus."

Changing the types and amounts of fats we consume can influence the fatty composition of brain cells and other cells in the body.

Why Are Fats Important?

The lining of every cell in the body—for instance, the lining of red blood cells that carry oxygen—is made of fats. The type of fats in a red-blood-cell membrane can change very quickly, often within hours, based on the type of fats present in a meal. This change influences the fluidity of the cell membrane. The more fluid a red-blood-cell membrane, the easier it is for it to squeeze through tiny capillaries and supply oxygen and nutrients to remote areas of the body.

The fats that make up brain-cell membranes are much more resistant to changes in diet than the fats forming the cell membranes of other tissues in the body. The brain has developed an excellent ability to preserve its fatty composition despite shortages of essential fats in the diet. However, it is possible to alter the fat content of the brain through diet.

We know this is true through animal studies. It has been demonstrated that manipulating the fatty-acid content of a rat's diet changes the fatty-acid composition of the brain-cell membrane within as brief a time period as three weeks (Yehuda 1998).

The types of fats that constitute the cell membrane influence how well brain cells interact and communicate with each other. Since the membranes of brain cells can be influenced by dietary composition, our objective should be to consume the correct types of fats and oils, and in their proper balance, which will guarantee that neurons function at their best.

Before I discuss what kinds of fats and oils you should be consuming and in what amounts, let's review some of the basic chemistry of fats. I hope this review will make it easier to understand the importance of omega-3 oils in brain health. It will also help you understand the role phospholipids play in cognition. (Phospholipids are discussed in Chapter 8).

The ABCs of Fats and Oils

Lipids is a general term that includes fats, oils, cholesterol and other substances that are fat-soluble. The simple difference between fats and oils is that fats are solid at room temperature, while oils are liquid. Fats and oils are triglycerides, which means they are made of a three-carbon molecule called *glycerol* attached to three long-chained carbon molecules called *fatty acids.*

There are dozens of common fatty acids present in the diet and the body. The length of these fatty acids varies, but most of them contain between four and twenty-four carbon atoms. Fatty acids are the building blocks for fats and oils and are divided into two groups—saturated and unsaturated.

Saturated fatty acids are found mostly in meat, animal fats, dairy products, lard and some tropical oils. Each carbon atom in these saturated fatty acids is attached to two hydrogen atoms.

In contrast, *unsaturated fatty acids* contain a double bond—which means that two neighboring carbon atoms have each lost a hydrogen atom. When fatty acids are unsaturated, they are more fluid and flexible. This is often a desirable trait.

Unsaturated fatty acids are in turn divided into two major groups…

1. Monounsaturated fatty acids are found in such vegetables as olives and avocados. They have one double bond. Mono, as you may know, means "one."

2. Polyunsaturated fatty acids have two or more double bonds. Poly means "many." The more double bonds present, the more fluid the fatty acid.

You can generally tell the degree of unsaturation of a particular food by how fluid it appears in the refrigerator or at room temperature. For instance, cheese contains mostly saturated fats and is hard. In contrast, olive oil is monounsaturated and it stays relatively liquid at room temperature, but hardens in the refrigerator. Fish oils and polyunsaturated oils, such as canola, can stay fluid even in very cold temperatures.

Many polyunsaturated fatty acids, called *nonessential fatty acids,* can be manufactured by the body. Others, called *essential fatty acids,* must be ingested through foods. *There are two types of essential fatty acids:* omega-3s and omega-6s.

Omega-3s

Omega-3 fatty acids are made from a fatty acid called *alphalinolenic acid* (ALA). *Omega* is the last letter in the Greek alphabet. In naming fatty acids, the last carbon of the chain is called *omega.* ALA is found predominantly in flaxseed oil (also known as linseed) and hemp-seed oil. Green leafy vegetables, soybeans, walnuts and canola oil have small amounts of omega-3 fatty acids.

Omega-3 fatty acids are beneficial because they provide fluidity to cell membranes and improve communication between brain cells. Omega-3s also reduce the clotting ability of platelets, thus potentially decreasing the incidence of heart attacks and strokes. Two very important omega-3 fatty acids are eicosapentanoic acid (EPA) and docosahex-anoic acid (DHA). They are found in seafood, especially mackerel, salmon, striped bass, rainbow trout, halibut, tuna and sardines. Supplements of fish oils that contain EPA and DHA are sold over-the-counter and DHA is also sold by itself. In the body, DHA is found mostly in the brain, retina and in sperm, and it plays an important role in vision.

Omega-6s

Omega-6 fatty acids are made from *linoleic acid,* a fatty acid found in vegetable oils such as corn, safflower, cottonseed and sunflower. Mayonnaise and salad oils normally contain a great amount of omega-6 fatty acids. Linoleic acid is eventually converted into arachidonic acid (AA), a beneficial fatty acid that, in excess, can induce inflammation, clotting, and have other unhealthy actions.

Unlike omega-3s, which are concentrated in the brain, omega-6s are found in most tissues in the body. Most Americans generally have a much higher intake of the omega-6s than the omega-3s. Up to 50 percent of the fatty acids in the gray matter in the brain is made of DHA and AA.

The mineral zinc and other vitamins and minerals help convert EPA to DHA. DHA has the ability to convert back into EPA (Hansen 1998). The human body is not able to make omega-3s from omega-6s, or vice versa.

The body uses omega-3s and omega-6s to produce several types of important substances such as prostaglandins, eicosanoids and leukotrienes. These substances have a number of effects on the brain and body. They can act as hormones and they are involved in the immune system, blood-pressure control, clotting and heart rhythm. These substances even influence tumor inhibition or formation. The types of fatty acids in the diet is known to influence the release of hormones by the pituitary gland.

Which Fats to Shun

Trans-fatty acids are new forms of fats that have been introduced over the past few decades. These are chemically altered and twisted fatty acids that are unhealthy and are not easily used by the body. Trans-fatty acids often result from hydrogenation, a process in which cheaper cooking oils are transformed to resemble better quality ingredients in taste and texture. Trans-fatty acids are generally found in margarine and many processed foods, pastries, donuts, corn chips and packaged foods.

Any type of fatty acid can be damaged and become harmful to the body if deep-fried. *Hydrogenated fats and oils,* commonly found in processed foods, are also unhealthy. Hydrogenation means adding hydrogen atoms, thus transforming a fatty acid from unsaturated to saturated.

A full explanation of fats can be quite complicated. I have listed several books in the bibliography that can give you a more detailed explanation. In this chapter it has been my goal to simply give you some background on the chemistry of these fatty acids in order to discuss the enormous importance of omega-3 oils to body and brain health.

Fish Oils and Mood

Over the past few years, scientists have attempted to determine whether the types of fats we consume have an influence on mental function. Many studies conclude that there is a connection. Dr. Andrew Stoll, of Harvard Medical School, has been a leader in this research, and he found in one study that a diet rich in fish (and fish oils) has a similar effect on people with depression as taking antidepressants (Stoll 1999).

In an earlier study, doctors compared fish consumption to the prevalence of major depression in eleven countries around the world. The study found that the more fish consumed in a country, the less the risk for depression. The doctors say, "Increasing rates of depression in the last century may be influenced by the consumption of increased amounts of saturated fatty acids and omega-6 fatty acids and the decreased consumption of omega-3 fatty acids."

Studies indicate that DHA levels in red-blood-cell membranes are low in depressed persons (Peet 1998). Other studies have shown that both eating fish regularly and supplementation with omega-3s can improve mood and memory (Hibbeln 1998, Benton 1998).

Manic-Depression

This condition is also known as "bipolar disorder." Patients with this condition go through cycles of experiencing mania (euphoria, racing thoughts, hyperactivity) followed by cycles of depression. The standard pharmaceutical approach to treating bipolar disorders is with lithium or drugs such as valproate and carbamazepine.

Dr. Stoll, director of the Psychopharmacology Research Laboratory at Harvard's McLean Hospital, has tested fish oils with bipolar patients. He conducted a four-month double-blind placebo-controlled study that administered about 10 grams a day of concentrated fish oils. Overall, nine out of fourteen patients responded positively to fish oils, compared to three out of sixteen patients receiving a placebo. Dr. Stoll concluded, "In cases of mild bipolar disorder, it would be

worthwhile to first try a therapeutic approach with fish oils before proceeding to pharmacological therapy."

Interestingly, Dr. Stoll reports that a preliminary study using flaxseed oil with fifty patients showed that the fatty acid found in flax (ALA) has mild mood-stabilizing and antidepressant effects.

Help for Schizophrenia?

Even relatively difficult mental conditions such as schizophrenia may partially be influenced by the fatty acid content in the brain. Studies show that schizophrenic patients have defects in certain brain receptors but they suggest that supplementation with concentrated fish oil can be helpful. In a study done at the Northern General Hospital in Sheffield, England, dietary supplementation of concentrated fish oil for six weeks with 10 grams per day led to significant improvement in patients with schizophrenic symptoms (Laugharne 1996). And a later study suggests that two months of omega-3 supplementation led to remission of all symptoms in some patients (Puri 1998).

Malcolm Peet, M.D., a professor at Northern General Hospital, has found that supplementation with fish oils as an addition to current antipsychotic drug treatment leads to significant improvement in treatment-resistant schizophrenic patients. Interestingly, he compared the effectiveness of the two omega-3 acids (EPA and DHA). Dr. Peet found that EPA was very effective, while DHA wasn't. This result was unexpected since EPA is not found in significant amounts in the brain. One can speculate that perhaps EPA is better transported through the blood-brain barrier than DHA, or perhaps EPA influences a set of immune and hormonal reactions that DHA does not. EPA can be converted into

DHA which then is incorporated into cell membranes. (Most fish-oil capsules contain both EPA and DHA, but supplements that contain only DHA are now available.)

Fish Oils and Learning

Long-term studies on humans have not yet been conducted to evaluate the effects of fish oil therapy and cognitive function. However, a one-year study in mice gives us some preliminary answers (Suzuki 1998). In the study, adult mice were fed a regular diet that included either 5 percent palm oil (containing mostly a 16-carbon saturated acid) or 5 percent sardine oil. At the end of one year, it was determined that the mice taking the sardine oil had a higher brain concentration of DHA. Their synapses and cell membranes were more fluid. Most significantly, the maze-learning ability of the mice taking fish oil was better than the mice that were fed palm oil.

Seeing Is Believing

The rods and cones of the retina in the eyes are very rich in DHA. It follows that a deficiency in dietary fish oils will reduce the photoreceptor activity of retinal cells, and therefore reduce visual acuity. Conversely, supplementation with fish oils (or flaxseed oil) could lead to improvement in vision and enhanced color perception.

Since levels of DHA in the brain decline with age, it is likely that the levels of DHA also decline in the retina. Is it possible that daily intake of fish oils can improve vision in older individuals? Hopefully future research can give us some answers. Chapter 20 discusses in more detail the effects of omega-3 oils and various nutrients on vision.

The Author's Experience: I have taken fish oils off and on for many years. I've experimented with very high daily dosages in order to determine whether these oils have any immediate effects. The highest daily dose I have taken is thirty capsules, each containing 300 mg of a combination EPA and DHA, totaling 9,000 mg.

When I took this dose in the morning, by late afternoon I noticed the onset of clarity in vision, with objects looking sharper and clearer. There was a slight improvement in my distance vision, and smaller details became more noticeable. Fine print on some documents became easier to read. The visual improvements continued and improved on subsequent days when I continued to take between ten to twenty capsules. Fish-oil supplementation also makes me more serene, focused and balanced. These effects, though, are subtle. I currently take about 600 to 1,200 mg of EPA/DHA per day except on days when I eat fish.

My experience with flaxseed oil has also been positive. When I take a tablespoon or more, I find that I have more energy and clarity of vision. These effects seem to increase over the following days if I continue taking the flaxseed oil. However, at higher doses, such as two tablespoons, I become overstimulated and experience insomnia.

The Simple "Brain Food" Plan

Dietary intake of omega-3 fatty acids varies significantly in the North American population. Generally, most Americans have a low intake of fish oils, perhaps as low as 200 mg per day of EPA and DHA. In other cultures where fish is a large part of the diet, such as with the Eskimo or Japanese people, the intake of fish oils can approximate 3,000 to 10,000 mg a day.

For optimal brain function, I recommend consuming fish at least two or three times a week. If your diet does not include enough of the omega-3 fatty acids or enough fish, you may consider taking supplements of fish oils or flaxseed oil. Vegetarians, or other people who don't eat fish, are good candidates for taking omega-3 supplements. As a rule, ingesting about half a gram to 2 grams of a combination of EPA and DHA daily should be sufficient.

There are dozens of different brands of fish-oil capsules sold in health-food stores, pharmacies and retail outlets. Each of them is likely to contain a different amount of EPA and DHA, but generally each capsule contains between 200 to 400 mg of a combination EPA and DHA. There are even small, fruit-flavored capsules for children. Fish oils are best stored in the refrigerator.

Which Formula to Look For

For many years fish-oil supplements were available as a combination of the two key fatty acids, EPA and DHA. Recently, DHA has been made available by itself. This algae-derived product does not contain EPA, but has 100 mg of DHA per capsule. A DHA capsule is much more expensive than a standard fish-oil capsule. The question arises as to whether DHA has benefits over that of fish oils. I had a discussion about this matter with Artemis Simopoulos, M.D., an expert on omega-3 oils, and President for the Center for Genetics, Nutrition and Health in Washington, D.C. She tells me, "…I do not see a need to take DHA supplements alone instead of fish-oil supplements that contain both EPA and DHA."

Based on all the information available to date, it appears that taking a DHA supplement by itself may not be necessary. At this time, I recommend to my patients that their supplements include a combination of EPA and DHA. Taking the combination is much cheaper than taking DHA by itself. It's possible, though, that future research may indicate that DHA alone may be helpful in infants, the elderly, in pregnancy, or other conditions. Algae-derived DHA supplements are also an option for strict vegetarians who do not wish to ingest fish oils.

Flax or Fish?

Since the fatty acid ALA in flax oil can convert into EPA and DHA, why not just take flaxseed oil supplements instead of fish oils? This might prove to be a good option for individuals like strict vegetarians who prefer flaxseed over fish oils. However, it is possible that some people may not have the adequate biochemical ability to convert ALA into EPA and DHA. The conversion is a difficult process and may require more than 10 grams of ALA to make 600 mg of EPA or 400 mg of DHA (Gerster 1998).

Lloyd Horrocks, Ph.D., Professor Emeritus of Medical Biochemistry at Ohio State University in Columbus, Ohio, is an expert on fish oils. He says, "The enzymes that convert shorter-chain and less-saturated fatty acids such as ALA into the longer-chain EPA and DHA may not work efficiently in everyone."

It has been suggested that several conditions or circumstances may lead to inadequate activity of the enzymes that convert ALA to EPA and DHA (Drevon 1992). These conditions include aging, diabetes, the person's intake of trans-fatty acids and a large amount of saturated fatty acids.

Norman Salem Jr., Ph.D., at the National Institutes of Health, tells me…

> Our research team has been studying omega-3 fatty-acid metabolism in humans. Our conclusion is that the conversion of ALA to DHA in most adults is adequate to maintain DHA status in the brain, but may not be adequate in newborns or individuals with certain metabolic disorders. A poorer DHA status associated with aging may occur due to dietary changes in essential fat, as well as low levels of antioxidant intake.
>
> We do know that the intake of omega-3 fatty acids is deficient in the Western diet. Most individuals are overdosing on *safflower, corn,* and *peanut oils.* These should be replaced by *canola, flaxseed,* and *olive oils.* In addition, it is important to consume the longer-chain omega-3 fats found in foods like fish and perhaps poultry. If chickens are fed foods high in long-chain fatty acids, the eggs will contain a higher proportion of these fatty acids. With time, eggs from better-fed chickens should become more widely available to consumers.

Based on the currently available evidence, it appears that most adults are able to convert flaxseed oil to EPA and DHA. But there may be some individuals who are unable to do so adequately. The reason for this may include genetics, medical conditions, excessive dietary intake of saturated or trans-fatty acids or simply the aging process. So, just to be on the safe side, it seems reasonable to include flax oil in the diet, as well as eat fish or take fish-oil supplements. This way, you will be ingesting all essential omega-3 fatty acids such as ALA, EPA and DHA.

 Cautions and Side Effects

There are few drawbacks in supplementing with omega-3 oils. However, because these oils can thin the blood, it is possible that very high doses could increase the risk of bleeding. When a bleed occurs in the brain, it is called a hemorrhagic stroke. *The incidence of bleeds is rare, but could be of clinical significance if a person is already taking high doses of aspirin, coumadin or other blood thinners.* The incidence of a hemorrhagic stroke is significantly less compared to the potential benefits from the reduction in heart attacks and strokes due to blood clots, and they generally only occur in doses over 1,000 milligrams per day.

 Recommendations

Individuals with a low intake of seafood or foods supplying omega-3 fatty acids are likely to benefit from supplementation with fish oils or flaxseed oil.

Added Health Benefit

You may reduce the risk of sudden death with omega-3s. An editorial in *Circulation: Journal of the American Heart Association* suggests that increasing dietary omega-3 fatty acids from fatty fish or flaxseed oil, and decreasing omega-6 fatty acids found in plant seed oils such as corn, safflower and sunflower, is a way to reduce the risk of sudden death from irregular heart rhythms or heart attacks.

At this point, it is difficult to suggest precise dosages of EPA and DHA that would apply to everyone. Individuals may vary in their requirement for these fatty acids, depending on their dietary intake as well as their biochemical ability to convert smaller-chain omega-3s to EPA and DHA. Generally, eating fish two or three times each week supplies about seven grams of EPA/DHA per week. A reasonable approach for someone who does not eat fish is to supplement with about one gram of a DHA/EPA combination on a daily basis. However, some individuals may require much higher doses to notice positive effects or to treat certain psychological, neurological or medical conditions.

EPA and DHA are important fatty acids in maintaining proper memory and cognitive function. Therefore, I consider fish oils to be a critical component of the mind-boosting program presented in this book. Taking a small amount of antioxidants, such as a few units of vitamin E, along with the fish-oil supplements seems prudent.

Over the next few years we may discover that omega-3-oil supplements have a positive influence on a number of neurological or psychiatric conditions. The influence may in some cases prove to be minor. But even a small benefit would be worthwhile since fish oils or flaxseed oils are inexpensive and do not have major side effects, as do some pharmaceutical drugs.

8

MEMORY BOOSTERS
PHOSPHOLIPIDS, CHOLINE AND
RELATED NUTRIENTS

Like omega-3 fatty acids, phospholipids are also important for optimal brain health. As the name implies, phospholipids are made of the combination of lipids (fats) and the mineral phosphorus. Phospholipids are found in high concentrations in the lining of practically every cell of the body, including brain cells. They help brain cells communicate and influence how well receptors function. Although present in many foods, phospholipids are found in higher concentrations in soy, eggs and the brain tissue of animals. There may actually be a biochemical rationale for the folk wisdom that eating brain makes one smarter.

The two most common phospholipid supplements sold over-the-counter are phosphatidylcholine (PC) and phosphatidylserine (PS). Phosphatidylcholine is also known as lecithin. This chapter explains the role and function of phospholipids, their clinical effects and practical recommendations for or against supplementation.

In addition to these phospholipids, I will also discuss choline, a nutrient that helps form phosphatidylcholine. Acetylcholine, the brain chemical involved with memory, is made from choline. Choline has been sold over-the-counter for many years. A new and more activated form of choline, called CDP-choline, became available in the United States in 1998.

Phospholipids and Healthy Cell Membranes

A lining called the "cell membrane" surrounds each brain cell. Without a healthy cell membrane, we cannot have optimum memory and mental function. Phospholipids play several roles in the brain. They not only determine which minerals, nutrients and drugs go in and out of the cell, but also influence communication between brain cells by influencing the shape of receptors and promoting the growth of dendrites.

Since phospholipids help form the cell membrane of the trillions of cells in the body, it makes sense that they would have an influence not just on the brain, but also on a number of organs and tissues, including the heart, blood cells, and the immune system. As we age, there's a decline in the amount of phospholipids making up cell membranes (Soderberg 1991).

WHAT BENEFITS DO CHOLINE AND PHOSPHOLIPIDS PROVIDE?

Individuals who don't have a good dietary intake of phospholipids may find that taking these nutrients leads to an improvement in learning and memory. Most young and healthy people who take PS or PC are not likely to notice any significant changes, although supplements could help some seniors. The effects from choline and its cousin, CDP-choline, are more noticeable.

WHICH CONDITIONS CAN CHOLINE AND PHOSPHOLIPIDS BENEFIT?

The clinical application of these nutrients has not yet been fully evaluated, but scientists have studied their role in age-related cognitive decline (ARCD), Alzheimer's disease, and Parkinson's disease. No firm conclusions are available yet as to whether PS and PC help improve these conditions. Choline and CDP-choline could potentially be beneficial in ARCD and Alzheimer's disease. In a recent study, researchers at the Rush Institute for Health Aging found that elderly people who regularly consumed fish or these nutrients in supplement form were 70% less likely to develop Alzheimer's than those who didn't. (Morris 2003)

The Making of Phospholipids

Phospholipids are compounds made of two fatty acids attached to glycerol, the mineral phosphorus, and an amine. An amine is a molecule that has nitrogen attached to a few carbon atoms. The two most common fatty acids attached to phospholipids in the brain are DHA and arachidonic acid (AA). You may recall from Chapter 7 that DHA is found in fish oils.

Phosphatidylcholine (PC) is the most abundant phospholipid in brain-cell membranes, comprising about 30 percent of the total phospholipid content, while phosphatidylserine (PS) makes up less than 10 percent.

The fatty-acid content of brain phospholipids can be altered by the composition of the diet, particularly just before and after birth, and the phospholipid composition of the brain can be manipulated even in adults.

Animal studies have indicated that omega-3 fatty acids added to the diet of rats are able to travel to the brain-cell membranes and become part of the phospholipids (Jumpsen 1997). If your diet includes seafood, then there will be an adequate amount of DHA present in the phospholipids forming the cell membrane of neurons.

The fatty-acid composition of phospholipids can deteriorate with aging and disease. As we age, many of the long-chained polyunsaturated fatty acids, such as DHA, can become shortened and more saturated. This can interfere with the optimal functioning of neurons.

In order to better understand how the nutrients in this chapter work, it helps to know how they are related to each other. As you can see from Figure 8.1, PS can be converted into PC; choline converts into CDP-choline and then PC.

Figure 8.1—Relation of Choline to Acetylcholine and Phospholipids

Choline   ←   →   Acetylcholine

↓

CDP-Choline

↓

Phosphatidylserine (PS)   →   Phosphatidylcholine (PC)

All of the nutrients listed in this figure, except for acetylcholine, are available over-the-counter as supplements. Acetylcholine is a brain chemical involved in memory and learning, among various other functions.

Now that you have the overview, I will discuss specific nutrients and the research evaluating their role in the therapy of cognitive disorders.

Choline

Choline helps form phosphatidylcholine, the primary phospholipid of cell membranes. Choline also helps form acetylcholine, one of the important brain chemicals involved in memory. This nutrient, usually as part of phosphatidylcholine, is widely available in a number of foods, particularly eggs, fish, legumes, nuts, meats and vegetables, as well as in human breast milk. Dietary intake of choline ranges from 300 to 900 mg a day.

Most individuals who have a normal diet are not deficient in choline. The importance of choline was emphasized in 1998 when the National Academy of Sciences classified it as an essential nutrient. Previously, it was believed that the human body made adequate amounts of choline when needed. However, a study by Dr. Steven Zeisel, from the Department of Nutrition at the University of North Carolina at Chapel Hill, demonstrated that volunteers on a choline-deficient diet were not able to produce enough of this nutrient (Zeisel 1991).

According to the results of several studies in rats, providing choline during pregnancy enhances memory and learning capacity in the fetus (Williams 1998). Dr. Christina Williams, a behavioral neuroscientist at Duke University in Durham, North Carolina, says her study findings demonstrate "that supplementation with choline during the last third of pregnancy has fairly dramatic and long-lasting effects on the memory of offspring."

Several other studies have been done administering choline to humans in order to evaluate memory function. The results have been mixed, with some showing positive results (Sitaran 1978) while others indicate no improvement (Mohs 1980).

Choline has also been tested in bipolar disorder, also known as manic-depression. When six patients already on lithium were given choline bitartrate, five of them had a substantial reduction in manic symptoms (Stoll 1996). More recent research suggests that choline helps lithium work better. (Moore 2000).

A 1997 study published in *Advances in Pediatrics* by Dr. Zeisel showed that choline reserves are depleted during pregnancy and lactation (Zeisel 1997). This depletion may affect normal brain development and memory in the offspring. The National Academy of Sciences suggests that pregnant women consume at least 450 milligrams of choline per day.

Availability and Dosage: Choline is sold in vitamin stores in doses ranging from 250 to 500 mg, and in a number of forms including choline bitartrate, choline chloride and choline citrate.

The Author's Experience: Within a few hours of taking choline, I notice an improvement in focus that lasts most of the day. I have not experienced side effects with dosages smaller than 500 mg. On a dosage of 1,500 mg, I experienced increased body warmth.

 Cautions and Side Effects

A high intake of choline is associated with mild gastrointestinal distress, nausea, sweating and loss of appetite (Wood 1982).

 Recommendations

Individuals whose diet includes a wide variety of foods are not likely to suffer from choline deficiency. Growing infants, pregnant or lactating women, and individuals with liver cirrhosis may be deficient in choline (Zeisel 1994). Whether choline supplements benefit older individuals with age-related memory decline has not yet been adequately determined.

Because of its relative safety and potential benefits, I recommend small amounts of choline for the elderly who have age-related cognitive decline (see Chapter 18 for specific recommendations). Choline can be taken occasionally by younger individuals on days when better concentration and focus would be helpful.

CDP-Choline

CDP-choline stands for cytidine 5-diphosphocholine. This nutrient is approved in Europe and Japan for use in stroke, Parkinson's disease and other neurological disorders (Secades 1995). In a way, you might consider CDP-choline as a more potent form of choline. Studies show that CDP-choline helps make phosphatidylcholine (PC) in human brain-cell membranes in older individuals (Babb 1996).

CDP-choline may also increase acetylcholine synthesis and improve mental performance in patients with Alzheimer's disease who have been given a daily dose of 1000 mg per day (Cacabelos 1996). The nutrient even improves memory in elderly patients with memory deficits (Alvarez 1997). A Belgian study has shown that administrating CDP-choline to dogs improves their ability to learn and remember (Bruhwyler 1998).

Dr. Vittorio Porciatti at the Institute of Neurophysiology in Pisa, Italy, tells me…

      66 CDP-choline is commercially produced in Europe under several product names. Neurologists have found this nutrient useful in Parkinson's disease, brain trauma and aging in general. It may surprise you that I mention Parkinson's disease. In addition to the understandable action on cell membranes, we have been somehow surprised that CDP-choline has dopamine-like effects. Interestingly, dopaminergic-like activity seems to be long-lasting, possibly due to stabilization of the effects at membrane level. We have found no significant side effects with CDP-choline even for long therapy cycles. In one study we gave a dosage of 1 gram a day for fifteen days to young individuals. They reported improvement in visual clarity. (Porciatti 1998). 99

Availability and Dosage: CDP-choline became available over-the-counter in the U.S. in 1998, but it's expensive and not widely distributed. Most pills come in a 250 mg dose.

The Author's Experience: Within an hour of taking a 250 mg CDP-choline pill on an empty stomach, I notice feeling more alert and motivated. The effects last a few hours. In addition, colors seem brighter and sharper, and occasionally I have noticed a slight libido enhancement. Because of the alertness it produces, I have difficulty sleeping if I take this nutrient in late afternoon or early evening.

 Cautions and Side Effects

Toxicology studies show that CDP-choline is safe and produces no serious side effects in doses ranging from 500 to 1,000 mg a day (Secades 1995). However, most of the studies lasted less than a few weeks. *Long-term safety is not known.*

 Recommendations

CDP-choline has been used successfully in Europe for many years, but clinical experience in the U.S. is limited. This nutrient appears to have a more direct and immediate effect on the brain than its cousin choline. However, it is difficult to predict at this time the long-term benefits or risks of regular use.

CDP-choline is a promising nutrient and I suspect that with time it will become more popular in the U.S. Eventually we may find that it has a role in the therapy of certain neurological conditions such as Alzheimer's disease and perhaps Parkinson's disease. Combining choline, lecithin and CDP-choline for therapeutic purposes is an interesting concept that has not yet been formally tested.

Phosphatidylcholine (Lecithin)

Lecithin is also known as phosphatidylcholine (PC), although lecithin is also a term loosely applied to describe a combination of PC with other phospholipids. Most people normally ingest 3 to 6 grams of lecithin a day through eggs, soy and meats. Vegetables, fruits and grains contain very little lecithin.

PC is the most abundant phospholipid component in all cells. PC levels in brain-cell membranes decline with age.

Several studies have been done with PC to investigate its effects on memory. The results of the studies have not been consistent. Some have shown positive responses (Labell 1998, Ladd 1993), while others showed no difference in memory or learning after lecithin administration (Gillin 1980).

Lecithin has even been evaluated in Parkinson's disease (Tweedy 1982). In this nine-week-long double-blind study, sixteen elderly patients took a daily dose of approximately 32 grams of a commercial lecithin preparation. Marked clinical improvement was not observed, but there was a slight improvement in memory, cognition and motility. And a review of 12 studies finds that using lecithin helps improve memory in those with Alzheimer's (Higgins 2000).

Availability and Dosage: Lecithin is sold in the form of liquid, capsules or granules. The amount of PC in each product varies between different brands. The lecithin you buy in a health-food store will generally include about 10 to 70 percent PC, along with other lipids. Different types of lecithin will differ in their lipid compositions depending on the source of the lecithin—soy or egg yolk—or the extraction process.

The Author's Experience: I have interviewed many individuals who have taken lecithin in order to improve cognition. The reports have not been impressive. The majority of users do not notice any obvious benefits from lecithin.

Lecithin does not provide me with cognitive effects. I have taken fifteen capsules a day of lecithin for a week without a noticeable effect on alertness, vision, or mood. Each capsule contained 1,200 mg of PC.

 Recommendations

Research findings regarding the role of PC in cognition have not been consistent. My professional and personal experience with PC does not indicate that this supplement has any dramatic effects on mental abilities. Based on the available evidence, it appears that the cognitive benefits of taking lecithin are likely to be minor.

As a rule, individuals who consume a wide variety of foods are not likely to suffer from PC deficiency. Whether lecithin supplements benefit a subgroup of seniors with age-related memory decline has not yet been adequately determined. It is certainly possible that there are those who may have a biochemical difficulty in making adequate amounts of PC and would benefit from additional supplementation.

If you are planning to take lecithin, keep your dosage low such as 3 grams a day or less.

Phosphatidylserine (PS)

Although lecithin (PC) has been available as a supplement for many decades, PS became available to the North American market in

the mid-1990s. In the past, PS was obtained from the brains of cows. In fact, when you read some of the research studies published on PS, it will identify this nutrient as BC-PS. The BC stands for "bovine cortex," or cow brain. The reason BC-PS is not sold is because of the fear of viruses or infectious agents being inadvertently introduced in the PS product when extracted from the brains of cows. The PS currently available over-the-counter is derived from soy.

Several studies have evaluated the role of oral administration of BC-PS in both animals and humans. In general, the results have shown positive benefits. However, we need to keep a very important point in mind. The studies with PS have used bovine cortex as the source.

Can we assume that the scientific results with soy-derived PS would be similar? Each PS molecule contains two fatty acids. The fatty acids in PS derived from soy are mostly 16- and 18-carbon molecules such as palmitic, oleic, linoleic and linolenic acids. These are small-chain fatty acids and have fewer double bonds than the fatty acids in PS derived from bovine brains, such as arachidonic acid and DHA, which are polyunsaturated and have longer chains of 20 and 22 carbons.

Human studies with soy-derived PS have not been published in reliable, peer-reviewed journals. However, there have been a number of studies evaluating the role of bovine-derived PS in cognitive function, particularly in age-associated memory impairment and Alzheimer's disease. Most of these studies have indicated that BC-PS improves memory and cognition in those with age-related cognitive decline (Crook

1991, Cenacchi 1993), and helps improve memory and recall in patients with Alzheimer's disease (Engel 1992, Crook 1992). However, other studies have found no improvement (Jorisse 2001).

Companies promoting soy-PS make positive claims about this supplement and defend their promotion by citing research studies done on BC-PS. I interviewed many experts on fats, including Drs. Simopoulos, Horrocks, Schmidt, Hibbeln and Salem, regarding their opinions on PS. All of these experts were unanimous in their assessment that the studies done with bovine-derived PS cannot automatically be used to claim the same benefits from soy-PS.

The Research: Dr. Arjan Blokland and colleagues from the Brain & Behavior Institute in Maastricht, The Netherlands, investigated the cognition-enhancing properties of different types of PS in rats. In the study, seventeen-month-old rats were treated daily for four weeks with a dose of 15mg/kg of PS derived from bovine cortex (BC-PS), soybeans (S-PS), egg (E-PS) or placebo. The substance was administered by injection into the abdominal cavity, whereas in humans it would be taken orally. The dose administered (15 mg/kg) is equivalent, by weight ratio, to about a 1,000 mg daily dose in humans.

The Results: It appeared that the cognition-enhancing effects of the soybean formula were not different from those of bovine formula. However, the egg-derived formula did not produce any improvement in cognition. The authors concluded that on the basis of their study, that soybean formula (S-PS) but not the egg-derived formula may have comparable effects on cognition as the bovine formula (BC-PS).

I interviewed Dr. Blokland regarding his findings. *He told me…*

" In our research group we have had lively discussions regarding the blood-brain barrier crossing of PS. Some of my colleagues did not believe that this molecule could pass the BBB….But others did not agree. Our human psychopharmacology unit also conducted a study with PS but did not find a positive effect on cognitive performance (unpublished data). They suggested that the PS was metabolized too rapidly and that not enough PS entered the brain. We are now planning an actual study in which we would like to apply radio-labeled PS in order to determine the activity of the labeled PS in the membrane fraction of rat brain tissue. That should answer our questions.

It is unclear to us why egg PS showed inactivity, whereas soy PS was active…. We can therefore only speculate that the egg PS may have lost bioactivity because of the breakdown of the bioactive compound during processing or storage. We were surprised by this finding but we do not have a clue for this behavioral observation. "

Availability and Dosage: Bovine cortex (BC-PS) is not available in the United States, but soy-derived PS is sold in vitamin stores. Each 500 mg gel capsule contains several phospholipids, with 100 mg consisting of actual PS. This is an expensive nutrient; each pill costs between 50 cents and one dollar. It is worth emphasizing again that the PS currently available is derived from soy products and thus has a different fatty-acid composition and chemical makeup than the bovine cortex-derived PS used in published studies.

The Author's Experience: I interviewed thirty individuals who have taken PS. The majority of them did not notice an effect from this nutrient. A majority reported minimal benefits in alertness and memory. Overall, in my opinion, the results were not impressive.

I have also taken soy-derived PS in dosages ranging from 100 to 1,400 mg. I do not notice an effect when taking a dosage lower than 300 mg. With higher amounts, I've noticed a mild enhancement in alertness, concentration and focus. These effects would persist late into the evening. No changes in my vision were apparent.

On the downside, I had a slight feeling of malaise and my mood was lowered. In my experience, the short-term effects from soy-PS are not as dramatic as those from choline and some of the other nutrients discussed in this book. Perhaps a person older than me, who lacks PS in his or her brain-cell membranes, may notice the effects of PS more clearly.

 Cautions and Side Effects

Short-term human studies have found few side effects from supplemental intake of PS. *The long-term effects are not known.* It's possible that PS could influence, positively or negatively, the immune system, the function of red blood cells or produce other effects. PS is found in the inner cell membrane of red blood cells and is involved in the process of blood-clotting. We don't know whether excess intake of PS will alter red-blood-cell membranes and increase the propensity for clots.

One Japanese study raises a concern (Uchida 1998). In that study, cells removed from Chinese hamster ovaries were incubated with PS and other phospholipids such as PC. The cells exposed

to PS became damaged, shrank and died, while those exposed to the other phospholipids were not affected. The clinical significance of this study is currently not known.

 Recommendations

Many human studies have shown BC-PS to have benefits in the therapy of cognitive impairment.

One study on soy-derived PS published in *Nutrition Neuroscience* in 2001 finds no improvement in memory from taking the supplement in either 300-milligram or 600-milligram doses (Jorisse 2001).

As to the effectiveness of soy-PS compared to BS-PC, I agree with the experts cited here that it is not scientifically acceptable to make claims regarding benefits of soy-PS using the results obtained from the bovine variety (BC-PS).

Since we only have soy-PS available over-the-counter, one interesting option is to take fish-oil capsules along with it. This way it's possible that we may more closely mimic the results of the studies done with BC-PS. Dr. Hibbeln says, "Available data in both rodents and in cell culture indicate that the rate of PS synthesis depends on the availability of DHA." However, whether taking fish oils along with PS will be advantageous is difficult to predict.

We need several studies published with soy-PS before we have a better grasp of its clinical uses. I have not yet established a firm opinion on whether the potential benefits of soy-PS supplementation will justify its cost. Most younger and middle-aged individuals who have a good diet that includes eggs, soy and other sources of phospholipids and omega-3 oils will not need additional PS. However, it's possible that a subgroup of older patients with age-related cognitive decline might potentially benefit from PS supplements.

With the availability of choline, CDP-choline, PC and PS, how do you decide which ones to choose? Unfortunately, not enough research is yet available to provide firm recommendations.

Of the four nutrients discussed in this chapter, I've personally noticed the clearest immediate effects from choline and CDP-choline. However, it is difficult to predict which of these nutrients provides the best long-term benefits with the least risk. Noticing an immediate effect from a nutrient does not mean that it is the best choice for long-term therapy.

Many of the nutrients discussed in this chapter may prove to have overlapping physiological functions and effects. One approach is to try each one separately to determine which one(s) provide the clearest benefit. ⬛

MOOD AND ENERGY BOOSTERS
B VITAMINS AND COENZYMES

A B-vitamin supplement is the cheapest, safest and most reliable way to improve your well-being and overall mental ability. I recommend the Bs to those who wish to improve their mood, mental clarity and energy. The effects of the B vitamins are subtle, especially in young people who normally have adequate dietary intake of these nutrients. Improvements in cognitive functions from the B vitamins are particularly noticeable in middle-aged individuals and the elderly.

In addition to discussing the B vitamins, this chapter will review coenzymes—the newer, more activated forms of the B vitamins—and make recommendations on how to reduce levels of homocysteine, an amino acid derivative that can be harmful to the cardiovascular and neurological system when present in excess.

The Bs in the Brain Get an A

B vitamins help in energy production and deficiencies in the Bs can lead to fatigue and poor mental functioning. The increased consumption of refined foods has decreased the amounts of B vitamins present in our diet.

However, on a more positive note, small amounts of B vitamins are regularly added to some food products, such as cereals.

The question of whether B-vitamin supplementation is necessary in healthy individuals who have a normal diet has been debated ever since vitamins were discovered. The results of several studies over the past few years have influenced my decision in favor of low-dose supplementation.

There can be cognitive improvements from taking B vitamins. Back in 1995, Dr. David Benton and colleagues from the University College Swansea in Great Britain gave ten times the recommended daily allowance of nine vitamins (mostly the B vitamins) to healthy college students (Benton 1995). The study lasted for one year. During that time, the students reported improvement in mood and feeling more agreeable. They also showed an improvement in cognitive functioning, especially in regards to concentration.

Many of my patients consistently report that B-vitamin supplementation improves their energy, concentration and mood while helping them handle everyday stress better. More recently, Australian researchers reported in the *Journal of Nutrition* that a daily vitamin B complex supplement helped improve memory and

59

BENEFITS OF B VITAMINS

Since B vitamins and their coenzymes play important metabolic roles in numerous biochemical reactions throughout the body, they can influence just about every aspect of brain and physical health. *As a rule, individuals who take B vitamins notice improvements in...*

- Mood and energy
- Alertness
- Learning and memory
- Speed of thinking

- Verbal fluency
- Concentration and focus
- Visual clarity

WHICH CLINICAL CONDITIONS DO THE Bs BENEFIT?

Because of their wide range of effects, B vitamins and their coenzymes can potentially be helpful in...

- Depression
- Age-related cognitive decline
- Anxiety disorders
- Alzheimer's disease

- Chronic fatigue
- Addiction disorders
- Parkinson's disease

mental performance in 211 healthy women, but not mood (Bryan 2002).

For individuals who are otherwise healthy, supplementation with one to three times the recommended daily allowance of the B vitamins is suggested. Higher dosages may be required for individuals with medical, psychiatric or neurological disorders.

Understanding Coenzymes

In the past few years, many of the B vitamins have become available in their more activated forms known as *coenzymes*. For instance, the B-vitamin niacin is now available in a coenzyme form known as NADH. An enzyme is basically a protein that promotes chemical changes in other substances, itself remaining unchanged in the process. A coenzyme is a substance that facilitates or is necessary for the action of an enzyme.

The brain, just like a car, needs fuel. Our primary source of fuel is through fats, proteins and carbohydrates in the diet. After digestion in the stomach, foodstuffs are absorbed into the bloodstream and circulate to various tissues and cells where they are broken down into even smaller particles. One of these particles is a two-carbon molecule known as acetyl. Enzymes help break down these fats, proteins, and carbohydrates into acetyl, and they then help extract the final energy from acetyl through a process called the Krebs cycle, named after the German biochemist who defined it. This energy is in the form of ATP (adenosine triphosphate).

Enzymes also need helpers, and these helpers are called coenzymes. Most of the coenzymes in the body are partly made from vitamins, such as vitamins E, C, lipoic acid and riboflavin (vitamin B-2).

The coenzyme form of a B vitamin often has a significantly more powerful effect than a regular B vitamin. The coenzyme forms of the B vitamins are an exciting addition to the field of nutrition. It is quite possible that the elderly or certain individuals with a particular biochemical deficiency may not be able to make adequate amounts of the coenzyme forms of the B vitamins despite adequate intakes of the individual B vitamins. Hence the coenzyme forms should be seriously considered as a supplement in those who do not respond to the regular B vitamins. Some companies include most of the Bs in their coenzyme form together in one pill. I think these products deserve serious consideration, especially for their use in the middle-aged and the elderly.

The Individual B Vitamins and Their Coenzymes

Thiamin (B-1) is necessary for the metabolism of carbohydrates and amino acids to adenosine triphosphate (ATP), the primary source of energy in the human body. Thiamin is found in good amounts in milk, lean pork, legumes, rice bran and the germ of cereal grains, but is lost during food processing and cooking. The current recommended daily allowance (RDA) by government advisory panels is about 1.5 mg.

Studies indicate that a thiamin deficiency may increase risk of cognitive problems, and that supplementation with thiamin provides benefits. In one study, researchers gave 50 mg of thiamin daily to young adult females for a period of two months (Benton 1997). The women reported being more clearheaded, composed and energetic. The taking of thiamin had no influence on memory, but reaction times were faster following supplementation. Prior to taking the thiamin, the women had normal blood levels of this vitamin.

Researchers at Princess Margaret Hospital in Christchurch, New Zealand, measured thiamin levels in elderly individuals before giving them 10 mg of the vitamin a day (Wilkinson 1997). Only the subjects with low thiamin concentrations showed benefits. They had an improvement in quality of life, with more energy and deeper sleep, along with decreased blood pressure and weight.

Thiamin is now also sold in its coenzyme form, called cocarboxylase or thiamin pyrophosphate (TPP). Human studies giving TPP to evaluate cognitive functioning have not yet been published.

Riboflavin (B-2) is a yellow-colored nutrient involved in dozens of metabolic pathways leading to energy production and the making of fatty acids and sterols. Good sources are lean meats, eggs, milk, certain vegetables and enriched cereals. The recommended daily intake is about 1.5 mg. You may notice your urine turning a deeper-yellow color after taking riboflavin.

Riboflavin is part of two larger activated coenzymes known as flavin adenine dinucleotide (FAD) and flavin mononucleotide (FMN). FMN is now available as a supplement. One product contains 25 mg of FMN per pill. Human studies giving FAD or FMN in order to evaluate cognitive functioning have not yet been published.

Niacin (B-3), also known as nicotinamide and nicotinic acid, plays essential roles in a large number of energy pathways. Perhaps as many as 200 enzymes are dependent on this nutrient.

Nicotinamide is part of the coenzyme known as nicotinamide adenine dinucleotide (NADH), which itself is sold as a supplement. I will discuss NADH later in this chapter since several studies have been published regarding this coenzyme. Good sources of niacin are meats, legumes, fish and some nuts and cereals. The recommended daily intake is about 15 to 20 mg.

Pantothenic acid (B-5) is essential for biological reactions involving acetylation and energy production. This vitamin helps in the formation of acetylcholine, the metabolism of fatty acids, and the incorporation of fatty acids into cell-membrane phospholipids. Pantothenic acid is also involved in making steroid hormones, vitamin A, vitamin D and cholesterol. Good sources are egg yolk and fresh vegetables. The recommended daily intake is about 5 mg. Pantothenic acid is sold over-the-counter in dosages ranging from 5 to 250 mg.

My patients report that pantothenic acid helps improve their mood and energy. Personally, I notice an improvement in alertness, concentration, energy, and visual clarity with dosages ranging from 100 to 250 mg. I do experience insomnia, though, when I take more than 250 mg, even if I take it in the morning. *Benita von Klingspor, a nutritionist in Marina del Rey, California, says...*

66 Pantothenic acid is one of my favorite nutrients. I know the effects of this nutrient extremely well, since I've been taking 100 to 250 mg most mornings for more than thirty years. I often recommend it to many clients with low energy. Pantothenic acid increases their alertness and focus, improves their mood, and enhances their joy in life. They begin to have more interest in whatever they're doing. However, if people take too much pantothenic acid, they can become overstimulated, wired, and easily aggravated. 99

Pantothenic acid is available in its activated form, known as pantethine. Pantethine itself is part of coenzyme A, a very important substance that participates in the metabolism of carbohydrates, amino acids, fatty acids and dozens of other important chemical reactions. The cognitive effects of oral administration of pantethine to humans have not been published. Pantethene is sold over-the-counter in doses ranging from 5 to 50 mg. In my experience, a lower dosage of *pantethine* provides similar effects as a higher dosage of *pantothenic* acid.

Pyridoxine (B-6), also known as pyridoxal, is widely available in most foods including vegetables, legumes, nuts, seeds and animal products. The coenzyme form of pyridoxine is pyridoxal phosphate (PLP), and at least 100 different metabolic reactions are helped by PLP. *PLP is a necessary coenzyme in the production of brain chemicals:* It helps the conversion of 5-HTP into serotonin, tyrosine into dopamine and norepinephrine and the production of other neurotransmitters such as histamine and GABA. The recommended daily intake is about 1.5 mg. Deficiencies in B-6 can lead to lowered mood.

Human studies with B-6 in mood disorders and depression have not yet been published. PLP is available in pills ranging from 5 to 20 mg. Some individuals notice the difference between regular B-6 and the coenzyme form. Joan, a fifty-three-year-old patient from Beverly Hills, California, says, "I've taken good-quality B vitamins for a few years. Recently I tried the pyridoxal phosphate form of B-6. It really has increased my energy, mood, and alertness."

Folic acid, also known as *folate,* generally functions in cooperation with vitamin B-12 in many metabolic reactions, including the synthesis of DNA. Folic acid helps reduce levels of homocysteine, a substance that can increase the risk for atherosclerosis (discussed later in this chapter). This vitamin functions as a methyl donor (see Chapter 10). Folic acid is found in almost all foods, and the recommended daily intake is about 400 micrograms. The coenzyme form of folate is called tetrahydrofolate.

Cobalamin (B-12), or cyanocobalamin, has a number of important roles in metabolism, including the synthesis of DNA. This function is particularly crucial when it comes to making new red blood cells. Therefore, a deficiency of B-12 leads to anemia. The formation of myelin—the white sheath surrounding nerves—is partly dependent on B-12. Deficiencies in B-12 intake lead to nerve damage, memory loss, poor coordination, lowered mood and mental slowness. This nutrient, along with folic acid and B-6 helps to lower levels of homocysteine. High homocysteine levels are suspected to be one of the factors causing hardening of the arteries.

The recommended daily intake of B-12 is about 3 micrograms, but much higher dosages are well tolerated. B-12 is found mostly in meats and fish. Vegetarians can become deficient in this vitamin if they don't take supplements. B-12 deficiency can occur in the elderly due to malabsorption from the intestinal tract.

If you have gastritis, absorption problems, autoimmune disorders, insulin-dependent diabetes, certain thyroid disorders or if you take antacids or other medicines that reduce stomach acid, you could have problems maintaining adequate B-12 levels. Hence, a monthly B-12 shot, in a dose of 1 mg

(1,000 micrograms) could well provide you with positive cognitive benefits. Sublingual forms of B-12 which dissolve under the tongue are also available.

There are two coenzyme forms of B-12, adenosylcobalamin and methylcobalamin. Adenosylcobalamin is sold over-the-counter as dibencozide, in a dose of 10,000 micrograms (10 mg), which is a large dose. Human studies evaluating its role in cognitive disorders have not been published. It's quite possible that with age, nutritional deficiencies, or enzyme deficiencies, some individuals may not be able to convert B-12 into its coenzyme forms.

Biotin is involved in the metabolism of carbohydrates and fats. It is widely available in foods, particularly egg yolk, soybeans, cereal, legumes and nuts. Bacteria in the gastrointestinal system also make it. The RDA ranges from 30 to 100 micrograms.

☑ Recommendations

All of the B vitamins are important, and supplementation would probably benefit most everyone. For healthy individuals, taking one to three times the RDA of the Bs would be sufficient. You will find B complex supplements that say "B-50" or "B-100" on the label. This means that many of the B vitamins, such as thiamin and riboflavin, are found in dosages of 50 or 100 mg per pill. The RDA for thiamin and riboflavin is about 1.5 mg. The average, healthy person does not need to take such high dosages. However, individual needs for supplements will vary.

Dr. David Benton, Ph.D., who researches the influence of B vitamins on cognition, says, "There can be enormous differences in the needs of vitamins. It wouldn't be unusual for some individuals requiring twenty times the amount of a particular vitamin compared to others in a similar age group."

In Part V you will find recommendations on B-vitamin dosages according to age groups, and Part VI has dosage suggestions for those with mood disorders, Alzheimer's disease or Parkinson's disease.

NADH (Nicotinamide Adenine Dinucleotide)

I remember my high-school biology class where I first tried to learn the complicated Krebs cycle and how energy was derived from sugars, amino acids and fats. I did recall coming across NADH (nicotinamide adenine dinucleotide), a coenzyme that helps in this complicated process of energy extraction. Although NADH is only one of the B-vitamin coenzymes discussed earlier in this chapter, it has been studied more thoroughly than the other coenzymes. NADH has been promoted very heavily through ads and magazine articles ever since it was introduced to the health industry in the mid-1990s.

One of the functions of NADH is to help convert the amino acid tyrosine into the important brain chemical dopamine. Dopamine is involved in regulating mood, energy, sexual drive, concentration, memory and muscle movement. NADH may also regenerate the antioxidant glutathione (see Chapter 11). NADH is normally found in meat, fish and poultry. Fruits and vegetables contain very little of the substance.

Most users report that NADH improves mood, energy, vision, alertness and sexual

interest. Mark, a fifty-six-year-old accountant from Oakland, California, is a satisfied consumer of NADH. He says, "I have been taking 2.5 mg of NADH three times a week for the last few months, and my brain's working again. I can think clearer and sharper."

Another case is Shelly, from Mission Viejo, California, who reports that "NADH makes me more alert and provides a sense of well-being. I currently take it about once a week."

According to Georg Birkmayer, M.D., an Austrian researcher whose family has been instrumental in developing a trademarked NADH product, "NADH energizes both body and brain activity, improves alertness, concentration, emotion, drive and overall mood enhancement." Dr. Birkmayer also says that no adverse or side effects have been reported with NADH. He further claims that NADH improves memory, slows the aging process and is helpful in a variety of conditions including Alzheimer's disease, Parkinson's disease, chronic fatigue syndrome, depression and overall lack of energy.

Are any of these claims true?

A small number of short-term studies done with NADH have shown that NADH has *slight-to-moderate* benefits in regards to depression, Parkinson's disease and Alzheimer's disease (Birkmayer 1991, 1993, and 1996). An eight-week double-blind study done at Georgetown University Medical Center found some patients with chronic fatigue syndrome to benefit from taking NADH at a daily dose of 10 mg (Forsyth 1998). However, long-term studies are required to determine if benefits from taking daily NADH continue with time, or whether tolerance develops.

Availability and Dosage: Most of the NADH pills come in doses of 2.5 and 5 mg. Individually sealed, airtight pills are a good option. One of the shortcomings with NADH is its cost, which can be close to a dollar a pill.

NADH is best taken in the morning, generally on an empty stomach. Alertness and mental clarity are often noticed within a few hours. Be careful when using multiple supplements that increase energy since their effects can be cumulative and lead to over-stimulation.

The Author's Experience: Does NADH really improve energy, concentration, and mood? I have taken NADH on numerous occasions. Within an hour or two of swallowing a pill on an empty stomach in the morning, I notice an increase in alertness, feelings of well-being, vitality, visual clarity and sexual interest. The effects last most of the day. However, I do develop a tolerance to NADH if I take it regularly.

 ### Cautions and Side Effects
Reports of untoward effects from the use of a 2.5 mg dose of NADH are infrequent. Higher doses can some-times lead to insomnia, anxiety, fatigue and overstimulation. George, a forty-two-year-old lawyer from Philadelphia, says, "I like the 2.5 mg dose of NADH because of the alertness it provides. However, when I take 5 mg or more, it makes me too stimulated, almost with a panicky feeling." As more individuals start taking NADH, we may find additional reports of side effects.

 ### Special Cautions
The risk of side effects increases when NADH is combined with other stimulants. A few patients have found that high dosages used daily for prolonged periods led to mood swings, anxiety and sleeplessness, which resolved when the NADH was stopped. Until we learn more about the long-term effects of NADH, I do not recommend its use on a daily basis for prolonged periods.

One user noticed that NADH helped her chronic fatigue, but had difficulty when she stopped. Betty, a thirty-six-year-old homemaker from Houston, says, "I have chronic fatigue syndrome [CFS], and was taking 10 mg of NADH daily. I know it really helped my energy level and mood. But I began to have stomach upset from it and stopped for a few days. I then fell quickly into a very bad CFS 'crash,' the worst one in months." I recommended that Betty only take 2.5 mg of NADH every other day.

 ### Recommendations
Studies with NADH have been short-term and therefore make it difficult to give definitive recommendations on its long-term benefits. Could side effects develop that we are not currently aware of? It is unlikely that NADH alone will be the magic bullet in Parkinson's disease, Alzheimer's disease, chronic fatigue syndrome and other conditions. However, if longer-term studies do confirm some of the minor benefits reported in preliminary findings, NADH could be an additional supplement doctors can recommend in the fight against certain chronic neurological diseases. And NADH, along with other B-vitamin coenzymes, could well be useful in age-related cognitive decline.

If you plan to take NADH on a regular basis, I would recommend you limit your frequency to no more than three

Figure 9.1—The Role of B Vitamins in Homocysteine Metabolism

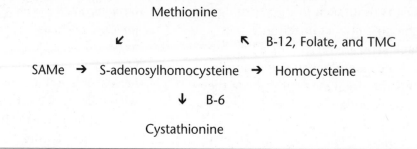

B Vitamins and Homocysteine

times a week. Please keep in mind, though, that the other B vitamins are also very important.

B Vitamins and Homocysteine

Homocysteine is a derivative of the amino acid methionine. It received a great deal of media attention in 1997 following publication of articles in medical journals indicating that a high blood level of homocysteine is a potential risk factor for atherosclerosis and heart disease.

Kilmer McCully, M.D., a pathologist at the Veterans Affairs Medical Center in Providence, Rhode Island, had been claiming for at least two decades that homocysteine is as important a risk factor for heart disease as cholesterol, but few in the medical profession paid serious attention to his claim. Dr. McCully was vindicated with the publication of additional scientific articles in the 1990s, most of which confirmed the dangers of elevated homocysteine levels. Fortunately, homocysteine levels can be easily lowered by taking supplements of B vitamins, particularly folic acid, B-6, and B-12 (see Figure 9.1).

In addition to contributing to cardiovascular conditions, homocysteine may also be detrimental to the brain since it can act as a toxin to brain cells. One study in *Neurology* finds that brain shrinkage is twice as likely to occur in elderly people with high homocysteine levels (Sachdev 2002). And another study in the *New England Journal of Medicine* suggests that increased homocysteine levels are "a strong, independent risk factor for the development of dementia and Alzheimer's disease" (Seshadri 2002).

Homocysteine is a reliable sign of vitamin B-12 deficiency, a common condition in the elderly, which is known to cause neurological deficits including cognitive impairment. Geriatric patients suffering from depression and dementia are often found to be deficient in folate. Furthermore, deficiencies in either of these vitamins (B-6 or B-12) lead to a decrease in SAMe and an increase in homocysteine, which can be critical in the aging brain." (I discuss SAMe in Chapter 10.)

Adequate intakes of folic acid, B-6 and B-12 will assure that homocysteine levels are kept low. Considering the possibility that there may be individuals, especially the elderly, who are deficient in B-6, folic acid, and B-12, an inexpensive and simple way to decrease the rate of damage to the brain from homocysteine would be by supplementing with these vitamins (Woodside 1998).

Nutritionists at Tufts University in Boston have also found a connection between B vitamins, homocysteine and memory. They investigated the relationship between blood concentrations of homocysteine and vitamins B-12, B-6 and folate, and scores from a battery of cognitive tests for seventy male subjects, 54 to 81 years old (Riggs 1996). The study showed that lower concentrations of vitamin B-12 and folate and higher concentrations of homocysteine were associated with poorer memory.

Summary

Because of the important role of each of the B vitamins in brain function, it makes sense that they should be consumed as a group instead of taking large amounts of one or two. As a general guideline, it would be reasonable to take a supplement providing at least one to three times the RDA for these vitamins. Perhaps higher would be even more beneficial in certain individuals. A multivitamin bottle will list on the label the percentage of the RDA (or PDV—percent daily value) contained for each of the different vitamins. Let's say the RDA for thiamin is 1.5 mg. A reasonable dosage for the pills you buy could be anywhere between 1 and 5 mg. Make sure that the B vitamins contained in the pill are balanced and that you are not consuming large doses of some while getting little or none of the others.

An exciting development over the past few years has been the introduction of the coenzyme form of the vitamins. It will take more research to evaluate many of these coenzymes and to determine who will best benefit from them and how they can be ideally combined for optimal brain function.

10

METHYL DONORS
FOR MORE ENERGY, BETTER MOOD

Unless your major in college was chemistry, chances are you don't remember learning about *methyl donors*. But if you find the field of brain nutrients and anti-aging health interesting, you will certainly want to learn more about these supplements.

A methyl donor is simply any substance that can transfer a methyl group (a carbon atom attached to three hydrogen atoms [CH3]) to another substance. Many important biochemical processes rely on *methylation,* including the metabolism of lipids and DNA. Scientists suspect that adequate methylation

of DNA can prevent the expression of harmful genes, such as cancer genes. It's quite likely that our body's ability to methylate declines with age, contributing to the aging process. Therefore, supplementation could well be beneficial for many people. The research in this area is still very new, and no firm answers are yet available. But one scientist is quite enthusiastic about methyl donors. Craig Cooney, Ph.D., Research Assistant Professor at University of Arkansas for Medical Sciences, Little Rock, Arkansas, is an expert on methylation and the author of scientific articles and a book on this topic. "I've been taking 250 mg of TMG a day since 1991," he says. "In my opinion,

WHAT CAN METHYL DONORS DO FOR YOU?

Methyl donors help in the production of several brain chemicals and hence improve mood, energy, well-being, alertness, concentration and visual clarity. A few people notice enhanced sexual enjoyment.

WHAT CONDITIONS CAN METHYL DONORS BENEFIT?

Methyl donors may be helpful in age-related cognitive decline, Alzheimer's disease, fighting depression and overall health maintenance. They may also be found to be helpful in Parkinson's disease.

methyl donors have the potential to slow the aging process."

In the preceding chapter, I explained that two of the B vitamins, folic acid and B-12, are also methyl donors. This chapter discusses four additional nutrients involved in methylation—TMG, DMG, SAMe and DMAE. All but SAMe have been sold over-the-counter for a number of years. SAMe became available in the U.S. in 1996. Interestingly, some vegetables, such as onions, garlic and beets, contain methyl donors (McCully 1997).

TMG (Trimethylglycine) and DMG (Dimethylglycine)

Trimethylglycine, or TMG, also known as betaine, is basically the amino acid glycine attached to three methyl groups. Dimethylglycine (DMG) is similar to trimethylglycine, except it has two methyl groups. You may recall that a "methyl group" is a carbon attached to three hydrogen atoms (CH_3). Both of these nutrients are powerful methyl donors. Methylation is an important factor in many biochemical processes in the human body.

In Chapter 9, I described how the B vitamins folic acid and B-12 reduce levels of homocysteine, the harmful substance in blood that can cause hardening of the arteries and possibly damage brain cells. By reducing homocysteine levels, you may reduce the risk for heart disease. TMG and DMG are also known to reduce homocysteine levels and therefore might be helpful in reducing the rate of heart disease. It's possible that supplementation with TMG or DMG may provide health and anti-aging benefits.

Methyl donors are also involved in the making of brain chemicals, which accounts for their cognitive effects. My clinical experience confirms that both TMG and DMG improve mood and energy.

As an example, Brian, a twenty-nine-year-old laboratory technician from Torrance, California, speaks for many when he says, "TMG gives me more energy and clearer thinking. There's a sense of well-being that comes on that lasts all day." *Paul Frankel, Ph.D., coauthor with Fred Madsen, Ph.D., of a book on methylation, says...*

> **""** I've been taking TMG since 1995 at a dose of 250 mg a day. Through my interviews with individuals who have taken TMG, I have come across many who report benefits—sleeping better, having more energy and experiencing less chronic fatigue. TMG could also jump-start some people and help them fight their depression. A woman whose daughter was suffering with depression told me, "TMG gave me my daughter back." **""**

Dr. Madsen adds, "I have taken TMG for more than ten years without any side effects. People who take TMG report that their mood is enhanced."

Availability and Dosage: TMG and DMG are sold in doses ranging from 100 to 500 mg. Beets, broccoli and shellfish are good food sources of TMG. In fact, the source of most of the TMG sold over-the-counter is often from the sugar beet. Some DMG products are available in sublingual form, which are dissolved under the tongue, for a quicker effect.

The Author's Experience: I definitely notice a sense of well-being, alertness and mental sharpness from either TMG or DMG, generally at doses between 100 and 500 mg. One morning I took three 750 mg pills of TMG (totaling 2,250 mg) on an empty stomach with an ounce of fruit juice just to see if there were any side effects. An hour later I felt the onset of mild nausea.

Drinking a few ounces of milk relieved the nausea. As the day progressed, I felt more energetic and my mood was enhanced. In the evening I took my routine three-mile walk and had a great deal of energy. I kept walking and ended up covering twice my normal distance. The drawback was that at bedtime I was still alert and couldn't sleep at all. I got out of bed several times throughout the night. I continued feeling the alertness well into the morning of the next day. Apparently 2,250 mg is a very high dose and can have effects on the brain lasting more than twenty-four hours. A positive effect from taking DMG or TMG that I hadn't expected was an enhanced libido. When I take a sublingual form of DMG, I notice the onset of alertness within thirty minutes.

 ## Cautions and Side Effects

TMG and DMG, if taken in high doses, can cause nausea, restlessness and insomnia along with elevated body temperature. According to Dr. Frankel, an additional side effect of high dosage can include muscle-tension headache.

I recommend not exceeding 250 mg of TMG or DMG or a combination on a daily basis until more is known about these supplements; dose of TMG and DMG should be reduced if you are taking B vitamins, SAMe, DMAE or choline since all of these nutrients have overlapping functions.

 ## Recommendations

TMG and DMG are underutilized nutrients that hold a great deal of promise, but unfortunately, few doctors are familiar with these nutrients. At this time, the clinical uses of TMG and DMG are not well defined, and whether they would be helpful in therapy for Alzheimer's and Parkinson's disease is not known. Since the body's ability to methylate declines with age, supplements of TMG or DMG in small amounts, such as 50 to 100 mg a day, may benefit middle-aged and older individuals.

SAMe (S-Adenosyl-Medthionine)

SAMe, a compound made from the amino acid methionine, is a methyl donor involved in the synthesis of dozens of important compounds in the body. SAMe has been available by prescription in Europe for many years as an antidepressant and has been available over-the-counter in the U.S. since about 1996.

A physician in Rome, Italy, Dr. Ascanio Polimeni says, "SAMe is a wonderful supplement. Some doctors prescribe it in Europe as therapy for many conditions, including depression, chronic fatigue syndrome and fibromyalgia. I have not found it to have any toxic effects even when I've prescribed it for several months in a row."

Unlike other methyl donors, where the research is scarce, there have been a number of studies with SAMe. These studies have shown that SAMe influences brain chemicals by helping to convert norepinephrine to epinephrine, and serotonin to melatonin. They help to make creatine, an important energy reservoir in muscle tissue and help to preserve glutathione, an important antioxidant. Furthermore, SAMe is involved in the formation of myelin, the white sheath that surrounds nerve cells and can improve the brain-cell membrane fluidity, thus potentially enhancing the function of receptors (Cestaro 1994).

SAMe and Mood

Because of its role in making neurotransmitters, SAMe has been widely researched as a depression treatment. Back in 1994, Dr. G. M. Bressa, from the University Cattolica Sacro Cuore School of Medicine in Rome, Italy, conducted a meta-analysis of the studies on SAMe (Bressa 1994). That is, he analyzed the results of already-published research papers. Dr. Bressa concludes, "The efficacy of SAMe in treating depressive syndromes and disorders is superior to that of placebo and comparable to that of standard tricyclic antidepressants. Since SAMe is a naturally occurring compound with relatively few side effects, it is a potentially important treatment for depression."

While some studies find that SAMe can offer relief and is more effective at lowering depression than placebo, the federal Agency for Healthcare Research and Quality (AHRQ) issued an evidence report in August 2002 based on 47 previous trials that suggests it is not better than conventional antidepressants.

SAMe has even been tested in depressed postmenopausal women. Researchers from the University of La Sapienza in Rome, Italy, gave 1600 mg of SAMe for one month to eighty women between the ages of 45 and 59 who had experienced depression following either natural menopause or hysterectomy (Salmaggi 1993). The result was a significantly greater improvement in depressive symptoms in the group treated with SAMe compared to the placebo group. Side effects experienced by the test group were mild and transient.

Availability and Dosage: A major drawback to the use of SAMe is the expense. The retail price of SAMe is about a dollar per 200-mg pill. The suggested dose of SAMe to treat depression ranges from 100 to 400 mg a day. Many nutrients work in a fashion similar to SAMe, particularly other methyl donors such as DMAE (discussed below), TMG, DMG and also some of the B vitamins. In fact, B-12 and folate help the body produce SAMe. Therefore, your dosage of SAMe should be reduced if you are taking other methyl donors.

The Author's Experience: I started with two 200-mg pills of SAMe one morning at nine A.M. on an empty stomach. Within an hour and a half I noticed an increase in concentration, energy, alertness and feelings of well-being. At eleven A.M. I took another 200-mg pill, and shortly thereafter ate my first meal of the day. An hour later, the alertness increased and my vision became slightly clearer. The sense of relaxed well-being continued all day and evening.

The highest dosage of SAMe I have taken is 800 mg, with no significant side effects.

 Cautions and Side Effects

Dr. Polimeni has extensive experience with this nutrient. He says, "I have prescribed SAMe for depression for many years. This nutrient is safe, but high dosages can cause dry mouth, nausea, restlessness and insomnia."

Kilmer McCully, M.D., from Veterans Affairs Medical Center in Providence, Rhode Island, has been researching homocysteine and methyl donors for the last three decades. He says, "High homocysteine levels can negatively influence cognitive decline. SAMe helps reduce homocysteine levels, and everything that I've read about it in scientific papers over the past three decades indicates that it is safe and beneficial.

We know that SAMe levels decline with aging, and perhaps replacement in older age may prove to be advantageous."

 Recommendations

SAMe has good potential to become a useful therapeutic agent for depression and age-related cognitive decline. Long-term studies are needed with SAMe before making widespread recommendations for its use. However, short-term human studies thus far have found it to be safe and effective. A major drawback to the long-term use of SAMe is its cost. Keep in mind that TMG and DMG are also powerful methyl donors. They work in a similar fashion, and are cheaper than SAMe.

Could TMG or DMG, taken with B vitamins, offer benefits similar to SAMe's at a fraction of the cost? It is known that TMG can help to regenerate SAMe (Barak 1996). Physicians from the Department of Veterans Affairs Medical Center in Omaha, Nebraska, have stated that TMG, being a SAMe generator, may become a promising therapeutic agent and a possible alternative to expensive SAMe.

Much more research needs to be done with SAMe to confirm some of the preliminary findings described here. Dr. Bottiglieri and colleagues from Baylor Research Institute in Dallas, Texas, published a review article on SAMe and other methyl donors (Teodoro Bottiglieri 1994). *They summarize...*

66 SAMe is required in numerous methylation reactions involving nucleic acids, proteins, phospholipids, amines and other neurotransmitters. The synthesis of SAMe is intimately linked with folate and vitamin B-12 metabolism, and defi-ciencies of both these vitamins have been found to reduce central-nervous system SAMe concentrations. Both folate and vitamin B-12 deficiency may cause similar neurological and psychiatric disturbances including depression, dementia, and peripheral neuropathy. Studies support a current theory that impaired methylation may occur by different mechanisms in several neurological and psychiatric disorders. 99

DMAE
(Dimethyl-Amino-Ethanol)

Known chemically as dimethyl-amino-ethanol, DMAE has been known in Europe by the product name Deanol for more than three decades. DMAE has two methyl groups and is chemically similar to choline. This nutrient has been popular for many years among those interested in improving mental alertness and clarity of thinking.

Studies on DMAE go back to the 1950s. One double-blind, placebo-controlled trial performed on twenty-seven patients with severe Alzheimer's disease did not show any significant benefits (Fisman 1981). Another study on twenty-one patients with memory deficits was also discouraging since no improvement was found in memory (Caffarra 1980).

In another study, DMAE was found to be helpful in patients with age-related cognitive decline (ARCD). This nutrient was given in a dose of up to 600 mg three times a day for four weeks to fourteen older patients (Ferris 1977). The result was that ten patients improved, and four were unchanged. The patients on DMAE had less depression, less anxiety, and increased motivation, but they had no improvement in memory. The researchers say, "The results thus suggest that although DMAE may not improve memory, it may produce positive behavioral changes in some senile patients." Dementia is a term that is now substituted for senility and is sometimes used to denote a severe case of age-related cognitive decline.

As you can see, limited studies with DMAE have not shown it to be effective with Alzheimer's disease or helping memory. However, DMAE does seem to help improve mood and motivation in older patients with dementia.

Availability and Dosage: DMAE is usually sold by the name of "DMAE bitartrate." A 350-mg pill of DMAE bitartrate yields 130 mg of actual DMAE. It is also available as liquid; one product contains 35 mg of DMAE per drop. Most users notice an effect from a dose of 100 to 200 mg of actual DMAE.

Users' Experiences: Audrey, a thirty-two-year-old patient from Hollywood, California, says, "I took a 350-mg pill of DMAE bitartrate at one P.M. By three P.M. I noticed a sharpened attention to detail, and a keener interest in observing my environment. DMAE definitely stimulated my thinking."

Most patients usually report similar effects, including the ability to focus better. However, higher doses can be counterproductive. For example, Jennifer, a thirty-five-year-old computer analyst from Santa Monica, California, says, "I have taken DMAE on numerous occasions over the last few months and have found that I get moody with high doses and start having arguments. Small doses are fine and help me become more alert and focused, but my problems come with amounts exceeding 350 mg of DMAE bitartrate."

The Author's Experience: Within two hours of taking 130 mg of actual DMAE, I notice a definite increase in alertness and slight mood and visual enhancement. I also get more motivated to work on projects and seem to work more efficiently. On higher doses I have experienced neck stiffness and anxiety.

 Cautions and Side Effects
High doses can induce irritability, over-stimulation, anxiety, headaches and stiffness in the jaw, neck and shoulder.

 Recommendations
DMAE can be helpful in the elderly who have cognitive decline. It can also be taken by an adult of any age who needs to be more focused and alert.

 Recommendations
Methyl donors are very interesting nutrients with a great deal of potential, particularly as antidepressants. Since our body's ability to methylate declines with age, it's possible that methyl donors someday may be found to have anti-aging benefits (Cooney 1993). These nutrients can also be taken on days when one needs to be more focused and alert.

In addition to their effects on the mind, methyl donors along with B vitamins can help lower homocysteine levels, thus reducing the risk for certain heart and neurological diseases.

11

KEEP YOUR BRAIN YOUNG
WITH OLD AND NEW ANTIOXIDANTS

Just about everybody has heard the word *antioxidant*. Over the past few years, the benefits of antioxidants—such as vitamins C and E—have been touted in countless magazine and newspaper articles. Yet even with all this press, most people don't have a good understanding of the concept of oxidation and antioxidation. I recently asked a number of my patients if they really knew what the word *antioxidant* meant. Although the majority of these patients were taking antioxidants, only a few understood what they were or how they really worked.

Understanding Antioxidants

A common image used to describe "oxidation" is a piece of metal in the process of rusting. The process that occurs in the body is obviously different since we are made of living tissue. During the normal metabolism or breakdown of carbohydrates, fats and proteins for energy production, certain molecules that can damage the contents within cells are generated. These destructive molecules often contain an unstable oxygen atom missing an electron. You may recall from chemistry class that atoms, such as hydrogen and oxygen,

have a pair of electrons spinning around them. An atom with only one electron in its orbit is very unstable. Chemists call this atom a *free radical*. This free radical can steal an electron from a neighboring molecule and cause that molecule to become damaged. The process of this damage is called *oxidation*. Cigarette smoke, fried foods, ozone, excessive sun exposure, car exhaust, certain drugs, radiation, toxins and air pollution lead to free radical formation or direct oxidation.

The body has developed ways to counteract these oxidants, by producing antioxidants. An antioxidant is any chemical, whether natural or synthetic, that has the ability to neutralize oxidants and thus protect our cells from being damaged. There's often a good balance between oxidation and antioxidation.

A certain amount of oxidation in the body is necessary in order to fight infections or to do repair work within cells. However, when a shift creates too much oxidation without adequate antioxidant support, the body undergoes what's called "oxidative stress." The body normally produces powerful natural antioxidants—such as superoxide dismutase, glutathione and catalase—to help fight these oxidants. Many antioxidants are also consumed through the diet, particularly fresh fruits and vegetables.

When excessive oxidation occurs for prolonged periods, it can take a toll on the system. Harmful changes may occur in cells including damage to fatty acids, inactivation of enzymes, deterioration of cell membranes, breakdown of proteins and damage to the DNA. For example, when oxidants damage DNA, the eventual consequence could be a higher likelihood of cancer. If the damage occurs in arteries that supply blood to the heart, the damage could lead to hardening of the arteries and a heart attack. All these changes lead to disease and premature aging.

Over the past few years, scientific evidence has slowly accumulated indicating that supplements could potentially reduce the risk of certain illnesses and help in maintaining brain health. There is currently no proof that ingesting antioxidants prolongs the life span in humans. However, enough evidence has been accumulated about the benefits of antioxidants that you should not casually dismiss their potential in improving quality of life and slowing the progression of certain chronic degenerative disorders.

But with the thousands of antioxidants available in our foodstuffs and the dozens available as supplements, which ones should you take, and in what dosages? This chapter will provide you with practical guidelines.

Brain Cells Can Get Oxidized

The cell membranes of neurons are made mostly of phospholipids, which contain fatty acids. Nerve fibers that travel from the brain to the spinal cord, and from the spinal cord to the rest of the body, are also insulated with a white-colored fatty substance called myelin. With time, these fats can become oxidized, interfering with proper nerve activity. The process of fats becoming oxidized is called "lipid peroxidation." The oxidation of fats contributes to brain aging and can accelerate degenerative disorders such as Alzheimer's disease. You may recall from Chapter 7 that the brain contains a great deal of polyunsaturated fatty acids, such as DHA and arachidonic acid, which are particularly susceptible to oxidation. As we age, many of these fatty acids in the brain become damaged due to oxidation. They lose some of their double bonds, thus becoming more saturated. Neurons in the brain become less efficient the more the fatty acids become saturated. Antioxidants can thus play a protective role in keeping the fatty acids in the brain healthy. After all, about 60 percent of the brain is made of fat.

Antioxidants and Memory

Although many antioxidant pills do not immediately influence cognition and memory, they very well may have a positive effect over time. In a study at the University of Bern, Switzerland, researchers evaluated 300 male and 130 female volunteers over a twenty-two-year period. At the start of the research, they measured blood levels of three antioxidants: vitamin E, vitamin C and beta-carotene and performed extensive memory testing. They found that higher levels of antioxidants, particularly vitamin C and beta-carotene, were associated with better performance in memory testing. The researchers concluded, "These results indicate the important role played by antioxidants in brain aging and may have implications for prevention of progressive cognitive impairments."

The Swiss researchers only tested blood levels of these three antioxidants. It is quite likely that a number of other antioxidants play a role in helping us preserve memory

WHAT CAN ANTIOXIDANTS DO FOR YOU?

As a rule, you are not likely to notice any immediate cognitive benefits from taking the antioxidants discussed in this chapter. So do not expect any immediate or dramatic changes in mood, energy, alertness or memory when you take them. Think of antioxidants as an insurance policy, in which the benefits will accrue over time. Antioxidants serve to protect your brain cells, proteins and DNA from the gradual damage that occurs with the aging process. However, Chapter 12 will discuss other nutrients that have antioxidant benefits, such as CoQ10 and lipoic acid, which are mind energizers—they have immediate cognitive effects.

WHAT CONDITIONS DO ANTIOXIDANTS BENEFIT?

Over the long run, it's quite likely that antioxidants could slow the progression of age-related cognitive decline, Alzheimer's disease, Parkinson's disease and perhaps other neurological disorders.

WHAT ARE EXAMPLES OF OXIDANTS?

There are quite a number of damaging oxidants that we are exposed to on a daily basis. The most common are hydroxyl (OH), superoxide (O_2), hydrogen peroxide (H_2O_2) and ozone (O_3).

and mental capacities in our later years. In another instance, an eight-month study in rats showed that administering extracts from strawberries and spinach, either alone or with vitamin E, was able to slow damage to brain cells due to the aging process (Joseph 1998).

Dozens of antioxidant products are available over-the-counter. Many foods, plants, herbal extracts, and other edible substances such as mushrooms, royal jelly, seaweed and others contain beneficial antioxidants and nutrients. In later chapters I discuss some nutrients and herbs, such as CoQ10, lipoic acid and ginkgo, that also possess good antioxidant properties.

In this chapter I will briefly discuss some of the well-known antioxidants and mention others that should be considered as part of a comprehensive antioxidant mind-preserving program.

Vitamin C

Also known as ascorbic acid, vitamin C was isolated in 1928. This vitamin serves as an excellent antioxidant and could protect brain cells, including those in the eye. The eye is highly susceptible to damage by sunlight, oxygen, various chemicals and pollutants. It's very important to have adequate antioxidants in the eyes. This is especially true for the aging population and because of continued depletion of the ozone in the environment. But how much vitamin C is enough to protect our cells?

Ever since Nobel Prize winner Linus Pauling extolled the benefits of mega-dosing with vitamin C, the medical community has debated the optimal dosage of this vitamin. Although many doctors for a long time asserted that the RDA of 60 mg for this vitamin was adequate, more and more doctors now realize that higher doses can confer additional antioxidant benefits. However, the optimal daily intake of vitamin C has not yet been determined, nor is it likely to be determined soon. Nevertheless, we now suspect that excessive intake of vitamin C, except perhaps in the therapy of a particular medical condition, may not be necessary.

A study published in the *American Journal of Clinical Nutrition* points that large doses of ingested vitamin C may be excreted without being utilized (Blanchard 1997). In the study, when the dosage of vitamin C given to a group of healthy men was increased from 200 mg a day to 2500 mg a day, blood levels increased only negligibly. James Blanchard, Ph.D., a professor of pharmacological sciences at the University of Arizona in Tucson, reports that the blood levels of vitamin C generally reflect the levels found in the rest of the body. Still, other studies find that when taken along with vitamin E, higher amounts of C seem to lower the risk of free radical damage associated with a decline in mental functioning (Grodstein 2003).

 Recommendations
Most people should have adequate antioxidant protection with vitamin C at a dose of 100 to 500 mg per day. The majority of our intake of vitamin C should be obtained from fruits and vegetables, which additionally provide hundreds of beneficial carotenoids and flavonoids that often work synergistically with vitamin C.

Many people take more than one antioxidant on a daily basis. Since antioxidants help protect each other from being destroyed, the amount required for each one would be less when taken together.

Vitamin E

Also known as tocopherol, vitamin E was isolated in the 1920s. There is general agreement that this fat-soluble vitamin can function as an excellent antioxidant, protecting cells from damage and specifically protecting polyunsaturated fatty acids. Epidemiological studies indicate that older individuals with high levels of antioxidants in their bloodstream, including vitamin E, may be one-third less likely to have memory problems (Morris 2002).

Several types of natural vitamin-E compounds are available, including alpha-, beta-, gamma- and delta-tocopherol. Alpha-tocopherol seems to be the most active, although we should not dismiss the importance of the others. It seems prudent to supplement with products that have mixed tocopherols as opposed to just alpha-tocopherol.

 Recommendations
The average American diet contains between 10 and 22 international units of vitamin E. Additional intake is likely to be beneficial. Most healthy adults should do well with supplementing with 20 to 100 units a day.

 Cautions and Side Effects
Very high dosages, such as 1000 units or more, can lead to an increase in bleeding risk, tiredness and possibly impaired immune function.

Carotenoids

These are a group of compounds that impart some of the orange color in vegetables and fruits. At least a few hundred of these carotenoids are found in our produce. Beta-carotene is the best known, but others are becoming more popular, including lycopene (found in tomatoes, watermelon, and much pink/red/orange-colored produce), lutein, zeazanthin and others. Many carotenoids have antitumor, antibacterial, antiviral, anti-inflammatory and antihistaminic actions. A diet rich in fruit and vegetables is likely to help prevent age-related mental decline.

 Recommendations

Most healthy individuals do not need to take supplements of carotenoids since they can be easily found in produce. I recommend consuming a variety of foods and vegetables on a daily basis. There is a potential risk of causing an imbalance when supplementing with high doses of only one carotenoid, like beta-carotene, at the expense of the others. It's possible that someday we may discover that certain medical conditions may respond to supplementation with specific carotenoids.

Flavonoids

Similar to the carotenoids, flavonoids are plant substances that have important antioxidant properties. Many of these also have antitumor, antibacterial, antiviral, anti-inflammatory and antihistaminic actions. Some of the well-known flavonoids include quercetin, apigenin, rutin and flavones. A certain type of flavonoids, called proanthrocyanidins, is found in extracts of pine bark and grape seeds. Polyphenols are another group of beneficial flavonoids. One such polyphenol, known as catechin, is found in green tea and other teas. You can find polyphenols in fruits, vegetables, herbs, wine and certain legumes.

 Recommendations

Flavonoid supplements are sold either individually, in combination with other flavonoids and carotenoids or in combination with other nutrients. Most healthy individuals do not need to take supplements of flavonoids if they consume a healthy diet. I recommend that you consume a wide range of fruits (citrus, berries), grains, herbs, nuts, seeds and vegetables (garlic, onions, broccoli).

We may someday determine that additional supplementation with specific flavonoids could potentially be beneficial in certain medical conditions.

Glutathione

This antioxidant, made from the combination of three amino acids, cysteine, glutamate and glycine, forms part of the powerful natural antioxidant glutathione peroxidase (GP) which is found in our cells. GP plays a variety of roles in cells, including DNA synthesis and repair, metabolism of toxins and carcinogens, enhancement of the immune system and prevention of fat oxidation. However, glutathione is predominantly known as an antioxidant that protects our cells from damage caused by the free-radical hydrogen peroxide. Glutathione also helps the other antioxidants in cells stay in their active form. Brain glutathione levels have been found to be lower in patients with Parkinson's disease.

Glutathione is found in foods, particularly fruits, vegetables and meats. Cyanohydroxybutene, a chemical found in broccoli, cauliflower, brussels sprouts and cabbage, is also thought to increase glutathione levels (Davis 1993). Although glutathione is available in pill form over-the-counter, its utilization by the body is questionable since we don't know if it can easily enter cells even after it is absorbed in the bloodstream.

Certain nutrients help raise tissue levels of glutathione, including NAC (see below), methyl donors, lipoic acid and vitamin B-12. However, if glutathione levels are excessively increased with the help of nutrients, the body may decrease its natural production. This situation is known as "feedback inhibition." The frequent use of acetaminophen (Tylenol) depletes glutathione levels.

Recommendations

Glutathione is sold in pills with doses ranging from 50 to 250 mg. Glutathione is a promising antioxidant. However, due to the inconsistencies in the medical literature on the ability of glutathione to enter tissues and cells when ingested orally, and the possibility of feedback inhibition, I can't confidently recommend supplementation with this nutrient until more information is published.

NAC
(N-Acetyl-Cysteine)

I might have included NAC in Chapter 13, on amino acids and related compounds, since it is made from the amino acid cysteine. However, NAC is such a strong antioxidant that placing it in this chapter is more appropriate. NAC donates the amino

acid cysteine to help form the antioxidant glutathione (Urban 1997).

An excellent review article in the April 1998 issue of *Alternative Medicine Reviews* summarizes the known effects of NAC (Kelly 1998). *The author writes…*

> " N-acetyl-cysteine is an excellent source of sulfhydryl (SH) groups, and is converted in the body into metabolites capable of stimulating glutathione synthesis, promoting detoxification, and acting directly as a free-radical scavenger. Administration of NAC has historically been as a mucolytic [mucus dissolving] agent in a variety of respiratory illnesses; however, it appears to also have beneficial effects in conditions characterized by decreased glutathione or oxidative stress, such as HIV infection, cancer, heart disease and cigarette smoking. "

The Author's Experience: Although large doses cause nausea and vomiting, NAC is a safe nutrient. I experienced a few minutes of nausea within an hour of taking three 600 mg pills on an empty stomach. I did not notice any effect on mood or energy that day. As a resident, I prescribed NAC intravenously to patients with liver damage due to acetaminophen (Tylenol) overdose. It protected the liver very well. One laboratory study indicates that while low dosages of NAC protect against oxidation, higher doses may have the opposite effect (Sprong 1998).

Recommendations

NAC is sold in dosages ranging from 250 to 600 mg. NAC can help form the powerful antioxidant glutathione, but the resulting increase in glutathione levels may cause a feedback inhibition that causes the body to decrease its natural production. Thus it is not clear

ANTIOXIDANT DOSAGE GUIDELINES

Here's an antioxidant dosage recommendation for the average person with no major medical problems. Please discuss with your health-care practitioner whether these doses are appropriate for you. Chapter 12 discusses additional nutrients—such as ALC, CoQ10, and lipoic acid—that are powerful antioxidants.

- Vitamin E—20 to 200 IU a day of the mixed tocopherols

- Vitamin C—100 to 500 mg a day

- Selenium—20 to 100 micrograms most days

- NAC—50 to 100 mg a few times a week

- Carotenoids and flavonoids are best obtained through fruits and vegetables.-

whether regular use of NAC can actually increase overall glutathione levels in healthy individuals who have normal levels of glutathione. The use of NAC certainly should be considered as an additional supplement in protecting various cells from damage in the elderly and those with Parkinson's disease.

 Cautions and Side Effects

If you are planning to use NAC along with other antioxidants, limit your daily dosage to 50 to 100 mg and don't take it all the time.

NAC could protect the livers of those who take acetaminophen on a regular basis.

Selenium

This mineral forms part of a very important enzyme normally present in our bodies, called glutathione peroxidase. The richest sources of selenium are organ meats and seafood, followed by meat, cereal products and dairy.

 Recommendations

The average intake of selenium in the American diet is 70 to 100 micrograms a day. Occasional supplementation with 20 to 100 micrograms of this mineral appears to be safe, and may be effective at reducing depression (Rayman 2000).

 Cautions and Side Effects

Selenium in amounts much higher than 20 to 100 micrograms can act as an oxidant and thus is counterproductive (Spallholz 1997). As with most supplements, low-dose use seems to be a cautious approach.

Summary

Pick up any health magazine and you are likely to see ads promoting dozens of different antioxidants. Many of them have a scientific basis to support their antioxidant properties. However, you can't just take all of them. What should you do?

First, keep in mind that there is no definite proof that antioxidant supplements will keep your brain young. However, there is enough promising evidence to convince me to recommend vitamins E, C, selenium and NAC.

Second, make sure you obtain the bulk of your antioxidants through fresh foods. Carotenoids and flavonoids can be easily obtained through fruits, vegetables, herbs and whole foods. If you do wish to take additional supplements, I recommend a multioxidant pill that contains small amounts of many antioxidants, instead of taking large amounts of just one or two. You could even have two or three different products on your kitchen counter and alternate their use so you don't get the same antioxidants in the same dosages all the time. Remember that the body needs some oxidation in order to fight certain germs and possibly to fight some cancer cells.

12

MIND ENERGIZERS
THINK FASTER, SHARPER AND LONGER

Just like all the cells in the body, brain cells or neurons need energy. In most children and young adults, the brain is able to metabolize glucose and other sources of energy very well. However, as we get older, the energy production system in neurons doesn't seem to work as well. This malfunction could contribute to mental fatigue and the age-related decline in learning and memory.

This chapter will focus on three nutrients that are directly and actively involved in energy production: Acetyl-L-carnitine (ALC), coenzyme Q10 (CoQ10), and lipoic acid. When used properly, these nutrients enhance mental function. CoQ10 is the best known of the three, and is used mostly in the treatment of cardiovascular conditions. ALC and lipoic acid have been available for several years and their popularity is gradually increasing. As an added benefit, all three of these mind-energizing nutrients also act as excellent antioxidants.

CoQ10 has become very popular over the past few years, as more people recognize the increase in energy it provides. Diane, a forty-six-year-old investment banker, says, "Ever since I started taking 30 mg of CoQ10

WHAT CAN MIND ENERGIZERS DO FOR YOU?

The most obvious benefits noted from this group of nutrients are improvements in...

- Alertness, arousal, and vigilance
- Mood, energy and motivation
- Concentration and focus
- Verbal fluency
- Mild visual enhancement

WHAT CLINICAL CONDITIONS CAN MIND ENERGIZERS BENEFIT?

Limited research indicates that these nutrients can potentially be helpful in...

- Depression
- Age-related cognitive decline
- Alzheimer's disease
- Parkinson's disease

each morning, I seem to be peppy all day. I used to have a very mild case of chronic fatigue with slight fogginess of the mind. CoQ10 helps a lot, but sometimes I need 60 mg." ALC has its share of fans, also. Renee, a fifty-five-year-old insurance agent, finds that this nutrient helps her stay focused all day. "I work with numbers all day," she says. "I take 250 mg of ALC on days when I want to be more alert and sharper. ALC improves my concentration and I actually feel smarter." Some diabetics currently take lipoic acid since this nutrient helps keep nerves healthier and stabilizes blood sugar levels. Few people are aware, though, that lipoic acid has cognitive benefits.

Carnitine and ALC (Acetyl-L-Carnitine)

Carnitine is a naturally occurring substance found in most cells of the body, particularly the brain and neural tissues, muscles and heart. It is widely available in animal foods and dairy products but plant-based foods have very small amounts. Most non-vegetarians consume about 100 to 300 mg of carnitine a day. The body is able to synthesize this nutrient when dietary intake is inadequate. When taken as a pill, carnitine is not able to cross the blood-brain barrier as well as its activated form ALC can. ALC has significantly more noticeable cognitive effects than carnitine. So, this section will focus on ALC.

How They Work
Carnitine and ALC play several important roles in the human body, particularly in energy metabolism. These nutrients shuttle acetyl groups and fatty acids into mitochondria for energy production. Without carnitine, fatty acids cannot easily enter into mitochondria.

The acetyl group of ALC is used to form acetyl-CoA, the most important intermediary in energy generation from amino acids, fats and carbohydrates. Therefore, ALC serves as an energy reservoir of acetyl groups. Both ALC and carnitine help improve energy production. Many adults who take carnitine pills notice an increase in their energy levels. The acetyl group of ALC is also used to make the important brain chemical acetylcholine. Some studies suggest that perhaps ALC can even act as a neurotransmitter itself.

In addition to producing energy, these two nutrients remove toxic accumulations of fatty acids from mitochondria, keeping these organelles healthy and functioning at their best (Carta 1993, Hagen 1998). Energy production in the mitochondria is not a perfect process, and toxic metabolites can often accumulate. This toxic accumulation and the resulting oxidative damage is likely to contribute to aging of cells (Shigenaga 1994). A waste substance called lipofuscin accumulates in cells as we age, and perhaps adequate ALC intake can help minimize this accumulation. It is theoretically possible that supplementation with carnitine or ALC can slow the aging process.

If these benefits weren't enough, studies show that carnitine and ALC stabilize cell membranes, protect synapses and protect neurons against damage from oxidation (Fariello 1988, Lyckesfeldt 1998).

Clinical Uses
ALC has been tested more often than carnitine in neurological conditions because it can cross the blood-brain barrier very easily when taken as a supplement (Parnetti 1995). ALC can potentially be helpful to many

individuals, particularly those with Alzheimer's disease, age-related cognitive decline and depression.

There are a few reasons why ALC may be helpful in Alzheimer's disease (AD). First, it helps form the important brain chemical acetylcholine, which is often deficient in Alzheimer's disease cases. Second, ALC can clear toxic accumulations of fatty-acid metabolites from mitochondria, allowing for more efficient energy production. Third, it can potentially help regenerate cholinergic neurons. A study in rats has found that administration of ALC can induce the production of nerve-growth factor, a type of protein that helps regenerate neurons (Piovesan 1994). Some patients with AD may be deficient in the enzyme that converts carnitine to acetyl-L-carnitine (Kalaria 1992); therefore, providing ALC is an easy solution to this problem.

There have been several trials of ALC in the therapy of Alzheimer's disease. The most extensive was a one-year-long double-blind, placebo-controlled study at the University of California San Diego in La Jolla, California (Thal 1996). The results were only slightly encouraging.

The Study: Subjects with mild-to-moderate AD, aged 50-plus, were treated with 3 grams a day of ALC or placebo for twelve months. Four hundred thirty-one patients entered the study, and 83 percent completed one year of treatment. Overall, both ALC- and placebo-treated patients declined at the same rate on all cognitive measures during the trial. When the researchers examined the data more closely, they found that those patients whose AD had started early (aged 65 years or younger at study entry) had a better response than those who were older than age 66 at the start of the study.

Here's a summary of additional research with ALC in Alzheimer's disease...

- ALC has been found to protect against several mechanisms associated with Alzheimer's. It protects against temporary cerebral ischemia (no blood flow) (Calvani 1999) and prevents against toxicity in the brain caused by glutamate and ammonia (Rao 1999).

- A double-blind placebo-controlled study with seven AD patients was conducted over one year at the University of Pittsburgh in Pennsylvania (Pettegrew 1995). The result was that acetyl-L-carnitine-treated patients showed significantly less deterioration than the patients on placebo.

- In a clinical trial, researchers from the Mario Negri Institute for Pharmacological Research in Milan, Italy, studied the efficacy of a one-year treatment with 2 grams of ALC a day in 130 patients with AD (Spagnoli 1991). After one year, all the patients had worsened, but the group treated with ALC showed a slower rate of deterioration than those who didn't receive it. They had better scores on logical intelligence, verbal and long-term verbal memory. Reported adverse events were relatively mild with no significant difference between the groups in incidence or severity of side effects.

- Investigators at Whittington Hospital in London, England, carried out a twenty-four-week double-blind clinical trial comparing treatment with 1 gram ALC twice daily and a placebo in twenty patients with AD (Rai 1990). There was apparent improvement in the ALC group in tests on short-term memory. Laboratory tests revealed no signs of toxicity.

- ALC has also been tested in age-related cognitive decline. A 1990 study at the

University of Parma showed that 2 grams a day of ALC improved memory, verbal fluency and attention among thirty patients over the age of 65 suffering from mild mental impairment (Passeri 1990). That same year, another Italian study on the effects of ALC on mildly impaired elderly was carried out on 236 subjects (Cipolli 1990). Each subject was treated for 150 days, and a battery of tests (investigating cognitive functioning, emotional state and behavior) was administered. The results showed that treatment with ALC significantly increased the effectiveness of performance on all the measures of cognitive functioning and mood.

- ALC has even been tested in the therapy of depression and shown to be helpful in improving mood. Out of sixty subjects with low mood aged 60 to 80 years, half were given 3 grams a day of ALC while the other half received a placebo (Bella 1990). The results showed that treatment with ALC induced a significant reduction in the severity of depressive symptoms and also a significant improvement in quality of life. ALC is a promising nutrient, particularly for Alzheimer's disease and age-related cognitive decline.

Availability and Dosage: ALC is usually available at doses ranging between 100 and 500 mg. It is expensive, and cost may slow its popularity. Carnitine is available in a variety of doses ranging from 250 to 750 mg and is also sold as a powder.

An Expert's Opinion: Dr. Ascanio Polimeni, M.D., a neuroendocrinologist from Rome, has used ALC in his practice with hundreds of patients. He says, "I like ALC very much, especially when it's combined with other cognitive enhancers. My patients notice increased attentiveness and alertness, and improved mood. Older patients find ALC helps them think clearer and learn easier."

The Author's Experience: I notice the effects of ALC within two hours after taking a 500 mg pill. These effects are arousal and vigilance, along with mood improvement, and they can last most of the day. The maximum dose I have taken is 1500 mg without experiencing a side effect. My patients report similar benefits.

 Cautions and Side Effects

ALC and carnitine are very well tolerated. However, high doses of ALC can induce nausea, restlessness and agitation.

 Recommendations

I believe ALC holds a great deal of promise and is currently underutilized, particularly in therapy for age-related cognitive decline. Its role in Alzheimer's disease is still not fully understood but there is a good possibility that ALC could be helpful to some patients.

Carnitine could be a beneficial supplement for vegetarians at a dosage of 100 to 250 mg a day. Carnitine is also a useful supplement for treating fatigue.

Coenzyme Q10

CoQ10, also known as ubiquinone or ubiquinol, is a naturally occurring nutrient in each cell. CoQ10 is found in foods, particularly in fish and meats. In addition to playing a significant role in the energy system of each of our cells, CoQ10 is an excellent antioxidant.

Studies of CoQ10 have mostly focused on its role in heart disease. However, CoQ10 has a role in brain function, too. Most of my patients who take CoQ10 notice that this nutrient provides energy and mental clarity.

How Does It Work?

Each cell in the body needs a source of energy to survive. Energy is produced from sugars, fats and amino acids in mitochondria. CoQ10 exists naturally in our mitochondria and carries electrons involved in energy metabolism. CoQ10 is essential in the production of adenosine triphosphate (ATP), the basic energy molecule of each cell.

In the bloodstream, CoQ10 is mainly transported by lipoproteins such as LDL (low-density lipoproteins) and HDL (high-density lipoproteins). It is thought that CoQ10 is one of the first antioxidants to be depleted when LDL is subjected to oxidation. Hence, CoQ10 is an extremely important nutrient that prevents the oxidation of lipoproteins, thus protecting arteries from forming plaques and getting damaged.

CoQ10 and the Brain

Studies evaluating the role of this nutrient in cognitive disorders are limited. Here are summaries of two important ones that have been published over the past few years.

- Parkinson's disease—In October 2002, researchers reported in *Archives of Neurology* that high doses of coenzyme Q10 slowed disease progression by as much as half (Shults 2002).

- Juvenile neuronal ceroid lipofuscinosis (JNCL) is an inherited, progressive neurodegenerative disease. In this study the levels of the antioxidants CoQ10 and vitamin E were measured in blood samples of twenty-nine JNCL patients and compared to forty-eight healthy controls (Westermarck

1997). A significant reduction of the CoQ10 level was observed in JNCL patients when compared to control subjects. The level of vitamin E was also markedly reduced in JNCL patients when compared to controls. The low levels of CoQ10 and vitamin E in JNCL patients may indicate an impaired antioxidant protection in this disease.

Availability and Dosage: CoQ10 is sold in 10 to 100 mg capsules and is also added to some multivitamin tablets.

The Author's Experience: The effect from 30 mg of CoQ10 is mild, mostly consisting of a slightly higher energy level. The effects become more noticeable with 60 mg. I have taken up to 120 mg in the morning. On this dose, I notice an increase in energy as the day goes on, with an urge to take a long walk or be otherwise physically active. There is a slight mood elevation with enhanced focus, motivation, and productivity, along with the desire to talk to people. The 120-mg dose is too much, since I still feel too energetic and alert in late evening when I want to slow down and get ready for sleep.

 Cautions and Side Effects

High dosages can induce restlessness and insomnia. *Since it has a chemical structure similar to vitamin K, patients taking blood thinners such as coumadin should probably avoid CoQ10, or keep their dosages low* (Landbo 1998).

 Recommendations

CoQ10 will likely be found to play a positive role in certain cognitive or neurodegenerative disorders, but more studies are needed. The results of short-term studies in Parkinson's disease have not been encouraging, although it is possible that the long-term use of CoQ10 in small doses may protect brain cells from oxidative damage. In the meantime, it would seem appropriate to supplement with this nutrient as part of a long-term health regimen. A daily dose of 10 to 30 mg seems to be a reasonable option for many individuals.

Lipoic Acid

Lipoic acid (LA) is a natural coenzyme important in the regulation of carbohydrate metabolism. Researchers are slowly recognizing its unique and powerful antioxidant abilities. LA is included here instead of the antioxidant chapter because it is more clearly involved in energy production, and provides noticeable cognitive effects. Over the past few years this nutrient has been tested in the treatment and prevention of a broad range of diseases, including diabetes and diabetic neuropathy.

LA is often mentioned in the medical literature as alpha-lipoic acid or "thiotic acid." Although LA is found in small amounts in foods (such as meats and spinach), full evaluations of LA in food contents have not been done as well.

LA has some particularly useful antioxidant properties. It can help preserve the function of vitamins C and E and increase the levels of glutathione, a very important antioxidant normally found in our cells (Busse 1992). Glutathione is especially important as an antioxidant in the brain, particularly for patients with Parkinson's disease.

Dr. Lester Packer and colleagues from the University of California at Berkeley have done extensive studies with LA (Packer 1997). *They say…*

66 This potent antioxidant can regenerate other antioxidants like vitamin C and vitamin E, and raises intracellular glutathione levels. Thus, it would seem an ideal substance in the treatment of oxidative brain and neural disorders involving free-radical processes. 99

However, Dr. Packer tells me that research on lipoic acid and the brain thus far has been done only with animals and no studies are available regarding the cognitive role lipoic acid plays in humans.

What is LA's role in neural disorders and memory? Nerves constantly use much energy and thus are vulnerable to oxidative stress. In order to produce energy, nerve cells have a large number of mitochondria. Energy production produces free radicals, which can damage the DNA within cells. It's possible that an inadequate antioxidant defense system can lead to degenerative disorders of the nervous system.

Studies with LA and cognition are limited. In research with aging mice given LA for fifteen days, they performed slightly better in a memory test than their younger counterparts that also received LA (Stoll 1993). Treatment with LA did not improve memory in young mice. LA has been also used therapeutically in the therapy of diabetic neuropathy with moderate success.

Availability and Dosage: LA is sold in dosages of 50 and 100 mg but most people do not need doses this high. You can open a capsule and take a small portion, such as 5 to 20 mg. You will also find lipoic acid added to certain multioxidant products in combinations with vitamins E, C, and CoQ10.

The Author's Experience: Unlike most antioxidants such as vitamins C, E and selenium, there is actually a noticeable effect from taking LA. I've observed a sense of relaxed well-being and slightly enhanced visual acuity. Higher dosages, such as 40 mg or more, even if I've taken them in the morning, cause me to have insomnia.

Cautions and Side Effects

There are no indications that low doses of LA, such as 5 to 20 mg, have side effects. Higher doses could cause nausea or stomach upset in addition to overstimulation, fatigue and insomnia. High doses could also potentially lower blood sugar. This effect is often beneficial to patients who have diabetes, but it requires close monitoring of blood-sugar levels.

Recommendations

Until long-term studies with LA are published on humans, I do not recommend taking more than 20 mg a day unless you're being treated for a particular condition under medical supervision. Since LA helps restore antioxidants, take less

vitamins C and E and other antioxidants when you take them along with LA.

Summary

There are a number of supplements available that influence energy production in brain cells. The research on nutrients is still very early and it's difficult to give precise dosage recommendations or combinations that would apply to everyone.

I am very confident that in time more doctors will realize the enormous benefit some mind energizers can provide to individuals with a number of neurological and psychological conditions. I believe that the medical profession is currently underutilizing CoQ10, ALC and lipoic acid.

Since carnitine and CoQ10 are mostly found in meat, fish and chicken, I recommend vegetarians supplement with 100 to 250 mg of carnitine and 10 to 20 mg of CoQ10 on a regular basis.

13

AMINO ACIDS
BUILDING BLOCKS FOR BRAIN CHEMICALS

 **S**haron is a thirty-four-year-old housewife who can't get going in the morning without a caffeine boost. It takes her a couple of hours before she feels alert and ready to function. Sharon asked me whether there were any nutrients that would provide the type of "wake-up" alertness equivalent to a cup of coffee. I recommended trying a small dose of an amino acid called tyrosine, which she found worked very well. She now takes this amino acid once or so a week in the morning on an empty stomach. It makes her more focused and alert, often within an hour.

Mindy is a forty-five-year-old health-food-store manager who takes 5-HTP a few times a month near bedtime. "Whenever I'm very tense and know that I'm going to have trouble sleeping, I take 50 mg of 5-HTP about an hour before bed on an empty stomach. 5-HTP helps me get a restful sleep," she says.

There are a number of amino acids and related nutrients sold over-the-counter. Some of these include tyrosine, phenylalanine, 5-HTP, creatine, GABA, pyroglutamic acid, taurine, glutamine and arginine. Sharon and Mindy are two individuals who have found that the occasional use of amino acids helps improve the quality of their lives. This chapter will discuss the appropriate use of tyrosine,

WHAT CAN AMINO ACIDS DO FOR YOU?

Tyrosine and phenylalanine are converted into the brain chemicals dopamine and nor-epinephrine. They lead to alertness, appetite control and slight mood elevation. 5-HTP is converted into serotonin and induces relaxation, controls appetite, helps with sleep and elevates mood.

WHAT CLINICAL CONDITIONS CAN AMINO ACIDS BENEFIT?

All three of these amino acids are useful in treating depression and obesity. 5-HTP can also be used in anxiety disorders and insomnia.

5-HTP and phenylalanine. I have chosen to focus on these three amino acids because there is ample research and much clinical experience supporting their use.

The other amino acids and related nutrients mentioned above are recommended for different purposes. For instance, creatine is a nutrient that increases muscle mass but has no cognitive effects. GABA, short for gamma-aminobutyric acid, is a brain chemical involved in relaxation but you won't notice much if you take a GABA pill because GABA cannot easily cross the blood-brain barrier. Pyroglutamic acid does increase alertness and focus but has very little published research. Taurine, glutamine and arginine have minimal cognitive effects.

What Is an Amino Acid?

The foods we eat contain proteins, fats and carbohydrates. Proteins are made from many amino acids assembled into long chains. There are about twenty different types of amino acids that make up proteins. An amino acid is basically a molecule that combines an amino group (NH3) and a carboxyl group (COOH) attached to a side chain. The side chain gives each of the twenty different amino acids its unique property.

Eight of the twenty amino acids are essential. This means that the body cannot manufacture them and they have to be ingested through foods. These essential amino acids include isoleucine, lysine, leucine, methionine, phenylalanine, threonine, tryptophan and valine. The nonessential amino acids are alanine, arginine, asparagine, aspartate, cysteine, glutamate, glutamine, glycine, histidine, proline, serine and tyrosine. In addition to the twenty common amino acids used to make proteins, there are others, such as taurine and pyroglutamate, that are not incorporated into proteins.

Phenylalaline and Tyrosine

Phenylalanine is an essential amino acid, but tyrosine isn't since it can be made from phenylalanine. These two amino acids are converted into dopamine and norepinephrine (see Figure 13.1). Supplementation with these amino acids leads to alertness, arousal and more energy.

Phenylalanine and tyrosine are sometimes prescribed as antidepressants, usually in combination with other nutrients and herbs that have mood-elevating properties. Some doctors also recommend these amino acids for appetite control. Phenylalanine may trigger the release of an appetite-suppressing hormone in the gut called cholecystokinin. Most individuals who take either of these amino acids notice improved alertness, arousal, and mood and a slight loss in appetite.

Figure 13.1—Conversion of Phenylalanine and Tyrosine to Dopamine and Norepinephrine

Phenylalanine
↓ (NADH)
Tyrosine
↓ Vitamin C
L-Dopa
↓ Vitamin B-6
Dopamine
↓ Vitamin C
Norepinephrine
↓ SAMe and methyl donors
Epinephrine

I have a few patients who occasionally take a small amount of these nutrients—such as 50 to 250 mg—in the morning as a substitute for caffeine.

Availability and Dosage: Phenylalanine and tyrosine are sold in dosages ranging from 100 to 500 mg. Tyrosine is also sold in its acetylated form as acetyl-tyrosine. No research on humans has been published regarding the mental effects of acetyl-tyrosine compared to plain tyrosine.

Always start with a low dose, such as 50 to 100 mg, in order to avoid side effects. If you can only find the 500 mg pills, you may have to open a capsule and take a portion. The effects of tyrosine and phenylalanine are more noticeable when taken on an empty stomach.

Be careful when you are adding either of these two amino acids to a regimen that includes other stimulants since the effects can be cumulative. Some of the nutrients that can act as stimulants include DMAE, CDP-choline, pantothenic acid, methyl donors, ALC, CoQ10, DHEA, pregnenolone, St. John's wort and ginseng.

The Author's Experience: I notice the effects from these amino acids with a dose as low as 100 mg when I take them on an empty stomach in the morning. In addition to enhanced alertness, arousal, focus and motivation, there is some appetite suppression and slight mood improvement. However, high doses make me anxious and restless. I have occasionally experienced brief episodes of heart palpitations when my dosage exceeded 750 mg.

I have taken acetyl-tyrosine twice, at a dose of 200 mg. The effects lasted most of the day and were similar to a higher dose of tyrosine.

 Cautions and Side Effects

In high doses, these amino acids cause anxiety, restlessness, irritability and insomnia. They also raise blood pressure, increase heart rate and may even cause heart irregularities in susceptible individuals. Those who have a defect in the enzyme phenylalanine hydroxylase cannot easily metabolize phenylalanine to tyrosine, and develop a condition known as phenylketonuria. Obviously, these individuals should avoid phenylalanine.

Avoid these two amino acids entirely if you are currently taking antidepressant drugs such as monoamine oxidase inhibitors (MAOs). I advise caution for those who take antidepressants such as Prozac, which are serotonin re-uptake inhibitors (SRIs). Both phenylalanine and tyrosine can have a stimulant effect when combined with energizing nutrients and drugs. Individuals with thyroid problems should consult their physician before using tyrosine because it is a precursor to thyroid hormones.

 Recommendations

Phenylalanine and tyrosine are useful in the therapy of depression and appetite control, especially when they are combined with other nutrients. I do not recommend their use for older individuals or for those who have high blood pressure, cardiovascular disease or a propensity for heart palpitations.

5-HTP (5-Hydroxytrytophan)

During the 1980s, consumers were using the amino acid tryptophan for sleep and as an antidepressant. Tryptophan was available until 1989 when the FDA prohibited its over-the-counter sale, because a contaminated batch from Japan caused a serious illness called eosinophilia myalgia syndrome. Tryptophan is now available only by prescription through compounding pharmacies. No further tryptophan contamination has been reported.

Since 1995, 5-HTP, the immediate precursor to serotonin, has been available without a prescription. Figure 13.2 shows that tryptophan converts into 5-HTP, which then readily converts into serotonin. Once serotonin is made, the pineal gland is able to convert it at night into melatonin, the sleep-inducing hormone.

The 5-HTP currently sold over-the-counter is extracted from griffonia seeds, which come from an African shrub tree grown in Ghana and the Ivory Coast. There are several European pharmaceutical companies that extract 5-HTP from these seeds.

Over the past three decades, scientists have tested 5-HTP for the following conditions…

- Anxiety disorders—Due to its conversion into serotonin, 5-HTP, when used occasionally, can induce relaxation and relieve anxiety.

- Depression—Most individuals find a slight mood elevation after using 5-HTP for a few days. Until more research is available, the regular use of 5-HTP as an antidepressant should be limited to a few weeks.

- Insomnia—The occasional use of 5-HTP in a dosage of 25 to 50 mg, about an hour before bed on an empty stomach, can help induce and maintain sleep.

- Obesity—5-HTP acts as a good appetite suppressant and, in combination with lifestyle and dietary changes, can help in weight reduction. Although 5-HTP can help you

Figure 13.2—Conversion of Tryptophan Into 5-HTP, Serotonin, and Melatonin

Tryptophan

↓

5-Hydroxytryptophan (5-HTP)

 Vitamin B-6

Serotonin

↓

N-acetyl-serotonin

 SAMe (and other methyl donors?)

Melatonin

lose weight, this nutrient should only be used temporarily (a few weeks at most) until new lifestyle habits are incorporated.

Availability and Dosage: 5-HTP is sold in 25 to 100 mg capsules. Most people notice the effects from 10 to 50 mg when taken on an empty stomach.

The Author's Experience: I have tried 5-HTP on numerous occasions and have noticed that it can induce relaxation, improve mood, and reduce hunger. It is effective for insomnia when used an hour or so before bed on an empty stomach. Tolerance to 5-HTP seems to develop rather quickly when it's taken frequently. The daytime side effects I've noticed on a dose greater than 50 mg include nausea and sluggishness. I've also had vivid dreams, including nightmares, on an evening dose of 100 mg.

 Cautions and Side Effects

Due to limited available research on this nutrient, caution is advised. 5-HTP should only be used for a brief period, such as a few weeks. After a break of a month or two, 5-HTP can be restarted again.

Do not take a dose exceeding 25 mg during the day if you expect to drive a car or operate heavy machinery since 5-HTP can make some people sleepy. High doses, greater than 100 mg, can induce nausea. A high dose at night can cause vivid dreams and nightmares. The risk for side effects increases with the dose.

 Recommendations

5-HTP can be helpful, most likely in combination with other nutrients, in treating obesity, anxiety, insomnia and depression. *Until more studies are available, I recommend not using 5-HTP more than four days a week, and continuously no longer than a few weeks without taking breaks.* It takes time to learn how to use 5-HTP well.

Summary

Amino acids and their derivatives have very important functions in the brain and body. When used appropriately, they can offer a number of benefits in the therapy of mood disorders, anxiety and appetite control. The medical profession has not taken full advantage of their potential uses.

14

BRAIN HORMONES
POTENT MEMORY AND SEX BOOSTERS

For many years we've heard about estrogen-replacement therapy and how it's supposed to fight osteoporosis, improve heart function and help with some of the changes in mood that occur in menopause. We've also heard that testosterone replacement can improve sexual function and feelings of well-being. It is becoming apparent that steroid hormones, which include estrogen, testosterone, DHEA, progesterone, and pregnenolone, not only play important roles in the body, but also have a significant influence on brain function. These hormones are made mostly in the adrenal glands, ovaries and testicles. However, many people don't realize that they are also made in the brain and have important effects on mental function. Since these hormones are made in neural tissue, scientists have proposed the name *neurohormones* to recognize and emphasize the importance of these hormones in the nervous system.

How hormones affect learning, memory, mood and libido is still being investigated, but researchers know that some hormones, such as DHEA, neutralize the effects of stress hormones such as cortisol. In addition to contributing to heart disease, cancer and other conditions, these stress hormones are linked to mental function and sexual desire. Scientists also discovered that hormones can influence the activity of brain chemicals, the structure of receptors and synapses, the release of other hormones, DNA formation within brain cells, and communication within nerve cells (Rupprecht 1999). These are all very important influences.

When we're young, particularly in our teens, we have adequate production of these hormones, but levels decline with age. Hormone supplements are generally reserved for those in their mid-forties and older. This chapter will focus on three hormones available over-the-counter: DHEA, pregnenolone and melatonin.

Cholesterol: The Source of Steroid Hormones

Cholesterol is one of the components of brain-cell membranes. It is also the precursor from which all steroid hormones are formed, not only in the adrenal glands, ovaries and testicles, but also in the brain. As you can see from Figure 14.1, pregnenolone, DHEA, progesterone, estrogen, and testosterone are all formed from cholesterol.

WHAT CAN BRAIN HORMONES DO FOR YOU?

DHEA and pregnenolone are very powerful. If you use them appropriately, you can expect improvements in learning and memory, sex drive and sexual enjoyment, mood and energy, speed of thinking, verbal fluency, concentration and focus, creativity, vision, hearing, awareness and sensory perception. Unfortunately, as you age, your body produces smaller amounts of both. Melatonin helps improve sleep.

WHAT CLINICAL CONDITIONS CAN BRAIN HORMONES BENEFIT?

Hormones have a broad range of effects, and if used properly, can have an influence in age-related cognitive decline, depression and perhaps Alzheimer's disease. They also help improve libido in those who have lost interest in sex.

Several studies over the past few years have indicated that drastically lowering cholesterol levels with drugs may lead to cognitive decline, depression and increased rates of suicide, homicide and accidents. Although the reasons for this are not completely clear, could interference with the production of neurosteroids be one of the reasons? Additional research will likely provide the answers to this question.

Estrogen and the Brain

Scientists are still determining how estrogen influences brain function. Studies in rats have shown that estrogens can regulate the formation of synapses, alter levels of brain chemicals, and influence various receptors (McEwen 1997).

As you likely know, there is a marked decline in levels of estrogen after menopause. Dr. Kristine Yaffe and colleagues, from the University of California in San Francisco, published a review article in the *Journal of the American Medical Association* evaluating the role of estrogen-replacement therapy in post-menopausal women and its effect on mental function (Yaffe 1998). Two of the studies showed inconclusive results, two reported no association between estrogen and cognitive function, and one found that estrogen use improved cognitive function.

Dr. Yaffe and colleagues conclude…

66 There are plausible biological mechanisms by which estrogen might lead to improved cognition, reduced risk for dementia, or improvement in the severity of dementia. Studies conducted in women, however, have produced conflicting results. Large placebo-controlled trials are required to address estrogen's role in prevention and treatment of Alzheimer's disease and other dementias. Given the known risks of estrogen therapy, we do not recommend estrogen for the prevention or treatment of Alzheimer's disease or other dementias until adequate trials have been conducted. 99

More recently, scientists at Rockefeller University discovered that estrogen is important in maintaining brain functioning (McEwen 2003) and actually serves to ensure

Figure 14.1—The Making of Steroid Hormones from Cholesterol

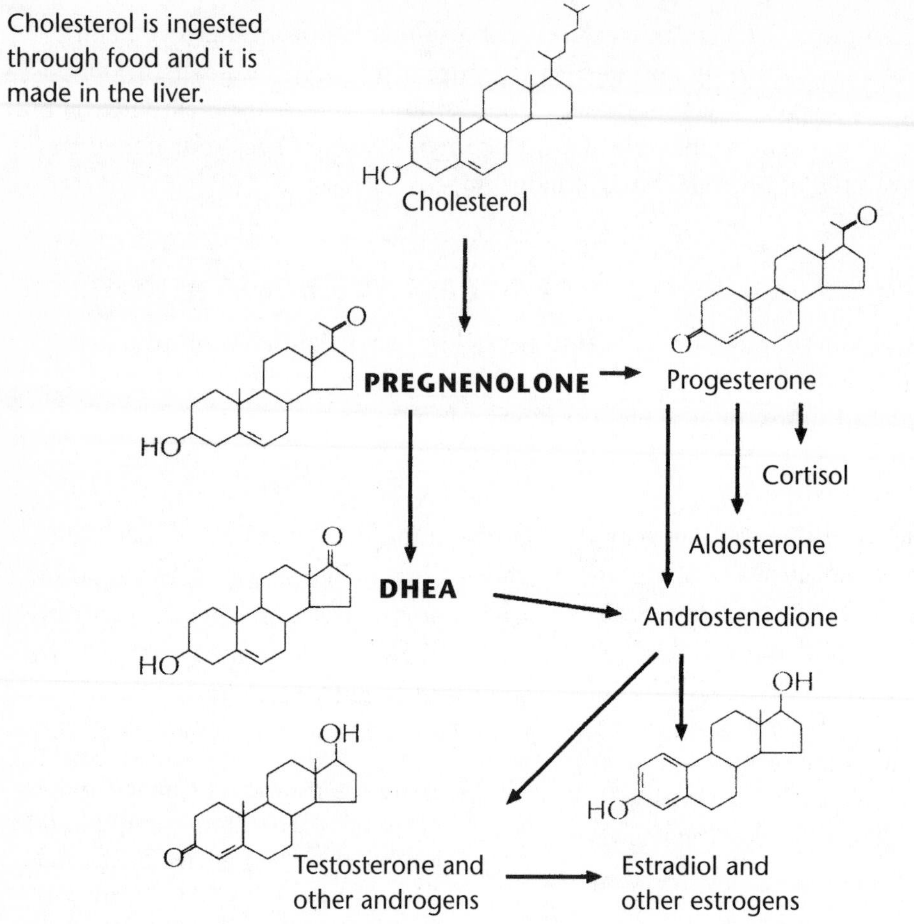

Cholesterol is ingested through food and it is made in the liver.

Cholesterol

PREGNENOLONE → Progesterone

Cortisol

Aldosterone

DHEA → Androstenedione

Testosterone and other androgens → Estradiol and other estrogens

Please note that some metabolic steps have been skipped in order to simplify this diagram.

---

that nerve cells remain active in the hippocampus, the part of the brain that controls memory.

Estrogens, unlike DHEA and pregnenolone, are available only through a doctor's prescription. Recently, plant estrogens, such as those found in soybeans or certain herbs, have become more popular. Further studies will determine whether a high intake of plant estrogens can reduce the required dosages of estrogen. In the meantime, the benefits and risks of estrogen replacement are still a matter of debate within the medical community, but most agree that a small dose of estrogen replacement may benefit some women.

Beyond Estrogen
During routine hormone-replacement therapy to postmenopausal women, doctors prescribe mainly estrogen (and sometimes progesterone or a synthetic progestin). Research

is slowly accumulating, which suggests replacing small amounts of other hormones could potentially be helpful—not only for women, but for men as well.

But not all the hormones in our bodies decline with age. Cortisol, made by the adrenal glands, and insulin, made by the pancreas, stay relatively the same, or even increase. Thyroid hormone levels vary. Pregnenolone, DHEA, growth hormone, progesterone, estrogens and testosterone all decrease with age.

The decline in the production of hormones due either to aging, or as a consequence of illness or chronic stress, can have a negative impact on a number of body tissues. All these hormones have the ability to enter most cells of the body, go to the DNA, induce the formations of a variety of enzymes and proteins, and significantly influence the function of cells and tissues.

Do Middle-Aged and Older Women Need Male Hormones?

Over the past two or more decades, women had been given estrogen or hormone-replacement therapy to treat menopausal symptoms. Recently some doctors have started using testosterone replacement in both men and women. Research indicates that there's a 30 to 50 percent decline in testosterone levels in women between the ages of 20 and 50 (Zumoff 1995). Furthermore, after menopause the ovaries stop making testosterone and estrogens. The decline in testosterone levels often leads to impaired sexual function, decreased feelings of well-being, loss of energy and thinning of bones. Therefore, some women are prescribed both estrogen and testosterone supplements.

The option of testosterone replacement should be given to postmenopausal women who suffer persistent loss of a sense of well-being, fatigue and most commonly, loss of libido, despite adequate estrogen replacement and after exclusion of other possible underlying medical conditions. However, the benefits and risks of testosterone replacement are currently not fully known. Side effects of excessive testosterone use include acne and hair loss.

As illustrated in Figure 14.1, DHEA is eventually converted into both testosterone and estrogen. Therefore, DHEA is potentially an alternative means of replacing testosterone in older women.

DHEA: The Parent of Estrogen And Testosterone

Judy, a fifty-two-year-old travel agent married for twenty-four years, was having problems with her marriage. *She told me...*

> 66 A few years ago, I noticed a distance develop between me and my husband. I just didn't have the urge to be intimate; and obviously, this hurt our closeness. The problem was getting worse and I really thought we were going to break up. I heard about DHEA, that it had the ability to improve sex drive. I started on 5 mg a day, and within a week, I couldn't keep my hands off my husband. He loved it. Now I only take the DHEA two or three times a week, and that seems to be sufficient. 99

What Benefits Does DHEA Provide?

DHEA is short for dehydroepiandrosterone, a hormone made mostly by the adrenal glands, which are located above the kidneys, but also made in the testicles, ovaries and brain. After production in the adrenal glands, DHEA travels in the bloodstream and enters tissues and cells where it is converted to testosterone and estrogens.

Most long-term studies indicate that this hormone is able to provide a sense of well-being and improve energy levels in the majority of the users (Huppert 2000, Labrie 1997). My clinical experience is consistent with the research findings. Owen Wolkowitz, M.D., from the Department of Psychiatry at the University of San Francisco, has been researching the role of DHEA as an antidepressant in middle-aged and older individuals. He tells me, "Our research has shown that DHEA supplementation improves mood."

In a double-blind German study published in the *New England Journal of Medicine,* twenty-four women with adrenal deficiency were given 50 mg of DHEA daily for four months (Wiebke 1999). They were selected because adrenal insufficiency leads to a deficiency of dehydroepiandrosterone. The result of the study showed that DHEA supplements helped improve their feelings of well-being and increased the frequency of sexual thoughts and sexual interest.

DHEA is converted in the body into testosterone and it is well known that testosterone increases sexual drive. In my clinical experience, at least a third of men and women who take DHEA report an increase in sex drive.

Availability and Dosage: DHEA is sold as pills, cream, sublingual tablets and time-release pills. Capsules and pills are sold in doses of 5 mg upward to 100 mg. Side effects (see below) are common on doses greater than 10 mg. I hope that more vitamin companies provide the 5 mg pills and will stop selling the higher doses.

Androstenedione is also available over-the-counter. I call it the "son of DHEA" since it is made from DHEA and has similar functions. Studies with androstenedione are much more limited than those with DHEA

and at this point it is difficult to predict which of the two is a better choice in hormone replacement.

A new form of DHEA, called 7-keto DHEA, was introduced in 1998. The companies that promote this product claim that it does not convert to testosterone and estrogen and consequently does not have androgenic and estrogenic side effects. On the other hand, they claim that 7-keto DHEA provides similar, or better, benefits than DHEA. If this substance does not convert into testosterone, as the manufacturers claim, then it is unlikely to have a significant effect on libido. No significant trials using 7-keto DHEA on humans have been published in peer-reviewed journals. Therefore, it is premature to make any definitive claims regarding the use of 7-keto DHEA.

 Cautions and Side Effects

Although DHEA can clearly improve mental function, users should be cautious. The influence of long-term DHEA supplementation on tumor initiation, promotion or inhibition is not known at this time. DHEA could increase the risk for benign prostatic enlargement.

High doses, generally more than 20 mg, may lead to heart palpitations in those individuals who are prone to arrythmias (Sahelian 1998). In order to reduce the risk for heart palpitations, make sure you have an adequate intake of fish oils and magnesium. If your medical condition requires that you take high doses of DHEA, have your doctor prescribe you a few pills of a beta-blocker such as propranol to carry with you. Take 40 to 60 mg of propranol if you suddenly develop a palpitation.

Cautions and Side Effects

Side effects can readily occur with the misuse of DHEA. These side effects are clearly dose-dependent, and generally begin at about 5 mg. Individuals prone to acne can get pimples on a dose as low as 2 mg. Women can experience hair growth in unwanted places such as the face and chin. DHEA could lead to accelerated scalp-hair loss due to this hormone's conversion into dihydro-testosterone (DHT), the hormone associated with hair loss. If you experience hair loss, stop the DHEA. Ask your doctor whether temporary therapy with finasteride (available in 5 mg doses as Proscar or a 1 mg dose as Propecia) might be appropriate. Finasteride blocks the conversion of testosterone to DHT and can regrow hair.

 Cautions and Side Effects

Anecdotal information indicates that high dosages of DHEA can lead to menstrual irregularities, overstimulation, occasional nervousness, irritability, aggressiveness, headaches and mood changes. Evaluation and supervision by a health-care provider is strongly advised when supplementing with hormones.

 Recommendations

There is little doubt that many individuals, especially those whose adrenal glands produce low levels of DHEA, notice an improvement in mood and sex drive when supplementing with this hormone. Some even report an improvement in energy, memory, and thinking abilities. However, due to its potential androgenic side effects such as hair loss and its unknown long-term effects, I urge individuals to use the least amount possible and to take breaks from use, which I call "hormone holidays." See the end of the chapter for dosage guidelines.

Pregnenolone: The Grandmother of All Hormones

Bill, a sixty-eight-year-old engineer from Park City, Utah, says, "I find pregnenolone to be a powerful memory booster. Ever since I started taking 5 mg three times a week, I remember phone numbers and names much easier."

Most users of pregnenolone (Preg) find this hormone to help with learning and memory, mood and energy, speed of thinking, verbal fluency, concentration and focus, creativity, vision, hearing, awareness and sensory perception. Some even report an enhancement in sex drive and sexual enjoyment.

Preg is primarily made in the adrenal glands from cholesterol, but it can also be made in other tissues, including the brain. I call Preg the "grandmother of all the steroid hormones" since the body uses it to convert into DHEA, progesterone and other steroid hormones (see Figure 14.1). Research on humans with Preg is very limited but several rodent studies have shown it to be a powerful memory enhancer (Flood 1995).

Availability and Dosage: Pills and sublingual tablets are sold in doses starting at 5 mg upward to 50 mg. Maximum regular, daily dosage should not exceed 5 mg. I recommend that you take "hormone holidays" from Preg as you would from DHEA. Both Preg and DHEA have overlapping functions. Therefore, if you plan to add Preg to your DHEA regimen, you need to reduce your dosage of DHEA. Preg is best taken in the morning, or at least no later than noon.

I'm often asked, if Preg, "the grandmother of all steroid hormones," can be converted into DHEA, progesterone, and the other steroid hormones, why not use it exclusively, and let the body convert it into the specific steroid hormones it requires?

Young people have the ability to easily convert Preg into all the other steroid hormones. As we grow older, the enzymes that convert Preg to DHEA, and Preg to progesterone, may not work as well. Nor would the enzymes that convert DHEA into androgens and estrogens be as effective. Therefore, in older individuals, giving Preg alone may not be enough.

Users' Experiences: I have recommended pregnenolone to dozens of patients. The majority reports that this hormone enhances alertness and arousal, and has a profound effect on memory and awareness. At least a third notice an enhancement in visual perception. A few find an increase in sexual enjoyment, but the sexual effects are not as consistent as that of DHEA.

Many older patients report that pregnenolone helps them recall phone numbers and names. One seventy-two-year-old patient says, "Before I started pregnenolone, I often found myself starting a sentence and forgetting what I was saying. Pregnenolone has been amazing. I never have problems with finishing sentences anymore. Both my short-term and long-term memory seem to be vastly improved."

The Author's Experience: I have taken pregnenolone on numerous occasions at doses ranging from 2 to 60 mg. Pregnenolone improves my visual and auditory perception along with providing a sense of well-being. I have also experienced side effects of headaches,

acne, insomnia, irritability and heart palpitations on doses greater than 20 mg. I use Preg only two or three times a month, on days when I need to be more alert and focused. Sometimes I take Preg if I wish to improve my visual appreciation, such as when I plan to visit an art gallery or an antique show. For instance, in March of 1999 I visited a Van Gogh exhibit at the Los Angeles County Museum of Art. That morning I had taken 10 mg of Preg along with ten capsules of fish oils. This combination certainly made my visit to the exhibit much more enjoyable.

 Cautions and Side Effects

High doses can lead to androgenic side effects similar to those of DHEA, including acne and accelerated hair loss. Irritability, aggressiveness, insomnia, anxiety, headaches and menstrual irregularities are also frequently reported in doses greater than 10 mg. *Heart palpitations can occur in doses greater than 20 mg, or even at 5 mg in individuals prone to irregular rhythms.*

 Cautions and Side Effects

In order to reduce the risk for heart palpitations, make sure you have an adequate intake of fish oils and magnesium. If your medical condition requires that you take high doses of pregnenolone, have your doctor prescribe you a few pills of a beta-blocker such as propranolol to carry with you in case you suddenly develop a palpitation.

 Recommendations

Preg is a fascinating hormone and there's still a great deal we need to learn about its potential. Eventually it could be found to play a role, either by itself or with other natural supplements, in arthritis therapy, seizure control, intelligence enhancement and a number of medical and psychiatric conditions. Caution is advised until we learn more. Keep your dosage level to a minimum. See the end of the chapter for guidelines.

Melatonin: Nature's Sleeping Pill

Melatonin is a hormone made in the pineal gland, a small, pea-sized gland located in the middle of the brain. This hormone is released at night and helps us get a deeper sleep. Cognitive improvements can occur when the proper use of melatonin improves sleep patterns and provides a deeper, more restful sleep.

Jerry, a sixty-eight-year-old retired policeman, says…

> ❝ I've had difficulty sleeping most of my adult life since work schedules kept changing. Sometimes I would do the night shift for a month and then switch to day shift. I think getting older made things worse, too. I find melatonin helps me tremendously. I take about 0.5 mg two or three nights a week. I sleep better, have more energy during the day, and feel more rested. I really like melatonin. I wish I knew about it years ago. ❞

Health Claims

Melatonin became very popular in 1996 because of media reports that, in addition to treating insomnia, melatonin could prolong life, act as an antioxidant, prevent tumors, improve sex and treat jet lag. Are any of these claims true?

A review of the published studies, and my clinical experience, indicates that melatonin works well as a sleep aid, does *not* improve sex drive, works well for jet lag, and can slightly improve mood by providing a deep sleep at night. No long-term human studies are available to indicate whether regular use prolongs life. A few trials have indicated melatonin also has antitumor potential, including a recent study presented at the American Association for Cancer Research suggesting it slows breast cancer growth as much as 70 percent (Blask 2003).

Laboratory studies have indicated melatonin to have antioxidant properties protecting brain cells from damage (Skaper 1998). Whether melatonin does so in the human body in the dosages normally consumed for sleep is not known.

Availability and Dosage: Melatonin is sold in regular pills, sublingual lozenges, under-the-tongue liquid, time-release tablets or capsules and even in a tea form. Dosages sold usually range from 0.3 to 3 mg. The time-release form is a good option and provides more consistent sleep throughout the night.

The Author's Experience: I have personally taken 0.3 to 1 mg of melatonin once or twice a week since 1995. Melatonin improves my sleeping patterns. But if I use it frequently, I notice the development of tolerance. (The serotonin precursor 5-HTP has sleep-inducing properties similar to melatonin.)

 Cautions and Side Effects
Amounts greater than 0.5 mg can produce vivid dreams, including nightmares. Even higher amounts can cause morning grogginess and lethargy and have been found to be no more effective at preventing jet lag than smaller "safe" dosages (Herxheimer 2003).

Recommendations

Until more research is available, limit your dosage to 0.3 to 1 mg. It can be taken from one-half hour to two hours before bedtime, preferably on an empty stomach. The time-release form is a good option. Small doses of melatonin can be combined with valerian, hops and other sedative herbs.

Do not use melatonin regularly for more than two nights a week because of the possible build-up of tolerance. Melatonin's effects are unknown when used nightly for prolonged periods.

The Multi-Hormone Replacement Solution

Many questions remain unanswered as to whether hormone replacement in middle-aged and older individuals is a proper medical approach to fighting the neuronal degeneration and cognitive decline that occurs with the aging process. I am certain that debate in this area will continue for a long time. It's quite likely that we'll eventually find that hormone replacement will benefit certain individuals but the required dosages may be much lower than are currently recommended. It may turn out that the best hormone-replacement regimen involves giving a small amount of Preg, DHEA and perhaps testosterone to men, and Preg, DHEA, and estrogens (and questionably, progesterone) to women. On the downside, it's possible that regular, high-dose hormone use could increase the risk of cancer in certain individuals.

Following are some guidelines on hormone-replacement therapy. Please discuss these with your physician if you're planning to take hormones on a regular basis. I wish to emphasize that these are suggestions only. In no way do I propose that these dosages are right for everyone. Each person has a unique biochemistry. Some may not need any of these hormones, while others may benefit from them. Also, your health-care provider may have a different opinion of whether these recommendations are appropriate for your situation.

Do You Need Physical Exams and Tests?

Your health-care provider should be consulted anytime you plan to regularly use hormone supplements. Taking hormones is not as simple as popping a multivitamin pill.

Here are some factors that should be considered while you're on long-term hormone-replacement therapy. You must involve your health-care practitioner in all decisions. These are guidelines for evaluations and you may consider having more or fewer tests done, depending on your particular circumstance. Remember that steroid hormones influence, or are metabolized in, many body tissues including the liver, fat cells, skin, endometrium, myometrium, intestines, breast, kidney, lung, muscle, heart, brain, prostate, testes, ovaries, eyes and others.

The Basics: Your health-care provider should perform a comprehensive medical examination, which includes weight, blood pressure, heart rate and rhythm, muscle mass, body fat, eyes and vision, hearing, skin (particularly for hair growth, moisture and pimples), hair (facial and scalp), and brain functions such as mood, alertness, memory, motivation and sleep patterns. Men should have their prostate glands evaluated routinely. Women need to have regular breast and pelvic exams.

Lab Tests: You will probably need a routine urinalysis, along with a blood panel that includes blood count, white blood cell count, kidney function, blood sugar, triglycerides, cholesterol, liver enzymes and thyroid tests.

If these evaluations are not enough to provide the necessary monitoring, your health-care practitioner may order more extensive testing.

Summary

I believe that with the right dosage and mix of hormone supplements, some individuals can improve the quality of their lives and enhance mental function. The trick is to find the right combination, frequency and dosages while minimizing potential side effects.

It will take us decades to learn the long-term effects of different hormone supplements and their combinations. In the meantime, as many of these hormones are readily available over-the-counter, consumers are looking for guidelines. I present the following charts merely as a guideline.

• If you plan to take these hormones, err on the side of taking less, not more. Take "hormone holidays." Please keep in mind that the dosages available over-the-counter are often too high and you may need to take only a tiny fraction of these pills. Have a health-care provider monitor you closely.

103

SUGGESTED REGIMENS BY AGE GROUP

READER NOTE: By "hormone holidays," I mean that you stop taking the hormones regularly. How often you stop, and for how long, is a decision you can make in consultation with your health-care practitioner. One reasonable approach is to "take off" one week or two weeks each month, or to take them every other day, or every third day. I recommend that you take hormones in the morning or before noon since taking them later in the day can lead to excessive alertness and insomnia. This is particularly true if you take high dosages.

Men—Ages 40 to 50

Melatonin:	0.2 to 0.5 mg once or twice per week, an hour or two before bedtime, especially if you have difficulty sleeping.
Preg:	1 to 4 mg every other day, taking frequent hormone holidays.

Or

DHEA:	1 to 4 mg every other day, taking frequent hormone holidays.

(Or the combination of Preg and DHEA, not exceeding 4 mg every other day, along with frequent hormone holidays).

Men—Ages 50 to 65

Melatonin:	0.2 to 1 mg once or twice a week, an hour or so before bedtime, especially if you have difficulty sleeping.
Preg:	1 to 5 mg every other day, taking frequent hormone holidays.

Or

DHEA:	1 to 5 mg every other day, taking frequent hormone holidays.

(Or the combination of Preg and DHEA, not exceeding 5 mg every other day, along with hormone holidays).

Men—Ages 65 and Older

Melatonin:	0.3 to 1 mg one to three times per week, an hour or so before bedtime, especially if you have difficulty sleeping.
Preg:	1 to 6 mg every other day, occasionally taking hormone holidays.

Or

DHEA:	1 to 6 mg every other day, occasionally taking hormone holidays.

(Or the combination of Preg and DHEA, not exceeding 6 mg every other day, with hormone holidays.)

Testosterone:	Optional, if DHEA by itself does not provide enough of an androgenic effect.

SUGGESTED REGIMENS BY AGE GROUP

Premenopausal Women—Ages 40 to about 50

Melatonin: 0.2 to 0.5 mg once or twice per week, an hour or two before bedtime, especially if you have difficulty sleeping.

Preg: 1 to 3 mg every other day, taking frequent hormone holidays.

Or

DHEA: 1 to 3 mg every other day, taking frequent hormone holidays.

(Or the combination of Preg and DHEA, not exceeding 3 mg every other day, with hormone holidays.)

Postmenopausal Women—Ages 50 to 65

Melatonin: 0.2 to 1 mg once or twice a week, an hour or so before bedtime, especially if you have difficulty sleeping.

Preg: 1 to 4 mg every other day, occasionally taking hormone holidays.

Or

DHEA: 1 to 4 mg every other day, occasionally taking hormone holidays.

(Or the combination of Preg and DHEA, not exceeding 4 mg every other day, with hormone holidays.)

Estrogen: Generally one-half to one-third of the dose normally recommended. For example, in the case of Premarin, 0.2 to 0.3 mg would be adequate, instead of 0.625. Women who take DHEA would need to reduce their dosage of estrogens because DHEA gets partially converted into female hormones.*

Women—Ages 65 and Over

Melatonin: 0.3 to 1 mg once, twice, or three times per week, an hour or so before bedtime, especially if you have difficulty sleeping.

Preg: 1 to 5 mg every other day, occasionally taking hormone holidays.

Or

DHEA: 1 to 5 mg every other day, occasionally taking hormone holidays.

(Or the combination of Preg and DHEA, not exceeding 5 mg every other day, with hormone holidays.)

Estrogen: See recommendations above.

Progesterone: See recommendations below.**

 * I recommend natural or plant estrogens instead of the synthetic versions or those collected from urine (Premarin). Synthetic versions and Premarin are available by prescription only. I also recommend consuming between one and four ounces of a soy product a day in the form of tofu, soymilk, or from other sources. Increasing soy intake or taking soy extracts reduces the need for estrogen.

** **Progesterone:** Since Preg converts into progesterone, the use of Preg makes the need for progesterone less essential. If you do take progesterone, use the natural form of micronized, sublingual or cream forms. You will need a much lower dose of progesterone if you're already on Preg since many of their effects overlap. Progesterone, in the appropriate strength, is available by prescription. Low-dose progesterone creams are also sold over-the-counter.

15

PSYCHOACTIVE HERBS
RECOMMENDED BY MOTHER NATURE

I was trained at Thomas Jefferson Medical School, a very conservative institution located in Philadelphia. During my four-year medical education in the early 1980s, I don't recall any of my teachers ever mentioning nutritional or herbal therapies. I graduated from medical school believing that if there *were* any effective herbal remedies, our teachers would have discussed them. Years later, when I first started reading about the potential uses of herbs for the treatment of medical and psychiatric conditions, I was skeptical. But over the past few years of studying herbs, reviewing the research, taking them myself and prescribing them to patients, I must say that I'm now a convert. Many herbs have very interesting compounds that have significant effects on the body and brain. In fact, there are countless chemicals found in herbs, and some of them are as powerful as pharmaceutical medicines.

Unfortunately, due to the fact that the natural chemicals in plants cannot be patented, funding for research with herbs has been slow. Only a few, such as St. John's wort, saw palmetto, kava, ginseng and ginkgo, have undergone extensive human trials. In this chapter I present some common herbs that you have probably read about. I also discuss some herbs imported from Asia and South America that seem to have an effect on brain function. The field of herbal medicine fascinates me since there are countless undiscovered chemicals within herbs that eventually might be found to have a therapeutic role in medical and psychiatric conditions. There are thousands of herbs and herbal combinations developed by healers from Asia, Africa and South America. With time, many of these will find their way into North America and Europe.

A common term you will find that describes herbs in this section is the word *adaptogen*. This is a nonspecific word indicating that the herb historically has been found to have several positive properties, particularly in increasing energy and improving resistance to stress and disease.

What Can Psychoactive Herbs Do for You?

There are thousands of different chemicals found within various herbs and I cannot make general statements regarding their effects on the brain. *There's a significant overlap in the cognitive effects of various herbs, but they can be loosely categorized in the following ways...*

- Herbs that increase energy—these include the adaptogens ginseng, maca and schisandra, and certain foodlike extracts such as royal jelly.

- Herbs that are particularly useful for anxiety disorders—kava is the most effective, although some of the adaptogens also work well. Ashwagandha and reishi are good options, too.

- Herbs that improve memory—ginkgo is the most well-studied herb in this category although bacopa, huperzine A and vinpocetine can be helpful.

- Herbs that improve mood—St. John's wort is the most consistent mood-elevating herb, although others have mild-to-moderate mood-elevating properties.

- Herbs that improve sex drive—many herbs, such as ginseng, have been promoted to have aphrodisiac qualities, but studies are limited. My clinical experience indicates ashwagandha is a good libido-enhancing herb.

Ashwagandha (*Withania Somnifera*)

Ashwagandha, also known as Indian ginseng, is a shrub cultivated in India and North America. The roots have been used for thousands of years as a folk remedy by Ayurvedic practitioners. It contains flavonoids and several active ingredients of the withanolide class (Elsakka 1990).

Several studies, mostly done on animals, have indicated that ashwagandha has antioxidant properties that may inhibit inflammation and cancer and influences brain chemistry. Specifically, it's believed to relieve stress by modulating metabolism of the stress hormone cortisol. When you are stressed, high cortisol levels can lead to anxiety and depression. Ashwagandha may also boost immunity and enhance the anti-tumor effects of chemotherapy.

Researchers from Banaras Hindu University in Varanasi, India, have discovered that some of the chemicals within this herb are powerful antioxidants (Bhattacharya 1997). They tested these compounds for their effects on rat brains and found an increase in the levels of three natural antioxidants—superoxide dismutase, catalase and glutathione peroxidase. They say, "These findings are consistent with the therapeutic use of *W. somnifera* as an Ayurvedic rasayana (health promoter). The antioxidant effect of active principles of *W. somnifera* may explain, at least in part, the reported anti-stress, cognition-facilitating, anti-inflammatory and anti-aging effects produced by them in experimental animals, and in clinical situations." Other studies confirm that extracts from ashwagandha have antioxidant properties (Mishra 2000, Dhuley 1998).

Ashwagandha may affect brain chemistry. It is used in India to treat mental deficits, including amnesia, in geriatric patients. Researchers from the University of Leipzig, Germany wanted to find out which neurotransmitters were influenced by ashwagandha (Schliebs 1997). After injecting some of the chemicals in ashwagandha into rats, the researchers later examined the rats' brains and found an increase in acetylcholine receptor activity. The researchers concluded, "The drug-induced increase in acetylcholine receptor capacity might partly explain the cognition-enhancing and memory-improving effects of extracts from *Withania somnifera* observed in animals and humans."

A study done in 1991 at the Department of Pharmacology, University of Texas Health Science Center, indicated that extracts of ashwagandha had activity similar to GABA, a substance in the brain that induces relaxation, analgesia and sleep (Mehta 1991). This may account for this herb's antianxiety effects. However, it is not the subject of much study in the U.S.

Availability and Dosage: Ashwagandha is sold in capsules of 500 mg, and is available as a dried root, powder or liquid extract. It is often combined with other herbs.

Expert Opinions: Dr. Shailinder Sodhi, N.D., an expert in Ayurvedic medicine from Bellevue, Washington, says, "Ashwagandha provides a sense of well-being with a decrease in anxiety. Users feel mellow. It is also a good aphrodisiac." Lise Alschuler, N.D., Chair of the Botanical Medicine Department at Bastyr University in Seattle, Washington, adds, "My clinical experience indicates that ashwagandha reduces anxiety and is helpful for insomnia. I recommend it for patients who are tense and need a calming herb. They can think more clearly after being relaxed."

The Author's Experience: I tried ashwagandha pills at a dose of 500 mg each at breakfast and lunch for a week. It made me calm and sleepy, and I am quite certain that it also increased my interest in sex. I find ashwagandha is better suited for me to take in the evening due to its sedative effects.

 Recommendations

Ashwagandha is an excellent herb for individuals who are tense and anxious, particularly if they suffer a loss of interest in sexual activity. Taking this herb in the evening is a good option since it can induce sleepiness in some people. However, if you have daytime anxiety or you are tense, you can take it at breakfast or lunchtime.

Ginkgo Biloba

Extracts from the leaves of the ginkgo biloba tree have been used therapeutically in China for millennia. According to fossil records, the ginkgo tree has been on earth for more than 200 million years and is one of the oldest still-existing tree species on earth. Individual trees live up to one thousand years. Ginkgo, like ginseng, is mentioned in the traditional Chinese pharmacopoeia. Ginkgo extracts are among the most widely studied and prescribed drugs in Europe to alleviate symptoms associated with a wide range of conditions. The main usages for these extracts are peripheral vascular disease and the therapy of age-related cognitive decline. Ginkgo contains many different substances, but most of them fall into two main categories: flavonoids and terpene lactones.

Flavonoids are natural substances that are also found in fruits and vegetables (see Chapter 11). Flavonoids act as antioxidants, have an influence on the immune system and interfere with tumor formation. Ginkgo contains many flavonoids, but the most concentrated are kaempferol, quercetin and isorhamnetin. Most ginkgo products on the market list a flavonoid concentration of 24 percent— you will often see "24%" printed on packages or bottles of ginkgo. Terpene lactones are what give ginkgo a bitter and strong flavor. The most important terpenes are the ginkgolides and bilobides. Ginkgolides have not yet been found in any other living plant species.

At least two-thirds of individuals I have treated or interviewed have noticed positive benefits from ginkgo. Gerry, a seventy-seven-year-old retired postal worker, says, "Ginkgo has helped my tinnitus [ringing in the ears]. It also works very well in keeping me alert and focused. I take 60 mg for breakfast and lunch." Mandy, a sixty-six-year-old actress, likes the effect of this herb. She reports, "I've been taking ginkgo for about four months now, and the improvement in my memory function is so much better I wouldn't even consider not taking it now."

However, not everyone notices benefits from ginkgo. Sandra, a thirty-seven-year-old, is disappointed. She says, "I took ginkgo for a period of six months after I heard all the positive benefits that other people were experiencing. Frankly, I haven't noticed any major difference."

How Does Ginkgo Work?

The active ingredients in ginkgo are believed to produce their beneficial effects by acting as antioxidants, preventing red blood cells and platelets from clotting, allowing more oxygen to reach neurons, and improving circulation in tiny blood vessels by inducing relaxation of the muscles surrounding blood vessels. One study found that even circulation to the eyes improves when subjects are given ginkgo (Chung 1999).

Clinical Uses

The primary indications for ginkgo use are age-related cognitive decline (ARCD) and Alzheimer's disease.

Age-related cognitive decline is a term that describes a collection of symptoms. These symptoms include difficulty in concentration and memory, absentmindedness, confusion, lack of mental energy and, in some instances, depressive mood. Some of these symptoms may be associated with an inadequate amount of blood reaching the brain. A potential justification for using ginkgo to lessen these symptoms is due to ginkgo's presumed role in enhancing blood flow to the brain. Ginkgo is licensed in Germany for the treatment of ARCD. Ginkgo may have promise in the treatment of Parkinson's disease and Alzheimer's when it is used together with other conventional medicines.

Several studies suggest that ginkgo extract may slightly improve Alzheimer's disease symptoms. In one study, patients who received between 120 and 240 milligrams daily for three to six months showed a 3 percent improvement in symptoms compared to those patients taking a placebo (Oken 1998).

What Dosages Are Best?

The majority of the studies done thus far with ginkgo have used total daily dosages of 120 to 160 mg (50:1 concentration, 24% flavonoids). Patients generally took their dosages as 40 mg three to four times a day. Treatment may be needed for a few weeks before positive results can be fully appreciated. Most manufacturers sell pills that contain 40 or 60 mg of ginkgo.

You may wish to start with one or two pills a day to see if there is any improvement in memory or thinking. Ginkgo is best taken early in the day, and no later than the afternoon.

The Author's Experience: I have found that I think faster, more clearly and am slightly more alert and talkative when I use ginkgo. The effects, however, are subtle.

 ### Cautions and Side Effects

Recent studies have shown that ginkgo biloba may interfere with the functioning of blood cells and could raise the risk of bleeding. There have been rare reports of internal bleeding when ginkgo was combined with other blood thinners such as aspirin or coumadin.

Ginkgo has antiplatelet activity and thus can prolong the time it takes to form a blood clot. In rare cases, mild stomach or intestinal complaints, headache and allergic skin reactions have been reported. Ginkgo users should tell their doctors that they're taking it.

 ### Recommendations

Ginkgo appears to be useful in memory loss due to aging or Alzheimer's disease. Because of its antioxidant properties, it may be useful in individuals with cerebrovascular disease. Because of its blood-thinning properties, do not take more than a dose of 60 mg a day on a long-term daily basis unless you are monitored by a health-care provider. Keep in mind that other nutrients and drugs have blood-thinning properties. They include coumadin, aspirin, fish oils and vinpocetine.

Ginseng

The root of the ginseng plant has been used in China, Japan and Korea for many centuries in the treatment of psychiatric and neurological disorders. There are several varieties of ginseng sold over-the-counter—Asian ginseng (*Panax ginseng*), American ginseng (*Panax quinquefolius*), and Siberian ginseng (*Eleuth-erococcus chinensis*) are the most common. Technically, Siberian ginseng does not belong in the same genus as Asian or American ginseng because it does not contain the same ingredients. As a rule, Chinese ginseng is more stimulating and raises body temperature while American ginseng is less heating and less stimulating. Siberian ginseng is neutral. Hundreds of ginseng products are available over-the-counter in different doses and combinations.

The roots of Chinese and American ginseng contain several saponins named ginsenosides that are believed to contribute to the adaptogenic properties. They are used in traditional Chinese medicine to improve stamina and combat fatigue and stress. Saponins are interesting natural compounds found in many plants, herbs, roots and beans. Saponins have potential in the prevention and treatment of diseases of the heart and circulatory system (Purmova 1995). For example, they inhibit the formation of lipid peroxides (fat oxidation) in cardiac muscle or in the liver. They decrease blood coagulation, cholesterol and sugar levels in blood and they stimulate the immune system. Some saponins may even have antitumor properties (Wakabayashi 1998).

The biochemical mechanisms of ginseng remain unclear, although there is extensive literature that deals with its effects on the brain (memory, learning, and behavior), neuroendocrine function, carbohydrate and lipid metabolism, immune function and the cardiovascular system. Reports are often contradictory, perhaps because the ginsenoside content of ginseng root or root extracts can differ—depending on the species, how it was extracted, subsequent treatment, or even the season of collection.

In a small study presented at the 2003 annual meeting of the American Stroke Association, Chinese researchers said that stroke patients had improvements in memory after taking daily ginseng supplements (Tian 2003). Another study presented before the American Academy of Neurology found the herb may be useful in improving mental function in those with multiple sclerosis (Kenney 2002).

Most patients who take ginseng notice an improvement in energy, vitality, feelings of well-being and mental clarity.

Laboratory and Human Studies

Let's examine some of the studies done with ginseng...

- Cognitive functioning—Various tests of mental performance were carried out in a group of sixteen healthy male volunteers given a standardized preparation of Asian ginseng (100 mg twice a day for twelve weeks, of a product called G-115). A similar group of subjects was given identical placebo capsules under double-blind conditions (D'Angelo 1986). A favorable effect of ginseng was observed in attention, mental arithmetic, logical deduction and auditory reaction time of those who were given ginseng.

- Researchers at Cognitive Drug Research Ltd., Reading, England, evaluated the effects of a ginkgo biloba/ginseng combination on cognitive function (Wesnes 1997). The study lasted ninety days and was performed in a double-blind, placebo-controlled manner with sixty-four healthy volunteers (aged 40 to 65 years) who had mild fatigue and lowered mood. Improvements were noted in memory and overall cognitive functioning. The treatment was well tolerated by all volunteers.

- In another study, ginseng root saponin at a dose of 50 mg three times a day was given for two months to 358 middle-aged and elderly individuals (Zhao 1990). The results showed that the herb improved memory and immunity.

- Diabetes and mood—To investigate the effect of ginseng on newly diagnosed noninsulin-dependent diabetes mellitus (NIDDM) patients, thirty NIDDM patients were treated for eight weeks with ginseng extract (100 or 200 mg) or placebo in a double-blind placebo-controlled manner (Sotaniemi 1995). The results showed that ginseng therapy elevated mood, improved psychophysical performance and reduced fasting blood glucose. A later study showed that blood sugar levels were 60 percent lower in diabetics who regularly took the herb (Vuksan 2000).

- Quality of life—The aim of this study was to compare the quality-of-life parameters in subjects receiving multivitamins plus ginseng with those found in subjects receiving multivitamins alone (Caso Marasco 1996). The study was randomized and double-blind, and it involved 625 patients of both sexes divided into two groups who took one capsule per day for twelve weeks. Group A received vitamins, minerals, trace elements, plus ginseng extract, while group B received vitamins, minerals, and trace elements only without the ginseng. At the end of the study, both groups tested positively on a questionnaire evaluating their quality of life, but group A, which had received the ginseng, had a higher score.

Availability and Dosage: Countless varieties and dosages of ginseng are available. One option is to buy a product that has a standardized extract of 3 to 7 percent ginsenosides. Use 100 mg of this extract in the morning a few times a week. You may require 500 to 2000 mg of crude extracts to feel the effects. It's best to cycle the use of ginseng. For instance, you can take it for two or three weeks and then take off a few weeks.

An Expert's Opinion: Lise Alschuler, N.D., Chair of the Botanical Medicine Department at Bastyr University in Seattle, Washington, says, "My favorite adaptogen is Siberian ginseng. I take it myself and recommend it to patients. I normally take it for a few weeks or months and then go off it for an extended period. This herb enhances well-being, increases alertness, decreases anxiety and provides more energy."

The Author's Experience: The effects from ginseng are subtle but definitely present. I have tried Asian ginseng on numerous occasions. I notice an enhancement in alertness, motivation, focus and mood, along with a sense of peacefulness. The effects seem to improve on subsequent days of use. High doses interfere with my sleep.

 ### Cautions and Side Effects

Insomnia is a common side effect from ginseng overuse, particularly with Asian ginseng—especially when it's combined in high doses with other herbs or nutrients that cause alertness.

Althea, a thirty-eight-year-old owner of a garden shop in Maui, says…

66 I tried taking a combination of kava and American ginseng that was recommended by a Chinese physician for fatigue. I took it for two weeks. I felt really better emotionally, mellow, and with increased energy. Then I started to have increased sleep problems and insomnia. I went three days being so mentally and physically overstimulated that I hardly got any sleep. I imagine this is what being on 'speed' must feel like. I stopped taking the herbs, and within two days I slowly returned to my normal state. 99

This story confirms my recommendation elsewhere in this book that dosages of nutrients and herbs have to be constantly evaluated since they can build up in the system cumulatively.

 ### Recommendations

Many people who take ginseng find this herb to be a good overall energizer and cognitive enhancer. Due to the tremendous variety of products sold, it is difficult to give definite dosage recommendations. You might try a few different products to see which one(s) give you a positive effect. In practical and simple terms, Asian ginseng raises body temperature and is more stimulating, while American ginseng is more cooling and calming. The effects of Siberian ginseng fall somewhere between these two. See this chapter's summary for additional recommendations.

Huperzine A

Huperzine A is an extract from a club moss (*Huperzia serrata*) that has been used for centuries in Chinese folk medicine. Its action has been attributed to its ability to strongly inhibit acetylcholinesterase, the enzyme that breaks down acetylcholine in the synaptic cleft (see Chapter 4). Acetylcholine is involved in memory and learning. By inhibiting the enzyme that breaks it down, more acetylcholine becomes available to stimulate neurons. Alzheimer's disease is a condition where there's a relative shortage of acetylcholine.

Several studies have been done over the past few years with huperzine A, both in China and the United States. These studies have shown that huperzine A is many times more effective and selective than tacrine (a cholinesterase-inhibiting pharmaceutical drug) in inhibiting cholinesterase (Cheng 1996).

Huperzine A has also been found to be beneficial in patients with Alzheimer's disease. In a study at Zhejiang Medical University, in Hangzhou, China, scientists administered 0.2 mg of huperzine A to fifty patients with

Alzheimer's disease for a period of eight weeks and compared the results to a group who received placebo pills (Xu 1995). The study was done in a double-blind, placebo-controlled, and randomized manner. The results showed 58 percent of the patients treated with huperzine A had improvements in memory, cognition and behavioral functions whereas only 36 percent of those on placebo improved. No severe side effects were found. Blood pressure, heart rate, electrocardiogram, electroencephalogram and liver and urine tests did not show any major abnormalities. The researchers say, "Huperzine A is a promising drug for symptomatic treatment of Alzheimer's disease."

This club-moss extract may also benefit older individuals with dementia. A study was conducted with fifty-six patients suffering from multi-infarct dementia (multiple small strokes) and one hundred patients with senile memory disorders (Zhang 1991). The dose used for multi-infarct dementia was 0.05 mg twice a day for four weeks, whereas that for senile memory disorders was 0.03 mg twice a day for two weeks. Most patients had an improvement in memory. A few reported slight dizziness, but this did not affect the therapeutic effects.

Huperzine was mentioned in the *Journal of the American Medical Association* as a possible herbal therapy for Alzheimer's disease (Skolnick 1997).

Availability and Dosage: Huperzine A is sold either by itself in doses of 0.05 mg, or in lower doses combined with other mind-boosting nutrients.

The Author's Experience: I took a capsule containing 50 micrograms (0.05 mg) of huperzine A at nine o'clock in the morning, on an empty stomach. Within an hour I could feel a subtle effect. This consisted mostly of feeling slightly more alert and focused. Over the next hour I took two additional capsules and then ate breakfast. My focus and concentration were slightly improved all day long and well into the evening. It didn't seem that huperzine A had any effect on mood, libido or appetite. No side effects occurred.

One study has shown that huperzine A is absorbed rapidly when taken orally and distributed widely in the body and eliminated at a moderate rate (Qian 1995). This rapid absorption and moderate elimination is consistent with my observation of the effects within an hour and the continuation of the effects late into the evening.

 Recommendations

Huperzine A appears to be a promising alternative to cholinesterase-inhibitor drugs used in Alzheimer's disease. More studies are required to determine its long-term safety and side-effect profile. Until we learn more about this herbal extract, I recommend its use only in the therapy of AD, and only under medical supervision.

Kava (*Piper Methysticum*)

More than 20 million Americans suffer from anxiety disorders, and countless others experience everyday stress. Since stress can interfere with mental clarity, the occasional use of kava can provide cognitive benefits.

Kava is a plant grown in the South Pacific Islands. The roots have been used by Polynesians as a psychoactive agent for centuries. The root of the kava plant contains a variety of chemicals known as kavalactones, which influence a number of the brain receptors involved in relaxation and mental clarity.

Until 1997, only a few short-term placebo-controlled studies on kava extract ingestion had been published. In 1997, Dr. Hans-Peter Volz, from the Department of Psychiatry, Jena University, Germany, published the results of the longest comprehensive human trial yet, which used extracts of kava in 101 patients who suffered from anxiety and tension. Many had a fear of public places (agoraphobia), social phobia, generalized anxiety disorder and related conditions. The dosage given was one capsule three times a day of 70 mg of kavalactones. The study lasted twenty-five weeks, and the results showed that the effectiveness of kava was superior to that of placebo. The specific areas that were improved included anxious mood, tension and fears. Patients tolerated kava well, and adverse reactions were rare.

In March 2002, the FDA issued a warning of potential liver damage from taking kava-containing supplements, which had been implicated in dozens of adverse events in other countries, including hepatitis, cirrhosis and liver failure.

Therefore, the FDA advises that anyone with liver disease or liver problems, or anyone taking drugs which can affect the liver should consult a physician before using kava-containing supplements.

The Kava Experience

Not everyone reacts exactly the same way to this herb because of individual differences in biochemistry. Furthermore, different products on the market may have varying amounts or constituents of kavalactones within them.

Most of the time, the effects of kava are noticed within an hour or two after ingestion and can last several hours. If you are already relaxed and have no muscle tension, you won't notice the calming effects of kava as much as someone who is anxious. Following are some common feelings that most users report. I have personally experienced these effects.

- A state of relaxation without interference in mental acuity, at least for the first few hours. Whether you feel more alert or sleepy from kava ingestion will depend on your individual biochemistry and from the product you are using. Often there's a feeling of alertness, followed by being drowsy and sleepy hours later. Many people have the misconception that kava is a sedative that will make one feel sleepy right away. In most cases the sedation follows an initial period of alertness.

- Less muscle tension.

- Feelings of peacefulness and contentment with mild euphoria.

- A few report a slight, temporary enhancement of visual acuity. Objects and people take on a sharper look.

The fact that kava causes relaxation, while keeping one mentally alert, distinguishes it from many drugs used for anxiety (such as Xanax and Valium), since these drugs have a tendency to interfere markedly with cognitive functioning.

Availability and Dosage: Kava is sold in a number of dosages and forms. A dose of 70 to 100 mg of kavalactones can be helpful in cases of anxiety. Try at least two or three different products before forming an opinion about kava's effectiveness.

 Recommendations

Kava is an excellent herb to use occasionally in order to relieve tension and stress. Many users find it to be a good alternative to antianxiety drugs. For more details, see my book *Kava: The Miracle Antianxiety Herb.*

The best time to take kava is in the late afternoon or early evening, unless you are very anxious during the day in which case you can take it in the morning or midday. Some individuals may need higher doses to notice an effect.

 Cautions and Side Effects

In view of the concerns about the effects of kava on the liver, it is best to restrict the use of kava to no more than a few days a month. If you have been taking kava regularly for a long period of time, consult your doctor. Your doctor will most likely recommend that you stop taking kava and have a routine liver enzymes test.

St. John's Wort (*Hypericum Perforatum*)

This simple herb took the media spotlight in 1997. What propelled St. John's wort to the status of superstar herbal antidepressant was a study published in the *British Medical Journal* (Linde 1996). The study was entitled "St. John's wort for depression—an overview and meta-analysis of randomized clinical trials." This study garnered such media attention because it was a *meta-analysis,* meaning the authors thoroughly reviewed twenty-three previous studies published on this herb and pooled the results together. Most of these studies were published in foreign journals and had not attracted the attention of the mainstream American media.

This herb has been popular in Germany and many other European countries for decades, prescribed more often than pharmaceutical antidepressants. Even the National Center for Complementary and Alternative Medicine says there is evidence it is useful in treating mild-to-moderate depression but not for major depression.

The *British Medical Journal* article showed that St. John's wort was as effective as pharmaceutical antidepressants and had fewer side effects. More than half of the patients on prescription antidepressant drugs reported side effects, compared to less than 20 percent of those patients taking the herb.

Extracts from this herb contain a number of groups of compounds, including hypericins and flavonoids. Many of the available preparations of St. John's wort are standardized, based on the hypericin content and not necessarily on the flavonoids.

How Does It Work?

Since there are a quite a number of compounds within St. John's wort extract, it is difficult to determine the precise ways this herb works in relieving depression. Some studies indicate this herb influences brain-chemical levels, such as dopamine, serotonin and norepinephrine.

Most of my patients who have taken St. John's wort have noticed a sense of well-being, increased alertness and energy, and an end to feelings of procrastination. They have a motivation to get things done, such as work projects and housecleaning. Some patients also report having a greater interest in being sociable, interacting with friends and meeting new people.

It may take one or two weeks to notice the antidepressant effects of St. John's wort. I recommend you take the herb for at least one month before forming an opinion on its effectiveness.

Availability and Dosage: Most of the extracts available over-the-counter contain 0.3 percent hypericins in a 300-mg dose because they are based on a European formulation that has been used as the standard in the various studies conducted over the years.

Many of the studies evaluating the effectiveness of St. John's wort have used a dosage of 300 mg of the extract three times a day. I find that patients experience a higher degree of insomnia when they take three pills a day. I recommend starting with one pill in the morning. If you feel no improvement in your mood after a few days, add a second pill when you eat lunch. Everyone has a unique biochemistry. Some may find that one pill in the morning, or one pill every other morning, is adequate. Other individuals may require three pills a day. If you have only a mild case of depression, I recommend starting with just one pill before increasing the dosage. (See Chapter 19 on how to use St. John's wort in combination with other mood-elevating nutrients.)

The Author's Experience: I notice the effects of this herb, such as an enhanced sense of well-being, the very first day of taking it. The effects become more pronounced over the next few days of use. I experience insomnia when my dosage exceeds two pills a day.

 Cautions and Side Effects
Fortunately, St. John's wort has few side effects. The side effects reported in scientific studies include dizziness, nausea, tiredness, restlessness, dry mouth and allergic reactions, including hives or itching. In most studies, these side effects occurred in less than 10 percent of users. These side effects are dose-dependent, meaning that they occur less frequently when you take lower dosages. It's very rare to experience side effects if you take a daily dose of 300 mg for less than two months.

Avoid excessive sun exposure while you are taking St. John's wort due to possible skin reactions.

 Recommendations
St. John's wort is definitely a good antidepressant and an effective alternative to pharmaceutical antidepressants in cases of mild-to-moderate depression.

Most cases of depression last only a few months. I advise that this herb be used continuously for no longer than six months. The majority of the human trials with this herb have lasted less than three months. We don't have long-term studies to know what kind of influence St. John's wort has on our bodies. If you find that your depression returns, you may consider restarting St. John's wort.

Vinpocetine

Vinpocetine is chemically related to, and derived from, vincamine, an alkaloid found in the periwinkle plant. Vinpocetine became available over-the-counter in 1998. It was introduced into clinical practice in Europe more than two decades ago for the treatment of cerebrovascular disorders and related symptoms. Experiments with vinpocetine indicate that it can dilate blood vessels, enhance circulation in the brain, improve oxygen utilization, make red blood cells more pliable and inhibit aggregation of platelets (Kiss 1996). Vinpocetine may even have antioxidant properties (Santos 2000, Orvisky 1997).

There have been quite a few studies with vinpocetine. Researchers at the University of Surrey in Guildford, England, administered vinpocetine to over 200 patients suffering from mild-to-moderate dementia (Hindmarch 1991). Every day for sixteen weeks, patients received either 10 mg doses of vinpocetine three times a day, 20 mg doses of vinpocetine three times a day, or placebo three times a day. The study found that statistically significant cognitive improvements were found in favor of those groups receiving the vinpocetine. The patients on 10 mg performed slightly better than those on 20 mg. There were no clinically relevant side effects reported.

In another study, fifteen Alzheimer's patients were treated with increasing doses of vinpocetine (30, 45, and 60 mg per day) in a pilot trial during a one-year period (Thal 1989). The study was done at Veterans Administration Medical Center, in San Diego, California. In this study, vinpocetine failed to improve cognition at any dose tested. There were no significant side effects from the therapy.

In a double-blind clinical trial, vinpocetine was shown to offer significant improvement in elderly patients with chronic cerebral dysfunction (Balestreri 1987). In the study, forty-two patients received 10 mg of vinpocetine three times a day for thirty days, and then 5 mg three times a day for sixty days. Matching placebo tablets were given to another forty patients for the ninety-day trial period. Patients on vinpocetine scored consistently better in all cognitive evaluations. No serious side effects were reported.

Twelve healthy female volunteers received pretreatments with vinpocetine in a dose of 40 mg three times a day or placebo for two days according to a randomized double-blind crossover design (Subhan 1985). On the third day of treatment, and one hour following morning dosage, subjects completed a battery of psychological tests. Memory was significantly improved following treatment with vinpocetine when compared to placebo.

Availability and Dosage: Vinpocetine is sold in 5 and 10 mg pills. Levels peak in the bloodstream within an hour and a half after ingestion.

Users' Experiences: Dennis, a seventy-two-year-old patient with age-related cognitive decline, says, "I take 5 mg of vinpocetine at breakfast and lunch. I feel more focused, and it seems that I can make decisions quicker. I also notice colors to be more vivid." Other patients report similar positive effects.

Dr. Polimeni, of Rome, Italy, says, "Vinpocetine is a good cognitive enhancer. It improves visual and auditory perception similar to pregnenolone. My patients appreciate the effects better after a few days of therapy."

The Author's Experience: I like the effects of vinpocetine. On 10 mg, I notice improvement in concentration and focus, and enhancement of color perception, peaking at about two hours after dosing. Thereafter the effects gradually decrease but persist for a few hours. I do not notice any significant changes in mood or energy levels.

 Cautions and Side Effects
The long-term effects of vinpocetine are not known. It does have blood-thinning potential. Therefore, those individuals taking warfarin or high doses of aspirin or other blood thinners need to inform their physician before use.

Recommendations

Vinpocetine appears to be beneficial in cognitive disorders that are due to poor blood flow to the brain. Therefore individuals with atherosclerotic vascular disease are probably most likely to benefit from vinpocetine. Until long-term studies are available, regular intake for prolonged periods should be limited to 2.5 or 5 mg once or twice daily.

Additional Herbs and Foodlike Supplements

There are many herbs that are reputed to influence mental function. A partial list includes bacopa monniera, cordyceps, gotu kola, rosemary, maca, Fo-ti, reishi and schisandra. There are also food-like supplements such as spirulina, blue-green algae and royal jelly. The research with many of these supplements is very limited. I am certain that some of them do have an effect since I have personally noticed increased alertness and energy levels when I've taken royal jelly, maca and gotu kola. I'll just briefly mention a few of these herbs.

- *Bacopa* is an Ayurvedic medicine used in India for memory enhancement, epilepsy, insomnia and as a mild sedative. This herb commonly grows in marshy areas throughout India. Some studies have shown that bacopa has antioxidant effects (Tripathi 1996), while a study on rats showed bacopa administration improves learning skills (Singh 1982).

Bacopa is sold either by itself or most commonly combined with other herbs. Dr. Shailinder Sodhi, an expert in Ayurvedic herbs, reports, "Bacopa is a brain tonic that provides relief from stress; it energizes but does not act as a stimulant. Bacopa is often taken in the morning and the effects can last all day. Users notice alertness, clarity of vision and stimulation of appetite. The dosage is 125 mg for 50 percent bacosides standardized extract, or 10 ml of the liquid extract." Bacopa has potential as a cognitive aid, but more studies are needed in order to determine which neurotransmitters this herb influences and to determine its long-term effectiveness and safety profile.

- *Gotu kola* is an herb commonly used in the Ayurvedic system of medicine. Traditionally gotu kola has been used as a nerve tonic to improve memory and clarity of thinking. It is sold in capsules and in liquid extracts. Most patients notice an increase in alertness and energy. However, a drawback is that it heats the body. In warm weather, users may sweat a little more than usual.

Dr. Sodhi believes that gotu kola improves circulation, causes alertness and helps in relaxation. The effects are similar to bacopa but milder.

I've taken gotu kola once at breakfast, four capsules of 500 mg each. Within one half hour, I noticed an increase in alertness and motivation that lasted most of the day. Some people take gotu kola occasionally as a substitute for caffeine in order to increase their alertness.

- *Maca* is a rootlike vegetable shaped like a radish that grows high in the Andes. Native Peruvians apparently used maca as a food and as medicine. Some people claim that maca is an adaptogen similar to ginseng. Maca has been used traditionally to increase energy and to promote endurance. Maca is available as capsules containing

500 mg of the herb or as a grain-alcohol extract.

I've only experimented with maca for a week, with doses ranging from 1000 to 5000 mg. Within a few hours of taking the higher dose of maca, there is an increase in arousal and energy levels. This lasts a few hours and then fades away. There is also a slight mood elevation.

- *Reishi* is a mushroom traditionally used in Asia to help calm the mind, ease tension, improve memory and sharpen concentration and focus (Teeguarden 1998). Reishi is available as an extract in capsules in a variety of dosages. You will often find it combined with other herbs. Patients report reishi gives them a sense of calmness. Dolores, a forty-four-year-old customer-service manager for a major airline, finds this herb helpful. She says, "I'm usually very stressed at work because we get a lot of complaints from customers. When I take reishi, I am able to respond to complaints in a poised and comfortable manner."

Rob Underhill, a nutrition educator from Scotts Valley, California, says, "Reishi gives me mental clarity and stamina. It provides a solid base to work from. I feel centered, stable and can easily access my mental power." Roy Upton, a herbalist from Soquel, California, reports similar effects: "I was burning candles on both ends while traveling, giving lectures and getting little sleep. Reishi helped me stay centered and focused. It gave me a solid physical and mental base to work from without being stimulated. I take up to three tablets a day of 750 mg each."

I've tried a product that contains 600 mg of reishi per capsule. I generally notice the effects when I take two pills. Within a couple of hours, there's a sense of relaxation and calmness, with the urge to take deep, relaxed breaths. My mind stays alert without much sedation or sleepiness. It appears that reishi is an herb that will undoubtedly become more popular with time. It is ideal for individuals who wish to handle stress better and need to stay calm throughout the day. This could apply to office workers and to moms at home taking care of hyperactive children.

With time we are likely to learn more about the effects on the central nervous system of these and many other herbs and foodlike substances.

 Recommendations

Here are some practical recommendations for those interested in taking herbs on a regular basis…

- Buy a bottle of one adaptogenic herb such as ginseng or maca and use it regularly for about two weeks. Note how this herb influences you.

- At the end of the two weeks, take a break for a week and purchase another herb. Try this one for two weeks. Again, record your impressions.

- Continue trying the several herbs discussed in this chapter and you'll eventually find out which one(s) you like most.

- Once you've determined the ones that are suitable for you, you can again try each one separately, or you can alternate their use on a daily or weekly basis. It's best not to take these herbs all the time, but instead to cycle their use. Take a break of a few days when you switch from one herb to another.

There are several advantages in alternating the use of different herbs.

1. You'll never find out how much you like the effects of a particular herb if you don't try it.

2. There may be nutrients or compounds within certain other herbs that could be beneficial to you and you will not get exposed to them if you take the same herb all the time.

3. The risk of potential side effects from a particular substance would be minimized. In case your body chemistry does not agree with the long-term exposure to a specific herb, alternating them would decrease the chance of an untoward reaction. Some herbs could have potentially toxic or harmful components if they are used for prolonged periods, but they may not be damaging if your exposure to them is limited.

4. Different herbs will influence different parts of the brain.

5. You may build a tolerance to a certain herb if you take it frequently. If you alternate the use of various herbs, you will continue noticing their cognitive benefits.

It takes time to learn about the different psychoactive herbs and how to best use them for different purposes. I consider learning about these herbs and other mind boosters an exciting, lifelong, enjoyable process.

Summary

As you have seen, there are a variety of herbs that have an influence on mood, memory, energy, libido, vision and cognitive function. How do you decide which one(s) to take?

It's important to differentiate between the herbs that can be taken regularly as adaptogens (such as ginseng) and ones that are used for a specific therapeutic purpose. For instance, St. John's wort is reserved for those with depression. Huperzine A is aimed for those with Alzheimer's disease. Ginkgo improves concentration and memory, and is also recommended for age-related cognitive decline and Alzheimer's disease.

You should also differentiate between the herbs that can cause increased energy, alertness and warmth—such as Chinese ginseng and gotu kola—and herbs that have a calming effect, such as ashwagandha, kava and reishi. 🍎

PART V

STAYING SMART
AFTER SCHOOL

16

THE MIND-BOOSTING PROGRAM FOR AGES 25 TO 40

Memory capacity and thinking abilities are excellent during our twenties and thirties. So many people in this age group would have little need to regularly supplement with mind boosters. However, there are occasions when supplements could prove to be beneficial. During this particular life stage, when many individuals are establishing their careers they need to be alert and focused at work to maximize performance and reap the rewards of accomplishment and success. The appropriate use of mind boosters can help in this regard.

Natural supplements can also be helpful in the therapy of mood and anxiety disorders and insomnia. Mood disorders are common in this age group, and depression can certainly interfere with optimal mental functioning. Many natural mood lifters can provide significant assistance, preventing the need for pharmaceutical antidepressants.

Alice, a thirty-one-year-old legal assistant, took frequent sick days off work. "I just couldn't make myself get up in the morning and go to work," she lamented. "Even though my boss liked my work, he was about to fire me for being absent so often." After only three weeks' therapy with a combination of St. John's wort, B-complex, and CoQ10, Alice's mood brightened and she has rarely missed work since.

Certain supplements can also be helpful in easing the stress and anxiety associated with work and family life. Michael, a respiratory therapist at a university hospital, found the occasional use of kava to be significantly helpful in relieving his stress. "I used to have a lot of arguments with the nurses," he recounts. "Since I've started kava, the nurses have commented that I'm much more cheerful and easy to get along with."

A third common problem that interferes with cognition and work performance is insomnia. Sleep difficulties can occur due to stress, lack of physical activity or anxiety. Many have benefited from the proper use of melatonin, 5-HTP, or certain sleep-inducing herbs such as ashwagandha and hops.

This chapter will provide practical suggestions that address the above issues and will recommend routine supplements for optimal mental functioning.

Routine Supplements for The 25-to-40 Age Group

Walk into a health-food store or any pharmacy or retail outlet that sells supplements, and you will find shelves and shelves of vitamins, herbs, nutrients and hormones. Most of these supplements have an effect on the mind. If you're planning to enhance your mental performance, how do you decide which of these supplements are appropriate for you, what dosages you should take, and in what combinations?

There are several factors you need to consider before starting a mind-boosting program. These factors include your age, sex, occupation, lifestyle, diet, medical status and the potential interaction of these supplements with medicines you may currently be taking.

Please review the top ten mind-boosting principles discussed in Chapter 2 before you start taking any supplements. I also suggest you follow as many as possible of the dietary and lifestyle recommendations for a healthy mind outlined in Chapter 5. Although it can sometimes be challenging, try to make these recommendations a normal daily habit for the rest of your life. You'll thank yourself many years from now.

If you don't like to take too many pills, I would suggest obtaining many of your basic nutrient needs through a multivitamin complex. There are countless daily multivitamin pills you can purchase over-the-counter. Each of these has a different combination and different dosages of vitamins and minerals.

As a simple guideline, look at the label and choose a product that contains about one to two times the RDA ("recommended daily allowance") or PDV ("percent daily value") for vitamins. For instance, if the RDA for vitamin B-1 is 1.5 mg, a product containing a range of 1 to 3 mg should be adequate for most people. The label will also show the percentage RDA contained in the product. For example, if the product contains 1.5 mg of B-1, the label will state that the dose is 100 percent of the RDA or PDV.

In the case of minerals, a product that contains a lower percentage than the RDA is usually adequate. Instead of one or two times the RDA, about half, or 50 percent, is all that would be necessary to take on a regular basis. That's because minerals have a tendency to accumulate in the body and lower amounts of mineral supplements are usually needed. This is in contrast to most vitamins, particularly the B-complex and C, which are easily flushed out of the system if larger-than-required doses are taken. You don't have to take these multivitamin and mineral pills every single day. A few times a week would be fine.

If you don't consume fish on a regular basis, I recommend taking fish-oil capsules that supply 500 to 1000 mg of the important omega-3 fats EPA and DHA. As an alternative, you could take about a teaspoon of flaxseed oil each day, which also contains omega-3 oils (see Chapter 7 for details). These oils are important for proper brain function and vision. Another option is to take both the flax and the fish oil daily.

One of my patients, James, is a twenty-eight-year-old strict vegetarian. As part of a mind-boosting program, I described to him the importance of omega-3 fatty acids. He noticed an improvement in mood and alertness within two days of taking a tablespoon of flax oil daily. "I realized that I wasn't feeling that midafternoon slump and sleepiness anymore. Even my vision improved," he says. He is currently taking a teaspoon of flaxseed oil every day.

Supplements That Improve Mental Performance

There are times when the demands of our modern society may require us to perform at an extraordinary level. For instance, during tax season accountants often labor through fourteen-hour days. Lawyers must grind through long nights in order to prepare for a courtroom appearance. Hospital interns and residents are routinely asked to work twenty-four-hour or longer shifts, and they must remain mentally alert and make life-and-death decisions. Writers, musicians, actors and other people in the arts may be required to create or perform for extended hours or during demanding situations. It is reassuring to know that there are natural supplements that you can rely on occasionally in order to enhance alertness, concentration, creativity and mental capacity.

Having supervised many patients who regularly take mind sharpeners, I have observed that individual responses vary significantly. Although I provide information on a number of supplements to select from, the only way to find out for certain how you respond is to try these supplements yourself. As a rule, it is desirable for your initial doses to be low. You can always increase the dose if you do not notice an effect.

I recommend that you have a thorough physical examination before trying new supplements and that a nutritionist or health-care practitioner adequately supervises you.

There is a large selection of mind-boosting supplements to choose from. The choice of a supplement would depend on a number of factors, including desired effect, cost and individual preference. The effects of many supplements overlap. Most commonly you will notice an enhancement in alertness, focus and motivation. Some supplements may also sharpen your vision, increase sex drive or sexual appreciation, or help you accomplish a particular project quicker and more efficiently.

The following is a list of natural supplements you can take *occasionally* to enhance your mental abilities. They are best taken in the morning or before lunch on an empty stomach, or with a small meal. As a general guideline, use these only a few days a month. If you take too high a dose, or a combination of two or more, you may feel overstimulated.

For full details on how each one of these works, see the appropriate chapter in Part IV.

- A B-complex supplement supplying five to ten times the RDA can provide an elevation in mood and energy. As I mentioned earlier in this chapter, I recommend taking one to two times the RDA on a daily basis.

- Pantothenic acid is one of the B vitamins. At a dose of 250 to 500 mg, it enhances energy, alertness and elevates mood.

- Coenzyme Q10 is an antioxidant that also plays a role in the energy-production system in each cell. A dose of 30 to 90 mg in the morning leads to increased energy that is most often noticed by late afternoon or evening.

- Trimethylglycine, or TMG, is a lesser-known nutrient that has very noticeable effects on mood. Many people like the increase in energy and elevation of mood that they feel a few hours after taking it. The usual dose is from 250 to 1000 mg. DMG, DMAE and SAMe provide similar effects.

- Acetyl-L-carnitine, or ALC, is a nutrient involved in the energy-production system of cells. A dose of 250 to 750 mg improves energy, alertness, and mood within one to two hours.

- Tyrosine and phenylalanine are amino acids that convert into a brain chemical known as dopamine. A dose of 100 to 300 mg in the morning on an empty stomach leads to alertness within an hour. Some people take a small dose of these amino acids as a substitute for coffee.

 Cautions and Side Effects

High dosages can lead to overstimulation, racing of the heart and irritability.

- Once you have experimented with the nutrients listed above, you may wish to try others. These would include NADH, lipoic acid, vinpocetine and pregnenolone. You can also learn about many of the energy-enhancing herbs such as ginseng, maca, gotu kola and others, in Chapter 15.

As you can see, there are quite a number of options available. It may take some trials to find the ideal nutrients that work well for your particular brain chemistry. It is likely that you will find other positive effects that are not mentioned above. For instance, some of these nutrients may make you feel more talkative, clever, humorous, creative or spontaneous.

It's also possible that too high a dose of some of these nutrients will interfere with your clarity of thinking or performance. It may take you several months to have a good understanding of how to best use these nutrients. Learning about mind boosters is a lifelong process. After years of research, I'm still constantly learning more myself. It's important to emphasize that these nutrients should be used only occasionally, such as a few times a month.

Mood-Improving Supplements

Depression or low mood occurs commonly in the 25-to-40 age group, especially among women. A thorough medical evaluation is necessary before taking mood-elevating supplements. As a rule, a good diet, exercise, and other positive lifestyle habits can make an enormous difference in your mood. Supplements that work very well in improving mood are the B vitamins and the herb St. John's wort. Chapter 19 provides a complete step-by-step nutritional approach to treating depression.

In cases of premenstrual syndrome, therapies that may be helpful include B-complex vitamins, calcium at 1000 mg a day, pregnenolone at 5 to 10 mg in the morning and 5-HTP or kava for anxiety. These supplements, except for the B-complex and calcium, are best reserved for the few days of the premenstrual stage. 5-HTP, or 5-hydroxy-tryptophan, is an amino acid-like nutrient that increases serotonin levels and works well for anxiety. A suggested dose is 25 mg on an empty stomach once or twice a day. Kava is an herb that effectively and safely reduces anxiety, and the suggested dose is 70 to 100 mg of the kavalactones (the active chemicals in kava) used occasionally.

Supplements for Stress

One potential problem that interferes with memory and clarity of thinking during one's twenties and thirties is stress, with severe cases leading to anxiety disorders. Herbal and nutritional supplements can address this problem.

Stress can occur on an occasional basis, or it can be ongoing. Kava, the anti-anxiety and anti-stress herb, can be very helpful when it is used occasionally and provided that you have no liver disease. The usual dosage is 70 to 100 mg of the kava-lactones (the active chemicals) once, twice, or three times a day. Kava helps in relaxation and does not significantly interfere with mental clarity. The best time to take it is in the late afternoon or early evening. Please see cautions regarding kava use in Chapter 15.

5-hydroxytryptophan (5-HTP), the serotonin precursor, is another supplement that can be used occasionally to induce relaxation. The dosage is 25 to 50 mg on an empty stomach. The effects are often noticed within an hour. A high daytime dose, such as more than 50 mg, can cause sedation and the urge to sleep.

Additional herbs that can help as stress busters include ashwagandha, American ginseng and reishi. The benefits from these herbs often become apparent to you after several days. If your diet is deficient in fish, fish oils or flaxseed oil, supplements might help you with your adaptation to stressful situations.

Strategies for Sleep

Insomnia and restless nights are common in any age group. See Chapter 5 for specific step-by-step suggestions on how to improve your sleep quality. Melatonin, 5-HTP, and herbs such as ashwagandha and hops can be used occasionally for a deeper sleep.

A Note to Vegetarians

I supervise many patients who are vegetarian. When I inquire about their dietary intake, I find that a significant number have a tendency to overconsume carbohydrates at the expense of protein. Some patients do well on this non-meat diet but many find an improvement in their energy and mood when they eat even small amounts of meat or dairy products. This improvement may be due to an increased protein intake, or to the restoration of certain nutrients that are mostly found in meats, poultry, and fish. These nutrients include CoQ10, creatine and carnitine. If you plan to continue on a vegetarian diet, I recommend taking supplements of these nutrients. The daily dosage would be about 10 mg of CoQ10, 250 mg of carnitine, and 1 g of creatine.

Fish contains important omega-3 fats, such as EPA and DHA, that are necessary for brain health. If you are vegetarian or if you don't consume fish on a regular basis, supplementation with fish oils may be beneficial for improved mood and clarity of thinking. A total of 500 to 1000 mg of DHA and EPA should be adequate. If you have an objection to taking fish-oil capsules, you could obtain omega-3 fats by consuming flaxseed oil, or DHA capsules that are derived from algae.

Pregnancy

Since most mind boosters have not been studied in pregnant women, no firm recommendations can be made. The addition of one to two times the RDA for vitamins is highly recommended, especially for folic acid. *A deficiency in folic acid can lead to neural-tube defects in the baby.*

After delivery some women suffer from a condition called "post-partum depression," as a result of major changes in hormones, fatty acids and neurotransmitters. See Chapter 19 on how to treat depression naturally.

Fish oils may be helpful for this condition since these fatty acids are depleted in the mother due to the enormous quantities transferred to the fetus. Choline could also be helpful during or after pregnancy since a placental transport system removes choline from the mother in order to supply the phospholipid requirements of the fetus.

Summary

As a rule, most young, healthy individuals do not need to take any mind boosters on a regular basis as long as they have a good diet, sleep well, and follow proper lifestyle habits. The use of mind-boosting nutrients for special situations can help you be more alert, focused and productive.

17

THE MIND-BOOSTING PROGRAM FOR AGES 41 TO 60

I hit age forty in November of 1997. I continue to be very productive and creative. However, when I don't take supplements, I feel less vital than I did a decade or two earlier. My energy level, memory ability and libido are slightly lowered. I suspect that over the next two decades there may be a gradual decline in my cognitive abilities. I plan to try to slow this process by following the positive lifestyle habits I discuss in Part III, and by taking some of the supplements mentioned in this book.

Men and women between the ages of 41 and 60 are often at the peak of their accomplishments and career advancement. Intellectual functioning during this time is still excellent, but subtle changes begin to become apparent. During these years, hormone levels start declining. Men and women alike often notice a dip in sexual drive, and perhaps a slight or moderate decrease in stamina. Some individuals will feel drowsy late in the day and have difficulty staying alert past dinner.

I have had many patients in this age group who, just like me, have benefited from the proper use of supplements. Gary, a fifty-one-year-old lawyer, had noticed a decline in alertness and focus for a number of years, as well as occasional insomnia. He was not as productive at work as he was in the past. Every afternoon he would feel sleepy and tired and have the urge to take a nap. His sex drive had also been gradually declining. After a thorough medical history and examination, I started Gary on a simple dietary and supplement program that led to a tremendous improvement. Gary responded particularly well to a B-complex vitamin, fish oils and ginkgo. Also, by substituting small frequent meals and snacks containing protein for a big carbohydrate lunch (he used to eat pasta regularly), he no longer had an afternoon slump. The twice-weekly use of small doses of nighttime melatonin improved his sleeping patterns. To help his sagging libido, I recommended the occasional use of DHEA at the times when he wanted to be more sexually active. It worked.

Victoria, a fifty-four-year-old interior designer, found that her energy levels, mood and cognitive abilities improved significantly with a combination of B vitamins, CoQ10, flaxseed oil and ginseng. She was able to stay alert and focused all day, accomplish her household duties, and still have enough energy to enjoy her interior-design work twenty hours a week. "I have a renewed sense of well-being and joie de vivre," she says.

In these two examples, the supplement programs used by Gary and Victoria were different, but the end result—more energy and greater focus—was similar. There are many different mind-boosting options and combinations available.

The mind-boosting supplements and lifestyle habits recommended for this age group are similar to the ones I recommended for the 25-to-40 group, but they are more extensive.

I separate these recommendations into three categories in order to accommodate individual preferences. Some people are reluctant to take many supplements, while others wish to take a dozen or more. If you are the former, the recommendations made in the "first-line" category should be sufficient for you. If you have an interest in taking more supplements, I have provided two additional categories. *Please consult a nutritionally oriented health-care provider before starting this mind-boosting program.* Make sure your provider is aware of the supplements you are taking, since some of them may potentially interfere with your prescription medicines. Read the top ten mind-boosting principles discussed in Chapter 2.

First-Line Supplements for The 41-to-60 Age Group

Begin with these simple suggestions…

- A multivitamin complex that contains one to three times the RDA or PDV is all that would be necessary to take on a regular basis. Your multimineral complex could include about 50 to 100 percent of the RDA for minerals. You don't have to take these multivitamin and -mineral pills every day. A few times a week would be fine. You might consider taking some of the B vitamins in their coenzyme form.

- In addition to the multivitamin pills, take additional antioxidants. I recommend vitamin C, between 100 and 250 mg, and vitamin E, between 20 and 100 IU. You don't have to take these antioxidants every day.

- Make sure you have enough fish in your diet —or taking fish-oil supplements providing a total of 500 to 1000 mg of DHA and EPA would be adequate. If you're a strict vegetarian, take one-half to one teaspoon of flax-seed oil each day to provide omega-3 oils.

- You can occasionally use an herbal adaptogen, such as ginseng, for additional mental and physical energy.

Second-Line Supplements

If the supplements recommended above are not enough for you, consider adding one or more of the following under medical supervision. Be careful when you start adding multiple supplements—their effects can be cumulative and overly energizing. In some cases the stimulation could cause you to feel irritable or anxious. Taking too many pills with energizing properties, even in the morning, can cause insomnia. I recommend that you learn the effects of each nutrient by itself before combining them. When you do combine, reduce the dosage of each.

Choose one of the following and learn its effects on your mind and body before trying another one…

- Ginkgo, at a dose of 40 mg, with breakfast or lunch, to improve memory and clarity of thinking. It may take several days before you notice the effects.

- CoQ10, at a dose of 10 to 30 mg, most mornings with breakfast, to increase energy levels.

- Pantothenic acid, at a dose of 100 mg. Take in the morning for enhanced energy and mood elevation.

- Trimethylglycine, or dimethylglycine, at a dose of about 100 mg. Take in the morning with or without food, to improve mood and energy.

- Acetyl-L-carnitine, at a dose of 250 mg, most mornings before or with breakfast, for enhanced alertness, clarity of thinking and mood.

As much as possible, try to have some physical activity during the day or evening that uses up the increased energy that the supplements provide. Even with all of these powerful nutrients, there's nothing like physical activity to help you feel good and give you a deep sleep at night.

Third-Line Supplements

Dozens of nutrients and herbs have an effect on the mind. You will notice significant mental improvement from the first- and second-line therapies suggested above. Most people will be quite content with these. However, it's possible that some of these recommendations may not suit your needs, or that you will eventually want to try additional supplements. Some users like to alternate between different nutrients. I have provided additional options for these reasons.

At this stage, it is very important that a health-care practitioner familiar with nutritional therapy closely supervise you. If you add these nutrients, you will need to stop or reduce the dosage of the ones you currently take.

It's always preferable to start a new supplement during a period when you are not taking other supplements to determine

its effects without interference. Try each nutrient individually for at least a few days to learn about changes in alertness, mood, concentration and potential side effects. If you plan to take these nutrients on a regular basis, I recommend using them only once or twice a week to avoid becoming tolerant.

- Choline helps with focus and concentration. A dose of 250 mg is a good start. If you don't notice any benefits, try 100 to 250 mg of the activated form, sold as CDP-choline.

- Lipoic acid, 5 to 25 mg, can be taken most mornings with breakfast. Lipoic acid provides a subtle relaxation and sharpness of vision. It is particularly helpful in regulating blood-sugar levels in diabetics.

- NADH at a dose of 2.5 or 5 mg once or twice a week in the morning, on an empty stomach, improves alertness, feelings of well-being and libido.

- There are additional herbs and nutrients, such as vinpocetine, DMAE and SAMe that you could explore with time. Remember that the effects of many supplements are cumulative. For instance, choline, CDP-choline and DMAE all affect the acetyl-choline system. Therefore, if you combine them, you will need less of each. The effects of TMG, DMG, DMAE and SAMe are also cumulative.

I do not recommend the amino acids phenylalanine and tyrosine in this age group since high doses increase heart rate and may cause palpitations.

Ask your physician whether it's appropriate for you to take a low dose of aspirin, such as a baby aspirin, or one-fourth of a 325 mg pill, a few times a week. This may help thin the blood and improve circulation to the brain and reduce the risk for strokes or heart attacks.

Hormone Replacement

It's well-known that the production of many hormones declines with age. A phenomenon called andropause has been defined as the gradual decrease in men of the production of androgens such as the hormones DHEA and testosterone. This decline in hormone levels happens very gradually in men, unlike menopause in women where there is a sudden drop in estrogen levels as the ovaries stop producing estrogen. Although hormone replacement in women has been well researched, male hormone replacement is still a new concept and no definite answers are yet available.

In my judgment, there would be little need for hormone replacement in men younger than their mid-forties. Toward the late forties, you might consider starting certain hormones in minute doses provided that your physician believes they would be beneficial. Hormones, especially DHEA and pregnenolone, are known to improve well-being and cognition and to increase sexual interest. Pregnenolone is a powerful memory booster. The question of estrogen and other hormone replacement in women continues to be a hotly debated issue. There are both benefits and risks from hormone replacement. If hormone replacement is instituted, the dosages used should be very low. See Chapter 14 for full details on the benefits and risks of hormone replacement and recommendations for both men and women.

 Cautions and Side Effects

Be very careful combining supplements if you have hypertension, heart disease, diabetes, thyroid problems or other chronic medical conditions. Powerful nutrients and hormones can interfere with medicines or alter the course of a medical condition, especially if you take many of them simultaneously.

Summary

Most individuals in the 41-to-60 age group do not suffer significant cognitive decline. However, many supplements can offer benefits in improving alertness, motivation, productivity, sex drive and clarity of thinking. If used properly, these supplements can also improve vision and mood, and help keep your mind youthful.

18

THE MIND-BOOSTING PROGRAM FOR AGES 61 AND OVER

With age, everyone experiences a decline in the ability to think, learn and remember. In addition, there is a decline in sensory perception—vision is not as sharp and hearing deteriorates. Is this cognitive and perceptual decline inevitable, or are there steps we can take to slow this decline—or even reverse it? Fortunately, we now have easy access to dozens of nutrients that have a positive influence on brain function. The challenge is to find the right combination and the right dosage to provide the greatest benefit with the lowest risk.

The use of mind boosters in the 61-and-over age group is complicated by the fact that many seniors have preexisting medical conditions. Although some of the nutrients discussed in this book do not influence the course of a medical disease, other nutrients can have a significant effect. Therefore, I will discuss some of the medical conditions common in this age group and suggest the best choice for supplements for each condition. This issue is further complicated by the fact that many older individuals are also taking pharmaceutical medicines to treat a particular condition. I'll discuss some of the potential interactions of drugs and nutrients, and even offer natural alternatives to some drugs.

The Encouraging Cases of Marge and Leonard

Marge is a seventy-one-year-old retired bookkeeper. "All my life I've worked with numbers," she said when she came to see me. "I used to have a great memory, but now I can't seem to remember simple things like phone numbers and where I put things. It's frustrating. I came home from shopping one afternoon and got the mail from the mailbox on the way into the house. There was a letter from my sister. I put the groceries in the kitchen and then I just couldn't remember where I put the letter. It took me twenty minutes, and I finally found it in the den."

Marge's case is typical of many people whose memory falters with the aging process. After a thorough medical and neurological evaluation, I started her on a program that included a multivitamin, B-complex and fish oils. She noticed slight benefits with these supplements. Two weeks later, I added ginkgo, at a dose of 60 mg each morning. Marge found that ginkgo helped her to be more alert and focused. However, she wanted additional supplements for further improvement. The next one I recommended was acetyl-L-carnitine. This nutrient proved to be extremely helpful. Marge felt that her thinking was as clear as it had been a decade or two earlier. Her memory improved and she was able to stay focused all day.

Leonard had a memory deficit similar to Marge's, but he also had noticed deterioration in his visual perception, energy levels and libido. A complete medical evaluation did not reveal any conditions that accounted for his symptoms. Leonard was already taking a daily multivitamin pill, with an additional 250 mg of vitamin C and 100 IU of vitamin E. My recommendations were to add a B-complex pill, a teaspoon of flaxseed oil daily (being a vegetarian, he did not want to take fish oils), 30 mg of CoQ10 and 60 mg of ginkgo. To help his sagging libido, I started Leonard on a combination of DHEA and pregnenolone, totaling 5 mg per day. Within two weeks, he noticed a marked improvement, and I recommended that he reduce the frequency of the hormones' dosage to three times a week. His visual perception has now improved, most likely due to a combination of the vitamins, flaxseed oil, ginkgo and pregnenolone. "Colors are sharper and clearer," he reports.

Age-Related Cognitive Decline

In Chapter 1, I discussed the concept of normal brain aging; this natural decline in mental functioning is known as *"age-related cognitive decline"* (ARCD). This term is applied to persons generally fifty years and older who continue on a steady course of memory loss or decline in thinking ability. The deficits seen in ARCD are minimal compared to those seen in Alzheimer's disease, but they can nevertheless impair work productivity and interfere with quality of life. Listening to music, looking at art, traveling and tasting food all become less enjoyable.

Several factors are involved in the gradual deterioration of mental capacities that accompanies aging. In order to slow down, stop or even reverse several aspects of this mental decline with adequate supplementation, we must look at all the factors involved. Here are specific recommendations on how to approach this decline from multiple directions.

Taking Care of Medical Problems

There are certain medical problems that commonly occur in the 61-and-over age group. Many of these conditions, or the medicines required to treat them, can accelerate cognitive decline. Be sure to have regular physical exams to rule out any cause of mental impairment that may be treatable. These conditions include thyroid disease, depression, elevated blood sugar or B-12 deficiency.

When vision and hearing are impaired, the brain receives less stimulation. Eye and ear checkups are essential to find treatable causes such as glaucoma, cataracts, or impacted wax in the eardrums. Proper glasses and hearing aids have a tonic effect on the brain. My father's mood and quality of life improved significantly after his eye doctor removed his cataracts and replaced them with new lenses. "I had forgotten how much pleasure is derived from seeing clearly," he tells me.

Let's discuss a few common medical conditions and see whether there are alternative therapies that do not interfere with cognitive function.

Cardiovascular and cerebrovascular diseases: Elevated blood pressure can damage large and small blood vessels in the brain and can lead to strokes. Strokes most commonly occur due to a clot that blocks blood flow to a specific part of the brain. Less commonly, they can be a result of bleeding into the brain; the latter type of stroke is called a brain hemorrhage. The use of aspirin and nutrients that have blood-thinning abilities can decrease the risk of a clot. However, caution is always advised. Taking many blood-thinning supplements in too-high doses excessively can interfere with coagulation, and increase the risk of bleeding (brain hemorrhage).

Blood pressure can often be controlled by anti-hypertensive drugs. A preferable way to control blood pressure is through healthy habits—including mild or moderate exercise, relaxation techniques, stopping smoking. You should also reduce body weight, incorporate fresh fruits and vegetables in your diet, and add magnesium, potassium, antioxidants and omega-3 oils such as flaxseed or fish oils.

Preliminary research indicates that fish oils reduce the risk of heart-rhythm irregularities. Calcium channel blockers and beta-blockers are often used to control high blood pressure, but they are known to interfere with optimal mental functioning.

If you have hypertension or heart disease, good choices for mind boosters include omega-3 oils, ginkgo, choline, B vitamins, methyl donors, CoQ10, lipoic acid and acetyl-L-carnitine. It is best to avoid the amino acids tyrosine and phenylalanine since they can increase blood pressure and cause heart-rhythm irregularities.

Elevated cholesterol: Many of the drugs (statins) used to decrease cholesterol and lipid levels in the blood can cause cognitive decline because they may also affect the production of cholesterol in the brain. Cholesterol is required for good brain-cell function, and is needed to make steroid hormones such as pregnenolone, DHEA, estrogen and testosterone. Excessively low levels of cholesterol in the brain, as a consequence of drug use or extreme dietary restrictions, can lead to lowered mood and disturbances in the thinking process.

If you have high cholesterol levels, many of the healthy habits that help reduce blood pressure also apply to lowering cholesterol levels.

In a recent study of omega-3 fatty acids, more than 11,000 patients who had experienced a heart attack were treated with a combination of omega-3 fatty acids or with vitamin E. Over a three-year period, no statistically significant benefit was observed with vitamin E, but those taking the omega-3 fatty acids experienced a 20 percent decreased risk of death and a 45 percent lower risk of sudden death (Harris 2003).

In a study conducted at the University of California at Irvine, adding fish oils (1800 mg of EPA, 1200 mg of DHA) and garlic powder (1200 mg) to the subject's diet for one month resulted in an 11 percent decrease in cholesterol levels and a 34 percent decrease in triglyceride levels (Morcos 1997). The effect of garlic supplements alone on cholesterol levels, however, is in dispute.

The mind boosters recommended for people with cardiovascular disease would also help those with high cholesterol levels.

Osteoarthritis: Although nonsteroidal anti-inflammatory drugs (NSAIDs) such as ibuprofen can potentially help reduce the risk for Alzheimer's disease, they can also have significant side effects, including stomach ulcers, hearing loss and kidney damage. A safer alternative for osteoarthritis would be taking 500 or 1000 mg of glucosamine three times a day. Glucosamine is a nutrient available over-the-counter. Chondroitin sulfate may also be helpful, at a dose of 400 mg three times a day. Vitamins C and D, omega-3 oils and methyl donors are also potentially helpful.

Benign prostate hypertrophy: Known as BPH, prostate enlargement is not fatal but can cause a significant reduction in the quality of life. The frequent nighttime awakenings to urinate interfere with the proper sleep necessary for full cognitive functioning. Doctors often prescribe the medicine finasteride (also known as Proscar) to block the conversion of testosterone to dihydrotestosterone (DHT), the hormone partly responsible for the growth of the prostate gland. However, finasteride may interfere with sexual drive and memory. You may wish to try the herbal extract saw palmetto, at a dose of 160 mg twice a day, which may potentially help in reducing your dose of finasteride. One advantage of finasteride, however, is that it can help preserve hair growth on the scalp.

Muscle wasting: As we age, we gradually lose our lean muscle mass. This decline can be partially reversed by the use of creatine. Creatine is a nutrient made of three amino acids. A dose of 3 grams a day can help increase muscle size (see Chapter 20). Be sure to take a week off from creatine use each month, and take a month off three times a year. Make sure your intake of protein is adequate for your weight because muscle tissue needs protein to maintain its mass.

Gastrointestinal problems: If you have a stomach ulcer or suffer from gastritis and take antacids and other medicines that reduce stomach acid, you could have problems absorbing certain nutrients, particularly B-12. Therefore B-12 shots might provide you with great cognitive benefits.

Regulating Circadian Cycles

As we get older, there is an increase in the likelihood of disturbances in circadian rhythm. These rhythms affect various body functions, such as sleep cycles, body temperature and hormone production. Exposure to sunlight or bright lights an hour or so a day can help assist in the regulation of these circadian cycles.

As a rule, if you tend to feel sleepy before your normal bedtime, expose yourself to late-afternoon or early-evening sunlight. If you normally tend to be wired late at night, expose yourself to light in the morning. You can benefit from light-exposure simply by sitting near a window or taking a walk outdoors.

The occasional use of melatonin, in a dose of 0.3 to 1 mg once or twice a week, an hour or two before bed, can be used to help regulate your sleep cycle.

Supplements for ARCD

The deterioration of mental functioning with age is a consequence of numerous factors. These factors include decreased blood flow to the brain, inefficient energy production by the brain cells, changes in levels of brain chemicals and hormones and deterioration of brain cells. Therefore, in order to keep the brain young, the body needs to slow down, stop, or even reverse as many of these processes as we can. First I will discuss how to deal with each of these processes, and then I will give you a step-by-step guide to a mind-boosting nutritional program.

Improving bloodflow to the brain: Anything that helps slow the progression of atherosclerosis (hardening of the arteries) is beneficial to mental functioning. Many people have the perception that atherosclerosis involves mostly the arteries of the heart—but hardening of the arteries with a reduction in blood flow occurs commonly in the arteries that supply blood to the brain. Therefore, a diet emphasizing fresh vegetables and fruits, whole grains, proper antioxidant use, and a good intake of omega-3 oils can be helpful.

Ginkgo and omega-3 oils are a good choice for improving blood circulation since they have antiplatelet (or blood-thinning) activity. Aspirin is also a powerful antiplatelet agent. A small amount, such as a baby aspirin, or one-fourth of a 325 mg adult dose, taken a few times a week should be sufficient. Keep your dosages low when you take ginkgo, omega-3 and aspirin at the same time.

Improving brain-cell energy metabolism: Brain cells need energy to function. They obtain most of this energy by metabolizing carbohydrates like glucose. B vitamins are known to assist in this energy production. Several additional nutrients are involved in energy production within brain cells. They include coenzyme Q10, acetyl-L-carnitine (ALC) and lipoic acid. In addition to their involvement in energy production, these nutrients also have good antioxidant properties. Many people notice cognitive improvements when they supplement with these mind energizers.

Studies have shown ALC to be beneficial in treating mild forms of cognitive decline. Arnold, a sixty-three-year-old engineer, says, "I take 250 mg of ALC on days when I need to keep focused. It helps me stay alert and helps me concentrate better. I think my work productivity has improved." CoQ10 also improves mental energy. Users find that they can think faster and stay more alert. A dose of 30 to 60 mg is generally adequate. Mary, a seventy-four-year-old patient with heart disease, finds that CoQ10 gives her more energy and improves her mood. Lipoic acid has not been tested in patients with ARCD, but small doses, such as 5 to 25 mg, sharpen vision and provide a relaxed sense of well-being.

Influencing neurotransmitter levels: Mood, behavior, memory, energy and sex drive are influenced by brain chemicals, including serotonin, dopamine, norepinephrine and acetylcholine. The levels of these brain chemicals can change with the body's aging. Fortunately, these levels can be manipulated with over-the-counter nutrients. For example, choline and CDP-choline have an influence on acetylcholine; phenylalanine, tyrosine and some of the B vitamins influence levels of dopamine and norepinephrine. 5-HTP is a direct precursor to serotonin.

The choice of nutrients depends on the specific condition being treated. For instance, Alzheimer's patients benefit from nutrients that influence acetylcholine levels, while patients with Parkinson's disease respond to nutrients that influence dopamine levels. Note that methyl donors increase the production of several neurotransmitters.

Influencing hormone levels: Similar to brain chemicals, over-the-counter hormones, such as DHEA and pregnenolone, influence mood, behavior, memory, energy and sex drive. Hormones can be very beneficial, but misuse can lead to side effects.

Rebuilding brain cells: Our brains are made of billions of cells (neurons) that often deteriorate with age. Each neuron is enclosed by a lining called the "cell membrane." This membrane separates the insides of the cell from the outside. The cell membrane serves as a barrier, allowing certain necessary nutrients to enter, while restricting the entry of undesirable substances. This membrane consists mostly of different types of fats. Manipulating the composition of these fats can significantly influence the function and efficiency of neurons. Several nutrients have the potential to do just this, including omega-3 oils and phospholipids.

Research on humans regarding the manipulation of brain-cell membranes with nutrients is still in its infancy. Therefore it is difficult to make specific recommendations regarding supplementation. Until we learn more, it may be appropriate to supplement with omega-3 oils and small amounts of phospholipids.

A Step-by-Step Guide to Supplements for the 61-and-Over Age Group

I separate the mind-boosting lifestyle habits and supplements recommended for the over-61 age group into three categories in order to accommodate individual preferences. Some people are reluctant to take many supplements, while others wish to take a dozen or more. If you are the former, the recommendations made in the "first-line" category should be sufficient for you. If you have an interest in taking more supplements, I have provided two additional categories.

Please consult a nutritionally oriented health-care provider before starting this mind-boosting program. Make sure your

provider is aware of the supplements you are considering because some supplements may potentially interfere with your prescription medicines. Before you take any supplements, review the top ten mind-boosting principles presented in Chapter 2.

Please note that it's impossible to provide guidelines that would be appropriate to every person reading this book. There are wide variations between individuals, in health status, mental function, the body's ability to absorb and metabolize nutrients, and efficiency of the organs of metabolism and elimination, such as the liver and kidneys.

First-Line Therapy

I recommend a daily multivitamin complex that contains two to three times the recommended daily allowances (RDA) for the B vitamins. Your multimineral complex might include about 50 to 100 percent of the RDA for minerals. Some seniors might have difficulty absorbing vitamin B-12 and they may respond well to monthly injections.

- In addition to the multivitamin pills, take additional antioxidants. I recommend between 100 and 500 mg of vitamin C and between 30 and 200 IU of vitamin E.

- If you don't eat fish, take fish-oil supplements. Look for a supplement that provides a total of 500 to 1000 mg of the fatty acids EPA/DHA. This should be an adequate amount.

- If you are a strict vegetarian and don't want fish oil, take one-half to one teaspoon of flaxseed oil a day.

- Women may consider adding more soy products to their diet. Soy contains compounds that have estrogenic properties.

Second-Line Therapy

Most seniors will notice benefits from the first-line therapy above. But if you feel you need more help, there are additional nutrients you can take. You don't have to take all of these supplements all of the time. If you are financially limited, or don't like taking too many pills, take only a couple of supplements a day. If you are interested in trying many supplements, start with one or two, and gradually add more. Remember that the effects of these nutrients are *cumulative*. If you're not careful, you could get overstimulated and experience insomnia, which would be counterproductive to good health.

As you add more supplements, reduce the dosage of the ones you already take. Ideally, I recommend that you learn the effects of each nutrient alone before you begin combining them.

- To improve blood flow to the brain, take 40 mg of ginkgo with breakfast or lunch.

- Energy metabolism can be improved by taking 100 to 250 mg of acetyl-L-carnitine, 10 to 30 mg of CoQ10, or 5 to 25 mg of lipoic acid.

- Hormone replacement with DHEA or pregnenolone can potentially benefit bone formation, mood, libido, memory and overall cognitive function. In some individuals, pregnenolone can improve hearing and vision. There are potential side effects to hormone replacement if they are misused. See Chapter 14 for full details and dosage guidelines.

- Melatonin can be used at a dose of 0.3 to 1 mg one or three times a week, an hour or two before bed, to improve sleep.

Third-Line Therapy

There are dozens of nutrients and herbs that have an effect on the mind. You will notice significant improvements from the routines suggested in the first- and second-line therapies. The majority of individuals will be quite content with these. However, I know other readers who are very curious to learn more about supplements. I have provided additional options for those with this inclination.

It's always best to start a new supplement when you are not taking other supplements. That way you can determine its effects without interference. Try each nutrient on its own for at least a few days to observe any changes in alertness, mood, concentration and potential side effects. If you plan to take the following nutrients on a regular basis, use them only once or twice a week to avoid developing tolerance.

- Choline helps with focus and concentration. A dose of 250 mg is a good start. If you don't notice benefits from choline, try 100 to 250 mg of its activated form, sold as CDP-choline.

- TMG, and its cousin DMG, at a dose of 100 mg, provide an improvement in alertness and mood.

- NADH, at a dose of 2.5 or 5 mg, improves mood, alertness and perhaps even sex drive. Limit the use of NADH to once or twice a week since tolerance to this nutrient can develop quickly. NADH is best taken in the morning on an empty stomach.

- There are additional nutrients, herbs and herbal extracts—such as DMAE, SAMe, ginseng, maca and vinpocetine—that you may eventually want to explore. Whether supplements of PS and lecithin improve cognitive abilities in the aged has yet to be determined.

 ## Cautions and Side Effects

Ginkgo biloba, feverfew, garlic, ginger, vinpocetine, aspirin and high doses of vitamin E may increase the risk of bleeding in patients taking antithrombotic (blood-thinning) agents.

Always take low dosages when you combine multiple supplements. This may require that you break a tablet into small portions, or open a capsule to take a fraction of the contents.

Summary

Although our bodies and brains are preprogrammed to aging, there are several steps we can take to slow this process. Many of the supplements I discuss in this book can have an enormous benefit in improving memory, vision, clarity of thinking, motivation, excitement for living and creativity. Let's be appreciative that these nutrients are readily available.

PART VI

NATURAL PRESCRIPTIONS
FOR DEPRESSION, VISION ENHANCEMENT, ALZHEIMER'S AND PARKINSON'S DISEASE

19

Supplements That Fight Depression

A happy, healthy mind can be compared to a pond with a high water level. There may be many rocks of all sizes and shapes at the bottom of the pond, but these rocks are not visible and they do not interfere with the pond's serenity and tranquility. The rocks at the bottom represent all the minor and major traumas that we have had or are currently experiencing, as part of living on this sometimes hostile and unforgiving planet. They represent embarrassments, emotional breakups, childhood traumas, past and current illnesses and all the other hurts that are the inevitable rites of passage that we all go through on our way to adulthood. *Yet a pond with a high water level covers up these rocks:* they are no longer visible and no longer interfere with the surface tranquility.

Now imagine the water level of this pond gradually depleting. Little by little, as the water level lowers, the tips of the larger rocks begin to show. As the water level drops even farther, medium-sized and even smaller rocks become apparent.

I sometimes share this analogy with patients who experience low mood or clinical depression. I usually tell them that even though it's very important to try to resolve as many past and current issues and hurts (the rocks) as possible through self-analysis, behavioral therapy, psychotherapy and other methods, it's just as important to bring the level of the water back up. The level of the water (i.e., brain chemicals) can often successfully be raised by using nutritional therapies. Once you restore the proper amounts and balance of your brain chemicals and provide the nutritional support for your brain cells to work more efficiently, many of the frustrations and hurts that you have experienced in the past, or currently experience, won't seem nearly as challenging or disturbing.

Nutrients to the Rescue

How good we feel is largely dependent on the levels and interactions of a number of neurotransmitters in the brain, including serotonin, norepinephrine and dopamine. Low mood or clinical depression is mostly due to an imbalance or shortage of some of these neurotransmitters at important sites in the central nervous system. However, disturbances in mood can also result from medical diseases, nutrient deficiencies, improper fatty-acid intake and inefficient energy production within cells.

Antidepressants were first introduced back in the 1950s. Since then, a number of different classes of antidepressants have been created. Many of these medicines have benefited countless patients by relieving their symptoms of despair. But there are nutritional factors that could be just as effective as drugs.

With the current availability of a number of natural supplements that influence mood, in my opinion, many people do not need to rely on pharmaceutical medicines for the therapy of mild—and probably moderate—depression. Perhaps some cases of severe depression could respond, at least partially, to a suitable combination of natural nutrients and herbs. Supplements can also be used in conjunction with behavioral and cognitive therapies, and even in combination with lower dosages of pharmaceutical antidepressants. Traditional psychiatrists are beginning to incorporate natural therapies in their practice. One of the first mood-influencing herbs to gain wide respect among medical doctors was St. John's wort.

There are different types of depression, and each person has a unique biochemistry. Some cases of depression are caused by low levels of serotonin, while other cases are due to low levels of dopamine or norepinephrine. Still other cases of depression may be due to abnormalities in the energy production of brain cells, abnormal cell membranes or nerve damage. It is unlikely that a single therapy will provide complete relief to patients who are clinically depressed.

Please keep in mind that the therapies discussed in this chapter are only my suggested guidelines. I recommend that you supplement with these natural nutrients only under the close supervision of a health-care practitioner. Your physician will look for and recommend a course of treatment for any obvious medical conditions that could account for your depression, such as thyroid disease, tumors or anemia.

First-Line Therapy

The health of the body is intricately involved with the health of the brain. I strongly recommend that you review the suggestions in Part III regarding diet, stress reduction, good sleep habits and physical activity. Taking control of these lifestyle factors can often be curative.

Many cases of depression may also be due to a person's feeling alone and unloved. If that's the case, try to find a community of caring individuals, where you feel part of a group. Pets are also wonderful companions. Relying exclusively on supplements to elevate mood, without making the effort to improve lifestyle habits or to develop loving connections, will not provide you with full relief.

Follow these step-by-step guidelines for feeling better…

- Eat frequent small meals throughout the day. They should consist of a well-proportioned balance between protein, fat and complex carbohydrates. I find that vegetarians sometimes suffer from low mood because they consume excess carbohydrates at the expense of adequate protein and the right kinds of fats. A large intake of carbohydrates can make one sluggish and sleepy.

- Take a multivitamin pill each morning that supplies about 100 percent of the RDA or PDV for most vitamins. In addition, take a B-complex pill that supplies five to ten times the RDA for the B vitamins.

- You might also consider the coenzyme forms of the B vitamins, especially if you are older or you do not respond to the regular B vitamins. After a month of taking five to ten times the RDA for the B vitamins, reduce your daily intake to two to three times.

- Take a combination of a few antioxidants in small doses, including 30 to 100 units of vitamin E and 100 to 250 mg of vitamin C. A multimineral pill that includes about 50 to 100 percent of the RDA for minerals is recommended.

- Take fish-oil capsules with meals, totaling about 2 to 4 grams a day of the omega-3 fatty acids EPA and DHA. After the first month, reduce the dosage to 1 to 2 grams a day. Strict vegetarians can take a teaspoon of flaxseed oil instead of fish oil.

Desiree, a thirty-eight-year-old homemaker with mild depression, is a typical example of someone who responded quite well to the nutrient supplementation described above. "I noticed the most dramatic effects from the B vitamins," she says, "although the addition of the flaxseed oil improved my alertness, too. I can now function all day without being tired and my husband mentioned that I was acting more cheerful."

Second-Line Therapy

If your depression has not been adequately treated after adopting the above regimen for two weeks, you can now include additional nutrients in your regime.

Take a St. John's wort pill with breakfast, at a dose of 300 mg, standardized to 0.3 percent hypericin content. This herb has a wonderful ability to improve one's outlook on life.

After a few days, if you don't notice any benefits, you can add a second St. John's wort pill either with breakfast or with lunch. Although most studies involving this herb have been done using three pills a day, I recommend the lower dosage. I have found that the risk for side effects such as insomnia increases when the dosage is increased to three pills a day. Instead of the third pill, it may be preferable to rely on different mood-elevating nutrients.

Michael, a forty-two-year-old systems engineer, suffered from a moderate case of depression following a divorce. The effects of St. John's wort were dramatic. "Within three days after starting the St. John's wort, I definitely noticed an uplifting of mood. It seemed like my emotional pain was not as intense." Michael stayed on St. John's wort for a period of four months, and successfully came off the herb without any further depression.

Third-Line Therapy

Let's assume you've tried the above therapies for four weeks, but you still feel that you need help. *Here are additional suggestions...*

- Start with tyrosine, at a dose of 100 mg, in the morning on an empty stomach. This amino acid is particularly helpful if you have difficulty staying alert. Many people find it to be a good substitute for caffeine.

 Cautions and Side Effects
Tyrosine is more suitable for those younger than forty-five, since older individuals, and those with heart problems, can develop heart palpitations with high dosages. If you're taking St. John's wort, do not take high doses of tyrosine; the effects are potentially cumulative.

- After one week, add a dose of 30 mg of CoQ10 in the morning. This nutrient can increase energy levels and is particularly helpful for those who have low energy levels associated with their depression.

- Additional nutrients that can be added over the next few weeks include TMG, DMG, SAMe or pantothenic acid at a dose of 100 to 250 mg, in the morning. All of these nutrients have excellent mood- and energy-elevating properties.

- Carnitine at 250 mg a day is another nutrient that increases energy levels.

    Daisy, a twenty-eight-year-old clothing-store manager, could not tolerate St. John's wort, due to an allergic reaction. But she found the combination dosage of 100 mg tyrosine, 30 mg CoQ10, and 100 mg pantothenic acid to be extremely helpful in "beating the blahs," as she called it. Her low mood was a consequence of a relationship breakup. She took these nutrients for three months and after that time she gradually eliminated the tyrosine. Now she occasionally takes only the pantothenic acid and the CoQ10, along with some of the nutrients described in the first-line therapy.

Fourth-Line Therapy

You have now been presented with several options. It's possible that your symptoms may have already responded adequately to the above regimen. However, if your depression has not improved significantly, it's time to consider additional supplements.

 Cautions and Side Effects

At this stage you must be very carefully and closely supervised by your health-care provider because the risk

of interactions between the nutrients can increase significantly.

There is also a possibility of over-stimulation when too many energizers are consumed. Some of these nutrients can slowly accumulate in the system, and you may find you need lower dosages with time. The treatment of depression is a dynamic process, and dosages of nutrients and medicines have to be adjusted up or down on a regular basis. If your depression lifts, don't continue adding more nutrients; instead try to minimize the dosages and the number of nutrients you are taking.

- There are quite a number of other options available. For instance, the herb ginseng can provide a sense of vitality and well-being.

- If your depression is associated with anxiety, the serotonin precursor 5-HTP can be helpful. The nighttime dosage is 25 to 50 mg, about an hour or two before bed, on an empty stomach. The daytime dosage for 5-HTP is 25 mg, which you may take at anytime. Taking 5-HTP at night will help you get a deeper sleep. At the maximum, 5-HTP should be used only four days a week, and for no longer than two months continuously. After a month's break, you can resume taking 5-HTP again. You can cycle 5-HTP two months on and one month off, if needed.

- For a deeper sleep, try the occasional use of melatonin, at a dose of 0.3 to 0.5 mg once or twice a week. Take it an hour or two before bed on an empty stomach. High doses of melatonin (more than 2 mg) can lower mood in some individuals if they use it every night. Since 5-HTP and melatonin work in similar ways to induce sleep, you must reduce the dosages of each if you're planning to take them together.

- Two additional supplements to consider are NADH and acetyl-L-carnitine. NADH can be taken at a dose of 2.5 or 5 mg two or three times a week, in the morning on an empty stomach. NADH improves mood, energy and sex drive. Since it is a relatively new nutrient, I recommend using it, at most, only three times a week until more research is available. Acetyl-L-carnitine has mood-elevating properties, and 100 to 250 mg is a good starting dose. As with most stimulants, it is best taken early in the day, before breakfast or lunch.

- Older people, especially those who have a sluggish libido, may find the addition of hormones, in conjunction with the nutrients, to be extremely helpful. DHEA or pregnenolone, or a combination of the two, can be started at a dose of 5 mg. For long-term use, I do not recommend

exceeding a dose of 2 to 5 mg a day. Be sure to take them no more than 3 weeks out of every month.

Summary

Combining supplements in the therapy of depression is a relatively new concept for most doctors trained in traditional medicine. Even doctors who practice complementary medicine are still in the early stages of learning the appropriate amounts to combine these nutrients. Due to the shortage of published information in this area, it is very important that the mixing of supplements be done in a cautious way—always starting with low dosages.

The intelligent combination of natural vitamins, nutrients, herbs and hormones can have powerful mood-elevating effects. At the very least, the use of nutrients could allow for a reduction in the dosages of pharmaceutical antidepressants.

20

SUPPLEMENTS THAT SHARPEN VISION AND HEARING

Do you remember how crisp, sharp and beautiful scenery looked years ago? Do you recall sitting for hours in your bedroom playing records or CDs over and over again, appreciating the melodies, rhythms and the musical contribution of each instrument? Do you now find that some of the enchantment from looking and listening has faded away?

As we get older, we lose some of our perceptive abilities. This is due in part to degeneration of nerve cells in the eyes and ears. Music and other sounds are no longer as delightful as they were in our teenage years. Going to a concert does not seem as exciting. A castle in Europe, a swan floating on a still pond, a delicate daisy or rugged mountain scenery may not impress us as much. We lose our ability to notice fine details and to differentiate subtle shades of colors. Has this enchantment disappeared forever, or are there ways to return the visual and auditory magic that life offers?

I am glad to report that the proper use of many of the nutrients can help restore, at least partially, the magic of seeing and hearing that you may have long forgotten. Most of this chapter will deal with visual enhancement because there is more information on how to improve vision with natural supplements than on how to improve hearing.

I will review two important parts of the eye: the lens and the retina. Then I will discuss nutrients that enhance vision and hearing.

The Lens

The lens and the retina are the two crucial parts of the eye involved in visual acuity. The lens is a disk-shaped transparent structure, about half the size of an M&M candy, that helps focus light on the retina, an area in the back of the eye. Excessive sunlight exposure, high blood-sugar levels (particularly in diabetics), smoking and a shortage of antioxidants can cause damage to the lens, leading to dark areas. Over time, these dark areas grow and become more prevalent, leading to the development of cataracts. When the doctor looks into the eye with a special flashlight called an ophthalmoscope, a cataract appears brownish or black. These dark areas interfere with vision because they block light from reaching the retina. Little can be done nutritionally to correct a cataract once it has formed, but a cataract can be removed surgically and replaced with an artificial lens.

The Retina

The retina lies in the back of the eye and is composed of cells called rods and cones. The retina gathers light and visual information from the outside world. This information is transmitted through a special nerve bundle, called the optic tract, to an area in the back of the brain called the visual cortex. The visual cortex, in turn, interprets this information. Thus, vision can be improved at the retinal level or at the level of transmission and interpretation of this optical information.

There's a small area in the retina called the *macula*, where vision is at its sharpest. Millions of elderly people suffer from macular degeneration, the leading cause of blindness in people over the age of fifty. Macular degeneration causes a gradual loss of vision and eventual blindness, and is caused at least partly by oxidation. Therefore antioxidants are helpful in keeping both the lens and the retina healthy.

Protecting Your Eyes

The lens, retina, macula and other parts of the eye can be protected with the proper intake of antioxidants. Almost all the antioxidants are likely to have a positive influence on eye health. In 1999, three studies showed a reduced likelihood of cataract surgery with increasing intakes of lutein and another carotenoid–zeaxanthin (Chasen-Taber 1999, Brown 1999, Lyle 1999). These substances are believed to protect eye tissue in the macula from damage by free radicals. Corn, eggs, green leafy vegetables, peppers, red grapes and pumpkins are some of the foods rich in lutein and zeazanthin. You can also find carotenoids and flavonoids in many herbs, including milk thistle and bilberry. Vitamins C and E, selenium and the carotenoids found in fruits and vegetables may also be beneficial.

For optimal vision protection, I recommend that you include a variety of whole foods in your diet and take antioxidant supplements. At this point, we don't know exactly what amounts and combinations of antioxidants will ensure optimal protection. You may wish to follow some of the suggestions provided in Chapter 11.

Nutrients That Sharpen Vision

Good eyesight requires more than just eating carrots. Most everything that you do to improve your overall health will ultimately influence the health of your eyes.

After years of supervising patients who take mind boosters, and trying various supplements myself, I have become aware of many supplements that have an immediate effect on visual perception. Unfortunately, very little information has been published regarding the influence of different nutrients on the visual system. Much of the information in this chapter is therefore anecdotal, based on my professional and personal experiences.

Here are some supplements that improve eyesight. You are likely to notice the effects the day you take them, and sometimes even within an hour or two. Generally, the higher the dose, the more obvious the visual improvement. However, the risk of side effects also increases as the dosage is increased. The combination of two or more nutrients often has a synergistic effect.

The mechanisms of action of these supplements can involve several pathways, such as raising levels of brain chemicals, improving blood circulation to the eye or altering the fatty-acid composition of rods and cones and brain cells. I find that vision changes are not as apparent when you are in broad sunlight. Going indoors—for instance, into a shopping mall—can help you notice the visual enhancement. Late afternoon, early evening and cloudy days are also good times to notice the visual changes.

Omega-3 oils: Just like the rest of the cells in the brain, the cells of the retina—the rods and the cones—contain long-chain fatty acids. The most prominent of these fatty acids in the eye is an omega-3 fatty acid called DHA.

In my experience, I have found that omega-3 oils, generally found in fish and flaxseed, enhance visual perception. I notice improved color perception and depth of vision, enhanced night and distance vision, and overall enhancement of visual awareness after several days of taking flaxseed oil or fish-oil capsules.

To see results more quickly—i.e., within two or three days—the dosages need to be significant. For example, most people need to take several grams of a combination EPA/DHA fish-oil supplement or a tablespoon or two of flaxseed oil. Once you notice an improvement, you can reduce your dosage of fish oils to one or two grams a day, or a teaspoon of flaxseed oil.

Burton J. Litman, Ph.D., at the National Institutes of Health in Rockville, Maryland, is an expert in the biochemistry of vision. *He says…*

❝ Each rod contains thousands and thousands of DHA molecules stacked up on each other. DHA is necessary for rhodopsin to function. [Rhodopsin is a protein in retinal rod cells that helps with perception of light.] Each day a small percentage of the DHA is taken away and replaced by new DHA. Dietary intake of fish oils [or omega-3 oils] could have an influence on these rods. As we age, we lose some of the phospholipids in brain-cell membranes that contain DHA and these are replaced by saturated lipids. ❞

Since we lose some of the DHA present in the retina with age, it's quite possible that someday we may discover that dietary replacement of the proper fatty acids, especially in the elderly, will improve visual and perhaps, auditory perception. I notice an enhancement in visual perception when I supplement with several grams of fish oils. Sometimes it takes me a few days of taking high doses of fish oils to notice a difference, although I have noticed an effect the first day if I take several grams.

Pregnenolone: This is an interesting hormone that not only improves vision, but also enhances awareness. I mean that you become more aware of your environment—scenery, artwork, clothing patterns, plants and architecture that you might normally overlook suddenly become eye-catching. I notice the effects within a few hours of taking a dose of 10 or 20 mg. However, it takes several days of supplementing with pregnenolone at a smaller dosage to notice the visual effects. Colors become brighter and clearer, and shapes and patterns are more obvious. Reports from patients indicate that about a third notice these dramatic effects. *Barbara, a television producer from Orange County, California, relates an interesting response…*

❝ I took 10 mg of pregnenolone in the morning for three days and didn't feel much. On the fourth day, while waiting at a traffic light, I noticed how beautiful the red color looked. The light turned green and I kept looking at it in amazement. I had never seen a traffic light look so beautiful. I had to move soon, though, because cars behind me started honking. I arrived at the shopping mall and now realized the beauty of the planted flowers. I kept staring at them for a long time. **99**

Ted, a physician from San Diego, says, "I had stopped at a gas station to fill up the tank when I noticed an American flag by the pump. I had never seen red and blue colors that intense. It came to mind that I had taken pregnenolone for the first time that morning, at a dose of 20 mg. I will always remember that flag at the gas station."

The improved visual appreciation can lead some individuals to a dramatic appreciation of art. I once ended up purchasing antiques on the spur of the moment, a few more than I really needed—they looked so beautiful. So don't take a high dose of pregnenolone and visit an art gallery or antique store while carrying a credit card!

The visual effects from pregnenolone can last from a few hours to a whole day.

 Cautions and Side Effects

Unfortunately, pregnenolone has a downside. High doses can lead to side effects, including overstimulation, irritability, headaches and acne. *Very* high doses, such as 30 mg or more, can cause heart palpitations in individuals prone to heart irregularities. Sensitive individuals may notice skipped beats on a dose as low as 10 mg. Until more is known about pregnenolone's long-term health effects, I recommend its use for

hormone-replacement therapy only in low dosages, such as 1 to 5 mg. Healthy individuals who have no major medical problems may take 10 or 20 mg occasionally, about once or twice per month. If you don't notice an effect from taking the oral pills, try the sublingual (under-the-tongue) form.

Pantothenic acid: This is one of the B vitamins (B-5). A dose of 100 to 500 mg taken in the morning improves clarity of vision. Its effect is usually noticeable in the late afternoon and continues until bedtime. As with other nutrients that cause alertness, high dosages, even when taken in the morning, can interfere with nighttime sleep. Pantethene, the coenzyme form of pantothenic acid, produces similar visual improvement on a much lower dose of 25 to 50 mg.

NADH: In August of 1998, I took a trip to Alaska. During my three-week sojourn in this beautiful state, I had the opportunity to try some new nutrients. On my second day, I was in a van with a group of people driving down from Anchorage to Homer. All around us were majestic snowcapped peaks and lush, green meadows dotted with spruce trees. The day was overcast and windy as we pulled up to a scenic point. The wind was creating small ripples over the dark blue waters of the Cook Inlet.

I had taken 5 mg of NADH, the coenzyme form of the B-vitamin niacin, before breakfast. Two hours later, the effects were becoming apparent. Not only did I have a pleasant sense of well-being, but the beauty of this Alaskan scenery was coming to life. I realized at that moment how fortunate we are to have access to many natural supplements that not only improve health, but also enhance our appreciation of life and the natural beauty of this planet. I became even more encouraged to continue my quest to learn as much as I could about nutrients that improve quality of life and to share this knowledge with the public.

I'm not sure exactly how NADH enhances vision. It likely is connected with raising levels of the brain chemical dopamine. In my experience, dopamine-enhancing nutrients and medicines improve visual perception. Any supplement or drug that enhances dopamine levels can improve vision, at least temporarily.

Phenylalanine, tyrosine and acetyl-tyrosine: convert into dopamine. Improvement in visual clarity is generally noticed within hours after taking a dose of 100 to 500 mg. However, be aware that high dosages induce irritability and anxiety.

Acetyl-L-carnitine: is an antioxidant involved in energy utilization within cells. A dose of 500 mg in the morning before breakfast works within two to three hours to induce a pleasant visual and mental clarity.

CDP-choline: enhances acetylcholine production, but may also influence dopamine levels. Visual clarity is apparent within a few hours after taking 250 or 500 mg.

TMG, DMG, DMAE and SAMe: are methyl donors that have similar effects of sharpening vision, most likely due to an increase in levels of brain chemicals. DMG is available in sublingual form and the visual effects are apparent within an hour of melting a pill under the tongue.

Lipoic acid: is an antioxidant that enhances glucose use in brain and eye cells. Usually a dose of 25 to 50 mg improves visual clarity. The effects are noticeable by late afternoon or evening.

Vinpocetine: is an herbal extract that improves blood circulation to the brain. A dose of 10 to 20 mg leads to visual clarity within one or two hours.

There are many other supplements that improve visual appreciation, but their effects are subtle. These nutrients and herbs include the *B vitamins, CoQ10, 5-HTP, ginkgo, kava, St. John's wort and some of the adaptogenic herbs, such as ginseng.* Lecithin, phosphatidylserine, creatine, and antioxidant vitamins such as C and E do not have an immediate effect on visual perception.

Auditory Enhancers

Formal research regarding the field of hearing improvement from the use of supplements is practically nonexistent. My experience with nutrients that improve hearing is limited compared to my experience with those supplements that improve vision. My eyesight is normally 20/30, with a slight astigmatism. Hence, I can appreciate even subtle changes in vision that some nutrients provide. My hearing is excellent, so it is difficult for me to notice subtle improvements. Nevertheless, I am quite certain that some nutrients have a definite influence on hearing; these include pregnenolone, NADH and pantothenic acid.

I first became aware of pregnenolone's effect on auditory appreciation while driving back to Los Angeles from a medical conference in Palm Springs, California. It was early evening, and I was changing the stations on the car radio when I realized that just about every song was pleasant to my ear, whether it was classical, jazz, rock, Celtic or country. That morning I had taken 20 mg of pregnenolone. I hadn't enjoyed listening to music that much since my teenage years. I have later noticed this auditory enhancement on multiple occasions.

The first time I noticed the effects of NADH on my hearing was while I was dining at a Peruvian restaurant. Andean flute music was playing in the background at a very low volume. I sat there mesmerized, in full appreciation of the gentle flute notes. My three friends at the table could hardly hear, let alone appreciate, the melody. My dose that morning was 5 mg.

Additional nutrients that may potentially enhance auditory appreciation include pantothenic acid, the amino acids phenylalanine and tyrosine, the methyl donors and some of the adaptogenic herbs such as ginseng. I am quite certain we will eventually discover many other supplements that improve hearing.

Summary

The use of supplements to improve vision and hearing is a relatively new concept in medicine. We are living in exciting times; it has only been in the last few years that we have had so many nutritional options available to us. It's comforting to know that we don't have to succumb to the ravages of time. We can see more sharply and hear more clearly by intelligently using nutrients and herbs.

However, I must add that not everyone notices visual effects from taking nutrients. Young people who already have excellent vision may not notice the subtle improvements that occur. The elderly, particularly those who have advanced cataracts or damaged retinas, also may not respond. Individual reactions may also differ depending upon how in tune they are with their senses. Some individuals can perceive very subtle improvements, while others require massive dosages before they realize that their vision is enhanced.

I have one thirty-year-old male patient who hardly ever notices any effects from supplements regardless of what he takes. Another patient, a forty-four-year-old woman, has excellent perception skills. This woman will notice a visual effect from 2 mg of pregnenolone. I, too, am very sensitive to subtle changes. Over my many years of taking different supplements in varying dosages, I have developed the skill of observing minute changes that occur in mood, energy, alertness and vision. This quality has helped in my evaluation of nutrients.

21

SUPPLEMENTS FOR PATIENTS WITH ALZHEIMER'S DISEASE

Alzheimer's disease (AD), a progressive deterioration in mental functioning first described by Alois Alzheimer in 1907, affects more than 4 million Americans. As many as one in 10 people over age 65 are affected, as well as at least half of people older than 85. AD has been known to start as early as age 30. One of the major cognitive problems with AD is the inability to acquire new knowledge. Loss of the sense of smell is common, and the mental deterioration proceeds to affect language and motor skills.

With the continued aging of the population, the prevalence of AD is expected to rise over the next few decades. One of the reasons medical therapies for this condition have generally been unsuccessful is that most research has focused on a "one pill" approach. It has been difficult to identify a precise area in the brain associated exclusively with AD. This is in contrast to Parkinson's disease, which is due to damage to a small, specific area in the brain. But growing evidence suggests that the memory and learning deficits associated with AD are due to

the degeneration of brain cells that rely on the brain chemical acetylcholine.

Several theories have been advanced in the past few decades regarding the causes of AD. These include genetics, vascular diseases such as heart disease and stroke, damage to brain cells by oxidation, infections, nutritional deficiencies, dysfunction of the blood-brain barrier and the side effects of medicines.

Treatment Strategies for Alzheimer's Disease

While scientists have not fully determined the actual causes of Alzheimer's disease, a number of treatment options have been proposed or tried over the years. *These treatments have included…*

- Exposure to sunlight and sleep-pattern restoration

- Therapy with B vitamins and lowering homocysteine levels

- The use of antioxidants

- Providing acetylcholine precursors

- Enhancing cellular energy with CoQ10 and acetyl-L-carnitine

- Hormone therapies with estrogen, testosterone and DHEA

- Providing anti-inflammatory agents such as aspirin or ibuprofen
- Blocking the breakdown of acetylcholine with pharmaceutical drugs
- Improving blood flow to brain cells
- Mood improvement through nutrients and herbs

I'll examine the potential benefit of each of these approaches. Later in the chapter, I provide step-by-step guidelines on how to best combine nutrients. Please keep in mind that no studies have been done on the combination of nutrients that I will discuss.

Scientific studies using combination therapies are rarely undertaken. We would have to wait a very long time to have scientists formally evaluate this approach. There are currently no effective pharmaceutical drugs for treating AD. I believe it is worthwhile for AD patients to explore nutritional therapies despite the fact that the necessary studies are not available. One can always resort to pharmaceutical medicines if this nutritional approach is not helpful.

A rational plan is to follow a multi-pronged and comprehensive approach in targeting the different problems that contribute to mental decline. This approach may perhaps stop, or at least delay, the relentless degeneration that occurs in AD. It is my hope that some individuals will be able to reverse their cognitive decline through this comprehensive approach.

Light Therapy

People afflicted with Alzheimer's often suffer disturbances in circadian rhythm, which affects body functions such as sleep cycles, temperature, alertness and hormone production. According to recent studies, exposure to sunlight or bright lights, for a few hours each day, could help correct sleep disturbances and assist in regulating the circadian cycles. This light exposure can be attained simply by sitting near a window or taking a walk outdoors. The occasional use of melatonin at night, in a dose of 0.3 to 1 mg, one or two hours before bed, can help reset the circadian rhythm and ensure a deeper sleep. Patients with AD produce much less melatonin than do other individuals of the same age (Liu 1999).

A recent study showed that providing Alzheimer's patients with several hours of sunlight each day helped them sleep longer and maintain a regular sleep schedule (Ancoli-Israel 2003).

Vitamin-B Therapy

Several studies have indicated that patients with AD have deficiencies in some of the B vitamins (McCaddon 1994). One B vitamin in particular—folic acid—seems to play a strong role. In one study on elderly nuns, those who had the lowest blood level of folic acid were most likely to develop Alzheimer's (Snowden 2000). A vitamin B-12 deficiency is common in older people, as their intestines can't absorb it from food as readily as they did previously. One symptom of this deficiency is memory loss.

Costing only pennies a day, the administration of a multivitamin supplement containing a few times the recommended daily allowance for the B vitamins is a cost-effective and safe first step in the therapy of AD.

All of the Bs are important because they function in multiple ways to improve brain function. B-6, folic acid and B-12 are helpful in reducing levels of homocysteine.

This is important because even moderate elevations in homocysteine are associated with a five-fold increase in stroke and a three-fold boost in Alzheimer's disease (McIlroy 2002).

Another study of hundreds of British patients also revealed a link between Alzheimer's and high levels of homocysteine (Refsum 1998). "It is a very promising finding," says Professor Helga Refsum of Norway's Bergen University. Like many scientists, Refsum is cautious about recommending supplements, stressing that the results so far have only revealed an association, not a direct cause and effect. She believes that, "We, as physicians, should refrain from recommending therapy before it has been scientifically proven to be effective in randomized controlled trials. This is not always practical to patients, though, since they wish to have therapy now."

Dr. Robert Clarke, from Radcliffe Infirmary in Oxford, England, adds…

66 Elevated homocysteine levels due to deficiencies of folate and vitamin B-12, and perhaps other nutrients, are common in the elderly and appear to increase with age. These deficiencies are even more common in patients with dementia. It is unclear whether or not these elevated homocysteine levels are a cause or a consequence of having dementia. We believe that this hypothesis should be investigated further. 99

In my opinion, based on the available body of knowledge, the potential benefits of vitamin-B supplements for the elderly are probably greater than their potential risks. Most patients with early-onset AD are not willing to wait years for additional research to be published. If they wait too long, in many cases their condition could deteriorate to an irreversible stage of AD.

In addition to the B vitamins, it is possible that methyl donors, such as TMG and SAMe, could be helpful.

Antioxidant Therapy

One of the first lessons I learned in pathology class in my first semester in medical school was that patients with Alzheimer's disease were afflicted with amyloidosis. Amyloidosis results from the deposit of protein fragments, called amyloid, around brain cells. Amyloid fragments join together to form small clumps, called amyloid fibrils. It is now fully accepted that the continued accumulation of amyloid leads to brain degeneration observed in Alzheimer's disease. Research indicates that amyloidosis may be a result of inadequate antioxidant protection.

Neurons in the hypothalamus, an area of the brain involved in memory and learning, are particularly susceptible to oxidative damage in AD patients. Vitamin E is the best-studied antioxidant in terms of slowing down the progression of AD. It's likely that quite a number of different antioxidants are also beneficial. In one well-publicized study in June 2002, Dutch researchers found that a diet rich in vitamins C and E seems to help prevent Alzheimer's disease (Engelbert 2002). However, the same effect was not seen from taking the supplements.

But a highly publicized article in the *New England Journal of Medicine* reported that the daily use of 1000 units of vitamin E was effective in slowing the progression of AD (Sano 1997). Researchers at the Rush Alzheimer's Disease Center, Rush University, Chicago, Illinois, found through an epidemiological survey that the use of vitamin E and C supplements reduces the risk of developing AD (Morris 1998).

Several studies have examined the antioxidant capability of patients with AD. Researchers at the New York University Medical Center have discovered that patients with AD have decreased levels of activity of two natural antioxidants that are normally produced by our bodies to protect cells from damage. These substances are called SOD (superoxide dismutase) and catalase.

In the same year, researchers at the University of Antwerp in Belgium also studied SOD activity in AD patients. They compared the cerebrospinal fluid (CSF) of patients with AD, patients with Parkinson's disease and healthy individuals. They found that patients with AD had significantly less SOD activity than the healthy patients. However, patients with Parkinson's disease had the same level of activity as the healthy patients. The researchers believe that their findings "may reflect impaired antioxidant defense mechanisms (in the AD patients)…and should further motivate others to pursue antioxidant neuroprotective treatment strategies." (De Deyn 1998).

In the next chapter I will discuss a study that found a decrease in glutathione activity in brain cells of patients with Parkinson's disease. It appears that these patients have problems with the glutathione antioxidant defense system, while those with AD don't have enough antioxidant protection due to a shortage of SOD.

Melatonin, the sleep hormone, is known to have antioxidant activity. Researchers at the University of South Alabama College of Medicine, in Mobile, Alabama, report that melatonin inhibits the progressive formation of amyloid fibrils (Pappolla 1998). *They say…*

66 Inhibition of fibrils could not be accomplished in control experiments when other antioxidants were substituted for melatonin under otherwise identical conditions. In sharp contrast with conventional antioxidants and available anti-amyloidogemic compounds, melatonin crosses the blood-brain barrier, is relatively devoid of toxicity, and constitutes a potential new therapeutic agent in Alzheimer's disease. 99

Providing Acetylcholine Precursors

There is a significant decline in levels of acetylcholine in patients with AD. Many approaches have been tried to elevate levels of this brain chemical. Studies providing precursors to acetylcholine such as choline, DMAE, CDP-choline and lecithin have not been successful to any large degree.

CDP-choline is a compound that helps make phosphatidylcholine. In a study with CDP-choline, AD patients who received a daily dosage of 1000 mg orally for one month showed slightly improved mental performance (Cacabelos 1996). It would seem reasonable for patients with AD to take small amounts of choline, CDP-choline, lecithin or a combination on a regular basis.

Improving Brain-Cell Membranes

Researchers from the Karolinska Institute in Huddinge, Sweden, have determined that the amount of polyunsaturated fatty acids present in the brain declines with age in AD patients (Soderberg 1991). Polyunsaturated fatty acids, such as DHA and arachidonic acid, were replaced by monounsaturated and saturated fatty acids in the brains of the Alzheimer's patients. This change was not as clearly observed in the brains of patients who did not have AD.

Although the reason for these changes remains unclear, the researchers speculate that brain cells in AD patients lose the ability to effectively unsaturate fatty acids. The result is that the cell membrane ends up with a preponderance of saturated and monounsaturated fatty acids. The loss of the long-chain polyunsaturated fatty acids, such as DHA, interferes with the proper function of the cell membrane. Dr. Soderberg and colleagues conclude, "The substantial decrease in polyunsaturated fatty acids may have serious consequences for cellular function. This could hamper the production of important active metabolites, such as prostaglandins and leukotrienes, which, in turn, could cause the changes observed in Alzheimer's disease."

The decline in polyunsaturated fatty acids, such as arachidonic acid and DHA, has been noticed in several studies (Conquer 1997, Prasad 1991). Perhaps oxidation damage reduces the amount of long-chain polyunsaturated fatty acids in the brain. It seems reasonable that therapy with polyunsaturated fatty acids, like fish oils, may benefit patients with AD, especially if they are combined with antioxidants. However, no long-term studies are available to determine whether providing fish oils to patients with AD would lead to benefits.

In addition to treating patients with AD with fish oils and antioxidants, using phospholipids should be considered. However, it is not clear at this time whether therapy with lecithin or phosphatidylserine would provide long-term benefits.

Improving Energy Production

Enhancing the ability of brain cells to produce energy is certainly an additional option to consider. Several nutrients are available that are involved in neuronal metabolism.

A one-year-long study done in 1996 indicates that some patients with AD would benefit from supplementation with acetyl-L-carnitine. Lipoic acid and CoQ10 may possibly be helpful, but no formal studies have been published regarding their use in patients with AD.

Providing Anti-Inflammatory Agents

Patients with AD have large amounts of neurofibrillary tangles in their brains. Neurofibrillary tangles result from the clumping of dead and damaged nerve cells. Many of these tangles contain a number of end products of inflammation. Studies have found that individuals who have used the non-steroidal anti-inflammatory drugs (NSAIDs) aspirin, ibuprofen and naproxen have a reduced risk of AD. The use of acetaminophen is not associated with reduced risk.

NSAIDs have potentially serious risks and hence are not recommended as therapy for AD (Aisen 2003). We should keep in mind that perhaps fish oils (or most omega-3 fatty acids) could be beneficial in reducing inflammation. The metabolites of these fatty acids have anti-inflammatory qualities not present in the fatty acid metabolites of omega-6 fatty acids. A low dosage of the common anti-inflammatory drug aspirin (i.e., 80 mg, a few times a week) should be considered.

Blocking the Breakdown of Acetylcholine

Another approach that has been tried in treating AD is to prevent the degradation of acetylcholine, the brain chemical associated with learning and memory. This can be achieved by providing drugs that block the activity of the enzyme cholinesterase, which breaks down acetylcholine. Two of these drugs are tacrine (Cognex) and donezepil (Aricept). Tacrine was first introduced in 1993, and donezepil in 1997. Although tacrine has shown modest benefits in treating Alzheimer's disease, it may induce liver damage.

A Chinese herbal extract called huperzine A has been shown in preliminary studies to block cholinesterase even more potently than tacrine (Xu 1995). Long-term studies with this herbal extract are not available.

Improving Blood Circulation

Any step taken to reduce atherosclerosis, or hardening of the arteries, is likely to improve blood circulation to the brain. A study in the *Journal of the American Medical Association* had good news about the herb ginkgo biloba (Le Bars 1997). Therapy with 40 mg of ginkgo three times a day for one year had a positive effect in patients with AD. There are several compounds in ginkgo that improve circulation and act as blood thinners and antioxidants.

Aspirin can also work as a blood thinner and improve circulation. Vinpocetine is another herbal extract that improves cerebral circulation.

Mood Improvement

Many patients with AD suffer from low mood or full-blown depression. Doctors sometimes prescribe Prozac and other serotonin reuptake inhibitors to these patients. It's possible that St. John's wort or other mood boosters, such as B vitamins or methyl donors, could be beneficial. No formal testing has been done with these supplements and AD.

Combination Therapies

As I said at the beginning of this chapter, we are not likely to find a single magic nutrient or drug that will treat AD adequately. The proper therapeutic approach to this disorder

will come from the intelligent combination of different supplements and medicines. Only a few trials have been conducted using combination therapy.

In a study done by Biopharmaceutical Research Consultants in Ann Arbor, Michigan, lecithin, when added to tacrine, was found to provide a small additional benefit (Holford 1994). Lecithin was estimated to provide benefits equivalent to about 40 mg of tacrine. Women with AD who were already on estrogen replacement therapy were found to get additional cognitive benefits when tacrine was added to their regimen (Schneider 1997).

Eat Less, Think Longer

One additional approach to improving brain health is caloric restriction. Mark Mattson, Ph.D., Professor of Anatomy and Neurobiology at the University of Kentucky, says, "Our findings in animal studies show that eating less makes nerve cells in the brain more resistant to deterioration and death. This suggests that reduced calorie intake may help shield the brain, and could present a lifelong preventative strategy for neurodegenerative disorders such as Alzheimer's disease."

First-Line Therapy for AD

The nutritional approach to treating patients with AD is still very new, and no standards have been developed. It may take much research and individual testing to find the ideal regimen for each patient. Here is a step-by-step guideline that you can review with your health-care practitioner and adapt to your particular situation.

- Therapy with the B vitamins should be the first approach. Use a B-complex that includes all the B vitamins, at about two to five times the RDA or PDV.

- Include plenty of fresh fruits and vegetables in your diet in order to obtain important carotenoids and flavonoids. Vitamin E, between 100 and 200 IU a day, preferably of mixed tocopherols, should be taken with a meal. You may recall that the *New England Journal of Medicine* study mentioned earlier used 1000 units of vitamin E.

- My mind-boosting program recommends including many antioxidants in your regimen. Antioxidants help protect each other from being destroyed, so combining many antioxidants would reduce the dosage required for vitamin E. The dosage for vitamin C can range between 100 and 250 mg twice a day. A small dose of lipoic acid, such as 5 to 20 mg, is recommended.

- Fish oils supplying DHA and EPA, at 500 to 2000 mg a day, taken with meals, could improve the composition of the cell membrane of neurons.

- Ginkgo biloba can sharpen thinking and improve memory. A 40-mg dose twice daily, with breakfast and lunch, is recommended. Ginkgo also provides antioxidant protection.

- Acetyl-L-carnitine is a nutrient that has shown promise in the therapy of AD. A dose of 100 to 250 mg before or with breakfast can be helpful in improving alertness and focus.

- CoQ10 at a dose of 30 mg with breakfast increases overall energy levels.

- Melatonin, in a dosage of 0.3 to 1 mg, one or two times a week, an hour or two before bed, can provide a deeper sleep in those who have mild insomnia.

Second-Line Therapy

These suggestions should be helpful, but you may require additional nutrients. I recommend that you consider nutrients that have a direct influence on acetylcholine levels. These include choline, lecithin, DMAE and CDP-choline. It is difficult to give precise dosages or combinations that would apply to all patients with AD. However, these proposed guidelines will help you and your health-care practitioner formulate the right program.

- Start with choline at 250 mg a day with breakfast or lunch. If choline itself is not effective, 100 mg of DMAE can be added. A new form of choline sold in health-food stores is CDP-choline. The dosage would be 100 to 250 mg in the morning. You may consider adding about 1 gram of lecithin (phosphatidylcholine) a day, with breakfast or lunch. Please note that these four nutrients work in a similar manner, and their effects are cumulative.

- Consider taking a small amount of the methyl donors TMG or DMG, such as 50 to 100 mg, as a way to reduce homocysteine levels and provide more energy and improved mood.

- An exciting addition to the nutritional armamentarium of natural therapies for AD is the Chinese herbal extract known as huperzine A. Huperzine A works in a manner similar to the drug tacrine, in blocking the breakdown of acetylcholine in the brain and making more acetylcholine available to brain cells. A dosage of 0.02 to 0.05 mg per day can be tried instead of the standard cholinesterase inhibitors—*this must be done under medical supervision.* The dosage of huperzine A should be reduced if it is combined with nutrients that elevate acetylcholine levels, such as choline, DMAE, PC and CDP-choline.

- Anti-inflammatory agents, such as ibuprofen and naproxen, have been shown in some studies to be beneficial, although the risks of stomach ulcers and kidney damage must be considered. Aspirin, at 80 mg a day, is a reasonable and safe amount to take as an anti-inflammatory agent—unless you are on anticoagulant therapy with coumadin or another blood-thinning agent.

- Some patients with AD have agitation or anxiety. The occasional use of kava or 5-HTP can be helpful in inducing relaxation. Vinpocetine is an herbal extract that improves circulation and could be considered in those who have poor circulation in the brain.

 ### Cautions and Side Effects

Ginkgo, vinpocetine, fish oils and aspirin are blood thinners. Therefore, be prudent if you combine them, especially in high doses. Sometimes it is difficult to predict the reaction of a patient who uses multiple nutrients.

I recommend that you constantly reevaluate the supplements you are taking. In time, you may need to adjust your dosages and take fewer nutrients or smaller dosages. Some patients may require the opposite approach. The therapy of chronic diseases is a dynamic process, and adjustment of dosages is required on a regular basis.

Summary

Finding an effective therapy for AD is very challenging. However, with a great deal of patience, and trial and error, you may find a combination of nutrients that can improve quality of life and cognitive function. Many nutritional options have been presented in this chapter, and it is important not to take all of these supplements at the same time. Gradually add one, and then another, in low doses, to determine the effectiveness of each nutrient. Sometimes you may build up tolerance to a particular nutrient and you may need to substitute another. The use of nutrients is especially appropriate in the treatment of AD since currently there is no effective pharmaceutical therapy for this condition.

22

SUPPLEMENTS FOR PATIENTS WITH PARKINSON'S DISEASE

Parkinson's disease (PD) is a common neurological condition afflicting about 1 percent of men and women over the age of seventy. Individuals with PD have tremor of the hands, rigidity, poor balance and mild intellectual deterioration. The tremor is most apparent when they are at rest and is less severe with movement.

In PD, a small region in the brain called the *substantia nigra* begins to deteriorate. The neurons of the substantia nigra make use of the brain chemical dopamine. When dopamine is lost, tremors begin and movement slows. Despite currently available drug therapies, PD remains a progressive and incurable condition. Many patients with PD may also suffer from age-related cognitive decline or the symptoms of Alzheimer's disease.

Although PD can be caused by viral infections or exposure to environmental toxins, in the majority of cases the causes are not well known. Scientists suspect that oxidative damage to neurons in the substantia nigra might be a major cause of Parkinson's disease, particularly because of the depletion of the antioxidant glutathione (Pearce 1997).

Treatment Strategies for PD

The nutritional therapy for Parkinson's disease is still uncharted territory. The most promising approach appears to be using antioxidants to slow the oxidation and damage to the substantia nigra. It's possible that additional nutritional approaches may be found in the future. In this chapter I have provided several options that PD patients might consider using, under the supervision of a medical provider.

Three types of drugs are commonly prescribed for patients with PD. First, doctors prescribe dopamine precursors, such as L-dopa, which converts into dopamine. Another approach uses drugs that block the breakdown of dopamine. A common medicine used for this purpose is selegiline (also known as deprenyl). As a third approach, drugs that influence dopamine receptors directly are prescribed. The two most commonly prescribed are bromocriptine and pergolide.

Over the past few decades, researchers have made important advances in the therapy of PD with pharmaceutical medicines. Several nutritional strategies should be explored further.

Increasing the Levels of Antioxidants

Of all the nutritional strategies available to treat PD patients, antioxidants appear to be the most promising choices to prevent or slow the progression of this condition. Individuals whose diets include plenty of healthy antioxidant-containing foods are less likely to develop PD. Patients should consume plenty of fruits and vegetables that contain glutathione or that can help produce it. Cyano-hydroxybutene, a chemical found in broccoli, cauliflower, brussels sprouts, and cabbage, is also thought to increase glutathione levels.

I recommend PD patients to consider taking the following antioxidants. It's important to take this regimen in addition to your standard pharmaceutical therapy and always consult with your physician.

- Vitamin E, between 100 and 400 international units each, preferably of mixed tocopherols, taken daily with any meal
- Vitamin C, between 100 and 250 mg twice a day. In addition to being an antioxidant, vitamin C also helps the production of L-dopa from tyrosine (Seitz 1998).
- Lipoic acid, 10 to 20 mg a day. Take in the morning, with breakfast. LA is a powerful antioxidant and helps generate glutathione.
- N-acetyl-cysteine is an antioxidant that can help regenerate glutathione. A dose of 250 mg of NAC can be taken most mornings before breakfast. However, I don't recommend the daily use of NAC until more is known about this nutrient.
- Selenium is an antioxidant that can help increase levels of glutathione. A dose of 50 to 100 micrograms can be taken daily with any meal. Selenium is also usually found in over-the-counter multimineral pills.
- Melatonin is the sleep hormone with antioxidant abilities. A dose of 0.3 to 1 mg can be taken one or two hours before bed in case you have occasional insomnia. Melatonin tolerance can develop with regular use. Since we don't know the long-term effects of nightly use, it's advisable to limit its frequency to once or twice a week.

In the 1980s, some individuals taking a synthetic drug called MPTP developed symptoms similar to Parkinson's disease. It was determined that MPTP causes an oxidative damage similar to what happens with PD. Interestingly, a study with rats determined that the administration of melatonin is able to almost completely prevent the neurotoxicity from MPP, a toxin very similar to MPTP. The rats on melatonin and MPP did not exhibit symptoms of PD while the the rats that did not get melatonin got the symptoms. The researchers from Kyong Hee University in Seoul, Korea, say, "The present results support the hypothesis that melatonin may provide the useful therapeutic strategy for the treatment of oxidative stress-induced neurodegenerative disease such as PD." (Byung 1998).

Providing Dopamine Precursors

L-dopa, the immediate precursor to dopamine, is a nutrient available by prescription. L-dopa (often combined with carbidopa) is the most commonly prescribed medication to treat PD. It is possible that the use of L-dopa for prolonged periods causes oxidation and toxicity to brain cells. If this turns out to be true, it's more justification for the recommendations that antioxidants be added to standard PD therapy. There is currently no clinical proof that antioxidant supplements help patients with PD live longer. All indications point to the possibility that the course of the disease can be slowed by providing adequate antioxidant support.

Tyrosine is an amino acid that can be converted into L-dopa. But there is no reason to take tyrosine if L-dopa is available. You can increase dopamine levels with the use of B vitamins, particularly NADH. Preliminary studies have shown some benefit with NADH in the therapy of PD. Although more research is needed, it would seem reasonable to add NADH at a dose of 2.5 mg. You may take NADH every other morning on an empty stomach. NADH may have another beneficial effect. It may help regenerate the antioxidant glutathione.

Be careful when you add NADH if you are already taking L-dopa or other medicines that treat PD, since the effects could be cumulative. The long-term effectiveness of NADH in patients with PD is currently not known. Taking from two to four times the RDA for the B vitamins seems to be a reasonable option.

Blocking Dopamine Breakdown

Dopamine is broken down in the brain by an enzyme called monoamine oxidase (MAO). When the activity of MAO is inhibited, dopamine is present for a longer period of time. This benefits patients with PD. Several drugs are available that block the activity of MAO. Selegiline is the most effective and the one used most commonly. The prescribed dosage is 5 mg a day.

No nutrients are currently known to prevent the breakdown of dopamine. However, a study conducted on rats at the College of Humanities and Sciences, Beijing Union University, in Beijing, China, indicates that the Chinese herbs codonopsis and astragalus can inhibit MAO type B and increase the activity of the antioxidant SOD (Jin 1997). We don't have any human trials to determine whether these two herbs would benefit patients with PD. Although selegiline is a very helpful

medicine, high doses may increase the risk of heart irregularities.

Additional Nutrients to Consider

The nutritional treatments for PD recommended thus far include antioxidants, B vitamins and NADH. There are additional options to consider.

Some of these other nutrients may not be directly involved in making more dopamine, but they may well improve general cognitive abilities. Many patients who have PD, especially the elderly, have additional age-related cognitive decline. I would recommend waiting one or two weeks after starting a supplement before you add another one.

- Fish oils are recommended, at a dosage of 500 to 1000 mg a day of EPA/DHA, taken with meals. The role of fish oils in PD is not known. But we do know that fish oils can generally improve overall brain health.

- Coenzyme Q10, at a dosage of 30 mg each morning, with breakfast. This nutrient improves the energy production in cells. In the first placebo-controlled trial sponsored by the National Institutes of Health, early-stage Parkinson's patients who received 1,200 mg supplements daily slowed their rate of disease progression by as much as half (Shults 2002).

- Ginkgo biloba, at a dosage of 40 to 60 mg most days, with breakfast or lunch. This herb has antioxidant properties and helps improve memory and alertness.

Summary

It's likely that the proper use of natural supplements can reduce the necessary dosage of L-dopa, selegiline and other drugs currently used to treat PD, or help slow the progression of the condition. There's still a great deal we need to learn about the nutritional treatment of PD.

APPENDICES

HOW TO BE A SAVVY SUPPLEMENT USER ADVICE FROM THE FDA

The U.S. Food and Drug Administration, and health professionals and their organizations, receive many inquiries each year from consumers seeking health-related information, especially about dietary supplements. Clearly, people choosing to supplement their diets with herbals, vitamins, minerals or other substances want to know more about the products they choose in order to make informed decisions about them. The choice to use a dietary supplement can be a wise decision that provides health benefits. However, under certain circumstances, these products may be unnecessary for good health or they may even create unexpected risks.

Given the abundance and conflicting nature of information now available about dietary supplements, you may need help to sort the reliable information from the questionable. Here are some guidelines and answers to frequent questions.

What Is a Dietary Supplement?

According to the FDA, a dietary supplement is a product taken by mouth that contains a "dietary ingredient" intended to supplement the diet. The "dietary ingredients" in these products may include vitamins, minerals, herbs or other botanicals, amino acids and substances such as enzymes, organ tissues, glandulars and metabolites. Dietary supplements can also be extracts or concentrates, and may be found in many forms such as tablets, capsules, softgels, gelcaps, liquids or powders. Supplements can also be in other forms, like bars. In that event, their label information must not represent the product as a conventional food or as sole ingredient of a meal or diet. Whatever their form may be, the government places dietary supplements in a special category under the general umbrella of "foods," not drugs, and requires that every supplement be labeled a dietary supplement.

How Do Supplements Fit into My Total Diet?

Dietary supplements are not intended to replace a balanced diet with a variety of foods from the major food groups. While you need to have adequate intake of nutrients, excessive amounts of certain nutrients can cause problems for some consumers. You can find information on the functions and potential benefits of vitamins and minerals, as well as upper safe limits for nutrients at the Institute of Medicine of the Academies Web site at *www.iom.edu.*

Should I Check With My Doctor or Health-Care Provider Before Using a Supplement?

This is a good idea, especially for certain groups of people. Dietary supplements may not be risk-free under certain circumstances.

1. If you are pregnant, nursing a baby, or have a chronic medical condition, such as diabetes, hypertension or heart disease, be sure to consult your doctor or pharmacist before purchasing or taking any supplement.

2. While vitamin and mineral supplements are widely used and generally considered safe for children, you may wish to check with your doctor or pharmacist before giving these or any other dietary supplements to your child.

3. If you plan to use a dietary supplement in place of drugs or in combination with any drug, tell your health-care provider first. Many supplements contain active ingredients that have strong biological effects and their safety is not always assured in all users.

   If you have certain health conditions and take these products, you may be placing yourself at risk.

• Some supplements may interact with prescription and over-the-counter medicines. Taking a combination of supplements or using these products together with medications (whether prescription or OTC drugs) could in certain circumstances produce adverse effects. For some people, these effects could be life-threatening.

• Be alert to advisories about these products, whether taken alone or in combination. *For example:* Coumadin (a prescription medicine), ginkgo biloba (an herbal supplement), aspirin (an OTC drug) and vitamin E (a vitamin supplement) can each thin the blood. Taking any of these products together can increase the potential for internal bleeding. Combining St. John's wort with certain HIV drugs significantly reduces their effectiveness. St. John's wort may also reduce the effectiveness of prescription drugs for heart disease, depression, seizures, certain cancers or oral contraceptives.

• Some supplements can have unwanted effects during surgery. You must fully inform your doctor about the vitamins, minerals, herbals or any other supplements you are taking, especially before elective surgery. You may be asked to stop taking these products at least 2-3 weeks ahead of the procedure to avoid potentially dangerous supplement/drug interactions—such as changes in heart rate, blood pressure and increased bleeding—that could adversely affect the outcome of your surgery.

• Adverse effects from the use of dietary supplements should be reported to MedWatch. Either you or your healthcare provider may report a serious adverse event or illness directly to the FDA if you believe it is related to the use of any dietary supplement product. Call the FDA at 1-800-FDA-1088, fax them at 1-800-FDA-0178 or file a report on-line at *www.fda.gov/medwatch/how.htm.*

   The FDA would like to know whenever you think a product caused you a serious problem, even if you are not sure that the product was the cause, and even if you do not visit a doctor or clinic.

Who Is Responsible for Ensuring That Supplements Are Safe and That They Really Work?

The Dietary Supplement Health and Education Act (DSHEA) was signed into law in October 1994. Prior to that time, dietary supplements were subject to the same regulatory requirements as were other foods. This new law created a regulatory framework for ensuring the safety of dietary supplements.

Under the law, manufacturers of dietary supplements are responsible for making sure their products are safe before they go to market. They are also responsible for determining that the claims on their labels are accurate and truthful. Dietary supplement products are not reviewed by the government before they are marketed, but the FDA has the responsibility to take action against any unsafe dietary supplement product that reaches the market. Except in the case of a new dietary ingredient, where the law does require a pre-market review for safety data and other information, a firm does not have to provide the FDA with the evidence it relies on to substantiate safety or effectiveness before or after it markets its products.

In June 2007, the FDA issued regulations on good manufacturing practices (GMPs) specific to dietary supplements. These regulations will hopefully ensure the identity, purity, quality, strength and composition of herbal pills, vitamins and other supplements. As of June 2010 all manufacturers are required to test all ingredients going into their supplements and to maintain production records. Testing methods and limits on contaminants within products are still determined by the manufacturers.

These GMPs give the FDA a stronger basis to question a supplement manufacturer. If the FDA can prove that claims on marketed dietary supplement products are false and misleading, the agency may take action against manufacturers making such claims.

Here are some considerations for you to think about when you're shopping for supplements.

First, Ask Yourself: Does It Sound Too Good to Be True?

Do the claims for the product seem exaggerated or unrealistic? Are there simplistic conclusions being drawn from a complex study to sell a product? While the Internet can be a valuable source of accurate, reliable information, it also has a wealth of misinformation that may not be obvious. Learn to distinguish hype from evidence-based science. Nonsensical lingo can sound very convincing. Also, be skeptical about anecdotal information from persons who have no formal training in nutrition or botanicals, or from personal testimonials (e.g., from store employees, friends, or on-line chat rooms and message boards) about incredible benefits or results obtained from using a product. Question these people on their training and knowledge in nutrition or medicine.

Think Twice About Chasing the Latest Headline.

Sound health advice is generally based on a body of research, not a single study. Be wary of results claiming a "quick fix" that depart from previous research and scientific beliefs. Keep in mind science does not proceed by dramatic breakthroughs, but by taking many small steps, slowly building towards a consensus. Furthermore, news stories about the latest scientific study, especially those on TV or radio, are often too brief to include important details that may apply to you or allow you to make an informed decision.

Look Carefully at Internet or E-mail Solicitations.

While the Internet is a rich source of health information, it is also an easy vehicle for spreading myths, hoaxes and rumors about alleged news, studies, products or findings. To avoid falling prey to such hoaxes, be skeptical and watch out for overly emphatic language with UPPERCASE LETTERS and lots of exclamation points!!!! *Beware of such phrases such as:* "This is not a hoax" or "Send this to everyone you know."

Beware of Some Common But Questionable Assumptions.

1. *Even if a product may not help me, it at least won't hurt me.*

   It's best not to assume that this will always be true. When consumed in high enough amounts, for a long enough time, or in combination with certain other substances, all chemicals can be toxic, including nutrients, plant components and other biologically active ingredients.

2. *When I see the term 'natural,' it means that a product is healthful and safe.*

   Consumers can be misled if they assume this term assures wholesomeness, or that these foodlike substances necessarily have milder effects, which makes them safer to use than drugs. The term "natural" on labels is not well defined and is sometimes used ambiguously to imply unsubstantiated benefits or safety. For example, many weight-loss products claim to be "natural" or "herbal" but this doesn't necessarily make them safe. Their ingredients may interact with drugs or

may be dangerous for people with certain medical conditions.

3. *A product is safe when there is no cautionary information on the product label.*

   Dietary supplement manufacturers may not necessarily include warnings about potential adverse effects on the labels of their products. If consumers want to know about the safety of a specific dietary supplement, they should contact the manufacturer of that brand directly. It is the manufacturer's responsibility to determine that the supplement it produces or distributes is safe and that there is substantiated evidence that the label claims are truthful and not misleading.

4. *A recall of a harmful product guarantees that all such harmful products will be immediately and completely removed from the marketplace.*

   A product recall of a dietary supplement is voluntary and while many manufacturers do their best, a recall does not necessarily remove all harmful products from the marketplace.

How Will I Be Able to Spot False Claims?

Be savvy! Although the benefits of some dietary supplements have been documented, the claims of others may be unproven. If something sounds too good to be true, it usually is. *Here are some signs of a false claim…*

- Statements that the product is a quick and effective "cure-all." *For example:* "Extremely beneficial in treatment of rheumatism, arthritis, infections, prostate problems, ulcers, cancer, heart trouble, hardening of the arteries, and more."

- Statements that suggest the product can treat or cure diseases. *For example:* "shrinks tumors" or "cures impotency." Actually, these are drug claims and should not be made for dietary supplements.

- Statements that claim the product is "totally safe," "all natural," or has "definitely no side effects."

- Promotions that use words like "scientific breakthrough," "miraculous cure," "exclusive product," "secret ingredient," or "ancient remedy." *For example:* "A scientific breakthrough formulated by using proven principles of natural health-based medical science."

- Text that uses overly impressive-sounding terms, like those for a weight-loss product. *For example:* "hunger stimulation point" and "thermogenesis."

- Personal testimonials by consumers or doctors claiming amazing results. *For example:* "My husband has Alzheimer's. He began eating a teaspoonful of this product each day. And now in just 22 days, he mowed the grass, cleaned out the garage, and weeded the flower beds; we take our morning walk together again."

- Limited availability and advance payment required. *For example:* "Hurry. This offer will not last. Send us a check now to reserve your supply."

- Promises of no-risk "money-back guarantees." *For example:* "If after 30 days you have not lost at least 4 pounds each week, your uncashed check will be returned to you."

Contact the Manufacturer for More Information About the Specific Product That You Are Purchasing.
If you cannot tell whether the product you are purchasing meets the same standards as those used in the research studies you read about, check with the manufacturer or distributor. *Ask to speak to someone who can address your questions, which may include…*

1. What information does the firm have to substantiate the claims made for the product? Be aware that sometimes firms supply so-called "proof" of their claims by citing undocumented reports from satisfied consumers, or "internal" graphs and charts that could be mistaken for evidence-based research.

2. Does the firm have information to share about tests it has conducted on the safety or efficacy of the ingredients in the product?

3. Does the firm have a quality-control system in place to determine if the product actually contains what is stated on the label and is free of contaminants?

4. Has the firm received any adverse events reports from consumers using their products?

What's the Bottom Line?

- Dietary supplements are intended to supplement the diet, not to cure, prevent, or treat diseases or replace the variety of foods important to a healthful diet.

- Supplements can help you meet daily requirements for certain nutrients, but when you combine drugs and foods, too much of some nutrients can also cause problems.

- Many factors play a role in deciding if a supplement is right for you, including possible drug interactions and side effects.

- Do not self-diagnose any health condition. Together, you and your health-care team can make the best decision for you.

What Consumers Want to Know About Botanical or Herbal Supplements

A botanical is a plant or plant part valued for its medicinal or therapeutic properties, flavor and/or scent. Herbs are a subset of botanicals. Products made from botanicals that are used to maintain or improve health may be called herbal products, botanical products or phytomedicines.

How Are Botanicals Commonly Sold?

Botanicals are sold in many forms: as fresh or dried products; liquid or solid extracts; and as tablets, capsules, powders and tea bags. For example, fresh ginger root is often found in the produce section of food stores while dried ginger root is sold packaged in tea bags, capsules, or tablets. Liquid preparations made from ginger root are also available. Sometimes a single chemical or a particular group of chemicals may be isolated from a botanical and sold as a dietary supplement in tablet or capsule form. An example is phytoestrogens from soy products.

How Are They Usually Prepared?

Common preparations include teas, decoctions, tinctures and extracts…

- A *tea,* also known as an *infusion,* is made by adding boiling water to fresh or dried botanicals and steeping them. The tea may be consumed either hot or cold.

- Some roots, bark and berries require more forceful treatment to extract their desired ingredients. They are simmered in boiling water for longer periods than teas, making a *decoction,* which also may be drunk hot or cold.

- A *tincture* is made by soaking a botanical in a solution of alcohol and water. Tinctures are sold as liquids and are used for concentrating and preserving a botanical. They are made in different strengths that are expressed as botanical-to-extract ratios (i.e., ratios of the weight of the dried botanical to the volume or weight of the finished product).

- An *extract* is made by soaking the botanical in a liquid that removes specific types of chemicals. The liquid can be used as is or evaporated to make a dry extract for use in capsules or tablets.

Are Botanical Dietary Supplements Standardized?

Standardization is a process that manufacturers may use to ensure the consistency of every batch of their products. The standardization process can also provide a measure of quality control.

Recent FDA regulations specific to dietary supplements (see page 169) may improve consistency of product from batch to batch, but, overall, dietary supplements are not required to be standardized in the United States. In fact, no legal or regulatory definition exists for standardization in the United States as it applies to botanical dietary supplements. Because of this, the term "standardization" may mean many different things. Some manufacturers use the term standardization incorrectly to refer to uniform manufacturing practices; following a recipe is not sufficient for a product to be called standardized. Therefore, the presence of the word "standardized" on a supplement label does not necessarily indicate product quality.

Ideally, the chemical markers chosen for standardization would also be the compounds that are responsible for a botanical's effect in the body. In this way, every batch of the product would have a consistent health effect. However, the components responsible for the effects of most botanicals have not been identified or clearly defined. For example, the genocides in the botanical senna are known to be responsible for the laxative effect of the plant, but many compounds may be responsible for valerian's relaxing effect.

Are Botanical Dietary Supplements Safe?

Many people believe that products labeled "natural" are safe and good for them. This is not necessarily true because the safety of a botanical depends on many things, such as its chemical makeup, how it works in the body, how it is prepared and the dose used.

The action of botanicals range from mild to powerful. A botanical with mild action may have subtle effects. Chamomile and peppermint, both mild botanicals, are usually taken as teas to aid digestion and are generally considered safe. Some mild botanicals may take weeks or months to be effective. For example, valerian often requires 14 days to alleviate insomnia. In contrast, a powerful botanical produces a fast result. Kava, as one example, is reported to have an immediate and powerful action affecting anxiety and muscle relaxation.

The dose and form of a botanical preparation also play important roles in its safety. Teas, tinctures and extracts have different strengths. The same amount of a botanical may be contained in a cup of tea, a few teaspoons of tincture, or an even smaller quantity of an extract. Also, different preparations vary in the relative amounts and concentrations of chemical removed from the whole botanical. For example, peppermint tea is generally considered safe to

drink but peppermint oil, which is much more concentrated, can be toxic if it is used incorrectly. Always follow the manufacturer's suggested directions for using a botanical and not exceed the recommended dose without the advice of a health-care provider.

Does a Label Indicate the Quality of a Botanical Dietary Supplement Product?

It is difficult to determine the quality of a botanical dietary supplement product from its label. The degree of quality control depends on the manufacturer, the supplier, and others in the production process.

FDA regulations known as Good Manufacturing Practices (GMPs) require all manufacturers to test ingredients going into botanical supplements (see page 169). Although these rules help ensure product quality and composition, they do not guarantee accurate label information. Some manufacturers voluntarily follow manufacturing practices used in the pharmaceutical industry, which are more rigorous than the ones for the supplement industry. Some companies in the dietary supplement industry have developed unofficial standards for GMPs.

What Methods Are Used to Evaluate The Health Benefits and Safety of a Botanical Dietary Supplement?

Scientists use several approaches to evaluate botanical dietary supplements for their potential health benefits and safety risks, including their history of use and laboratory studies using cell or animal models. Studies involving people (individual case reports, observational studies, and clinical trials) can provide information that is relevant to how botanical dietary supplements are used. Researchers may conduct a systematic review to summarize and evaluate a group of clinical trials that meet certain criteria.

ARE THERE SPECIAL CONCERNS FOR SENIORS? MORE ADVICE FROM THE FDA

Even if you eat a wide variety of foods, how can you be sure that you are getting all the vitamins, minerals, and other nutrients you need as you get older? If you are over 50, your nutritional needs may change. Informed food choices are the first place to start, making sure you get a variety of foods while watching your calorie intake. Supplements and fortified foods may also help you get appropriate amounts of nutrients.

To help you make informed decisions, talk to your doctor and/or registered dietitian. They can work together with you to determine if your intake of a specific nutrient might be too low or too high. They can help you decide how you can achieve a balance between the foods and nutrients you personally need.

Today's dietary supplements are not only vitamins and minerals. They also include less-familiar substances, such as herbals, botanicals, amino acids, enzymes and animal extracts. Some dietary supplements are well understood and established, but others need further study. Whatever your choice, supplements should not replace the variety of foods important to a healthful diet.

Unlike drugs, dietary supplements are not pre-approved by the government for safety or effectiveness before marketing. Also, unlike drugs, supplements are not intended to treat, diagnose, prevent or cure diseases. But some supplements can help assure that you get an adequate dietary intake of essential nutrients; others may help you reduce your risk of disease. Some older people, for example, are tired due to low iron levels. In that case, their doctor may recommend an iron supplement.

At times, it can be confusing to tell the difference between a dietary supplement, a food or over-the-counter (OTC) medicines. This is because supplements, by law, come in a variety of forms that resemble these products, such as tablets, capsules, powders, energy bars or drinks. One way to know if a product is a dietary supplement is to look for the *Supplement Facts* label on the product.

The illustration on the following page shows you what to look for on a dietary supplement label.

174

WHAT YOUR DIETARY SUPPLEMENT LABEL MUST TELL YOU

Statement of Identity

GINSENG
A DIETARY SUPPLEMENT

Net quantity of contents

60 CAPSULES

Structure-function claim

Directions

Supplement Facts panel

Other ingredients in descending order of predominance and by common name or propriety blend.

"When you need to perform your best, take ginseng." This statement has not been evaluated by the Food and Drug Administration. This Product is not intended to diagnose, treat, cure, or prevent any disease.

DIRECTIONS FOR USE: Take one capsule daily

Supplement Facts
Serving Size 1 Capsule

Amount Per Capsule

Oriental Ginseng, powdered (root)   850 mcg*

*Daily value not established

Other Ingredients: Gelatin, water, and glycerin.
ABC COMPANY
Anytown, USA 00001

Name and place of business of manufacturer, packer, or distributor. This is the address to write for more product information.

Source: Food and Drug Administration—Web site

The Special Risks for Older Consumers

While certain products may be helpful to some older individuals, there may be circumstances when these products may not benefit your health or when they may create unexpected risks. Many supplements contain active ingredients that have strong biological effects in the body. This could make them unsafe in some situations and hurt or complicate your health. *For example...*

- Are you taking both medicines and supplements? Are you substituting one for the other? Taking a combination of supplements, using these products together with medications (whether prescription or over-the-counter), or substituting them in place of medicines your doctor prescribes

could lead to harmful, even life-threatening results. Be alert to any advisories about these products. Coumadin (a prescription medicine), ginkgo biloba (an herbal supplement), aspirin (an over-the-counter drug), and vitamin E (a vitamin supplement) can each thin the blood. Taking any of these products alone or together can increase the potential for internal bleeding or stroke. Another example is St. John's wort that may reduce the effectiveness of prescription drugs for heart disease, depression, seizures, certain cancers or HIV.

- Are you planning surgery? Some supplements can have unwanted effects before, during, and after surgery. It is important to fully inform your health-care professional,

175

including your pharmacist, about the vitamins, minerals, herbals, and any other supplements you are taking, especially before surgery. You may be asked to stop taking these products at least 2-3 weeks ahead of the procedure to avoid potentially dangerous supplement/drug interactions— such as changes in heart rate, blood pressure or bleeding risk that could adversely affect the outcome of your surgery.

- Is taking more of a good thing better? Some people might think that if a little is good, taking a lot is even better. But taking too much of some nutrients, even vitamins and minerals, can also cause problems. Depending on the supplement, your age, and the status of your health, taking more than 100% of the Daily Value (DV) (see the *Supplements Facts* panel) of certain vitamins and minerals, e.g., Vitamin A, vitamin D, and iron (from supplements and food sources like vitamin-fortified cereals and drinks), may actually harm your health. Large amounts can also interfere with how your medicines work.

Remember: Your combined intake from all supplements (including multivitamins, single supplements, and combination products) plus fortified foods, like some cereals and drinks, could cause health problems.

Getting the Right Amount Of Vitamins and Minerals Through Your Diet

Vitamins and minerals are nutrients found naturally in food. We need them to stay healthy. The benefits and side effects of many vitamins and minerals have been studied. The best way to get vitamins and minerals is through the food you eat, not any supplements you might take.

Use the Food Guide Pyramid, developed by the USDA, to help you choose a healthful assortment of foods. Twelve new individualized food pyramids have replaced the old one most people were familiar with.

The new pyramids feature vertical bands that represent different food groups instead of the old horizontal bands and they follow the new dietary guidelines, developed, in part, by the American Dietetic Association, which recommends eating two cups of fruit and two-and-a-half cups of vegetables a day, along with three ounces of whole grain foods and three cups of fat-free or low-fat milk. The USDA says people should choose lean meats and poultry. The USDA recommends choosing more fish, beans, nuts and seeds.

In addition, a person is shown climbing steps on the outside of the pyramid to illustrate the new slogan, "Steps to a Healthier You," and support the recommendation of at least 30 minutes of exercise a day as an essential component of good health. Today, two in three adults in the country are overweight or obese, while 15% of adolescents and 15% of children aged 6 to 11 are overweight.

For more information, please visit *www.mypyramid.gov*.

Remember that all calorie sources are not created equal. Carbohydrate and protein have about 4 calories per gram, but fat has more than twice that amount (9 calories per gram). Most weight-conscious consumers should aim for a daily fat intake of no more than 30 percent of total calories.

Keep your intake of saturated fats (fats that increase your risk of high cholesterol and heart disease) at less than 10 percent of your total calories. This means avoiding, or eating only occasionally, or very small portions of foods like high-fat dairy products (like cheese, whole milk, cream, butter and regular ice cream), fatty fresh and processed meats, the skin and fat of poultry, lard, palm oil and coconut oil.

If you drink alcoholic beverages, do so in moderation. Alcoholic beverages supply calories but few nutrients. For example, a 12-ounce regular beer contains about 150 calories, a 5-ounce glass of wine about 100 calories, and 1.5 ounces of 80-proof distilled spirits about 100 calories.

Limit your use of beverages and foods that are high in added sugars—those added to foods in processing or preparation, not the naturally occurring sugars in foods such as fruit or milk. Foods containing added sugars provide calories, but may have few vitamins and minerals. The major sources of added sugars include non-diet soft drinks, sweets and candies, cakes and cookies and fruit drinks and fruit-ades.

If you can't eat enough, ask your doctor if you should be taking a multivitamin and mineral supplement. *And remember…*

- The supplement doesn't need to be a "senior" formula.

- It shouldn't have large or "mega-doses" of vitamins and minerals.

- Generally store or generic brands are fine.
  How much should you take? Check the label on your supplement bottle. It shows the level of vitamins and minerals in a serving compared with the suggested daily intake.

For example, a vitamin A intake of 100% DV (Daily Value) means the supplement is giving you the full amount of vitamin A you need each day. This is in addition to what you are getting from your food.

Some people might think that if a little is good, a lot must be better. But, that doesn't necessarily apply to vitamins and minerals. Depending on the supplement, your age and your health, taking more than 100% DV could be harmful to your health. Plus, if your body cannot use the entire supplement you take, you've wasted money. Finally, large doses of some vitamins and minerals can also keep your prescription medications from working as they should.

Anything Special for People Over 50?
Even if you eat a good variety of foods, if you are over 50, you might need certain supplements. Talk to your doctor or a registered dietitian. *Depending on your needs, he or she might suggest you get the following amounts from food and, if needed, supplements…*

- Vitamin B-12—2.4 mcg (micrograms) of B-12 each day. Some foods, such as cereals, are fortified with this vitamin. However, up to one-third of older people can no longer absorb natural vitamin B-12 from their food. They need this vitamin to keep their blood and nerves healthy.

- Calcium—1200 mg (milligrams), but not more than 2500 mg a day. As you age, you need more of this and vitamin D to keep bones strong and to maintain the bone you have. Bone loss can lead to fractures, mainly of the hip, spine or wrist, in both older women and men.

- Vitamin D—400 IU (international units) for people age 51 to 70 and 600 IU for those over 70, but not more than 2000 IU each day.

- Iron—extra iron for women past menopause who are using hormone-replacement therapy (men and other postmenopausal women need 8 mg of iron). Iron helps keep red blood cells healthy. Postmenopausal women who use hormone-replacement therapy may

WHAT FOODS HAVE CALCIUM?

- Dairy products such as milk and cheese and foods made with them

- Canned fish with soft bones such as salmon and sardines

- Dark green leafy vegetables

- Calcium-fortified products such as orange juice

- Breads and cereals made with calcium-fortified flour

still experience a monthly period. They need extra iron to make up for that loss of blood.

- Vitamin B-6—1.7 mg for men and 1.5 mg for women. This vitamin is needed for forming red blood cells and to keep you healthy.

What About Antioxidants?

You may have heard about the possible benefits of antioxidants, natural substances found in food. Right now, there is no proof that large doses of antioxidants will prevent chronic diseases such as heart disease, diabetes or cataracts. Eating fruits and vegetables (at least five servings a day) rather than taking a supplement is the best way to get antioxidants. Vegetable oil and nuts are also good sources of some antioxidants. Non-dairy calcium sources are especially good for people who cannot use dairy products.

Should I Consult My Health-Care Provider About Dietary Supplements?

You and your health professionals (doctors, nurses, registered dietitians, pharmacists

and other caregivers) are a team working toward a common goal—to develop a personalized health plan for you. Your doctor and other members of the health team can help monitor your medical condition and overall health, especially if any problems develop. Although they may not immediately have answers to your questions, these health professionals have access to the most current research on dietary supplements.

There are numerous resources that provide information about dietary supplements. These include TV, radio, newspapers, magazines, store clerks, friends, family or the Internet. It is important to question recommendations from people who have no formal training in nutrition, botanicals or medicine. While some of these sources, like the Web, may seem to offer a wealth of accurate information, these same sources may contain misinformation that may not be obvious. Given the abundance and conflicting nature of information now available about supplements, it is more important than ever to partner with your health-care team to sort the reliable information from the questionable.

Keep a Record of Your Supplement Intake

If you take dietary supplements, you may find it helpful have a record and share it with your health-care advisors, who could include your doctor, nurse, registered dietitian, pharmacist and/or caregiver. They need this information to help develop a personalized plan for you.

List all supplements you take and how often you take them. Include all multiple, single or combination vitamins, minerals (like calcium and iron), or any herbal or botanical supplement you may have on the

WHAT TO ASK YOUR HEALTH-CARE PROVIDER

Ask the following questions when you talk to your doctor about dietary supplements.

Question	Yes	No
Is taking a dietary supplement an important part of my total diet?	❏	❏
What is this product for?		
What are its intended benefits?		
How, when and for how long should I take it?		
Are there any precautions or warnings I should know about (e.g., is there an "upper limit" I should not go above)?	❏	❏
Are there any known side effects (e.g., loss of appetite, nausea, headaches, etc.)? Do they apply to me?	❏	❏
Are there any foods, medicines (prescription or over-the-counter), or other supplements I should avoid while taking this product?	❏	❏
If I am scheduled for surgery, should I be concerned about the dietary supplements I am taking?	❏	❏

kitchen or medicine cabinet shelf. Because supplements come in so many forms that resemble other food and drug products, check to see if there is a *Supplement Facts* label on the product to be certain it is a dietary supplement.

Complete the chart on the following page by including the amounts and reasons for taking supplements. Have this information handy when you meet with your health-care team to discuss the best decisions for your overall health.

PERSONAL SUPPLEMENT AND MEDICATION RECORD

Name: _____ Age: _____ Date: _____

1. Please list below which supplements you take, how often, and why you take them.

Supplement	How Often?	How Much?	I Take It for These Reasons:
Example: Calcium	Once a day	500 mg	Support healthy bones
Example: Multivitamin	Once a day	1 tablet	Supplement my diet
1.			
2.			
3.			
4.			
5.			
6.			
7.			
8.			

2. Are you currently taking or have you recently taken any over-the-counter medications (e.g., aspirin, cold medicine, stool softener, pain reliever, etc.)?

❏ Yes (Which ones?)   ❏ No

1. _____
2. _____
3. _____
4. _____
5. _____

3. What prescription medication(s) are you currently taking, if any?

1. _____
2. _____
3. _____
4. _____
5. _____

Other: _____

_____

Sources: FDA/Center for Food Safety & Applied Nutrition
The Administration on Aging (Department of Health and Human Services [DHHS]), Food and Drug
Administration (DHHS), Office of Dietary Supplements (National Institutes of Health, DHHS)

How to Research Dietary Supplements on the Web

Start with the Web sites of organizations, rather than doing blind searches using a search engine. *Here are some questions to consider…*

Who Operates the Site?

Is the site run by the government, a university, or a reputable medical or health-related association (e.g., American Medical Association, American Diabetes Association, American Heart Association, National Institutes of Health, National Academies of Science, or U.S. Food and Drug Administration)? Is the information written or reviewed by qualified health professionals, experts in the field, academia, government or the medical community?

What Is the Purpose of the Site?

Is the purpose of the site to educate the public objectively or just to sell a product? Be aware of practitioners or organizations whose main interest is in marketing products, either directly or through sites with which they are linked. Commercial sites should clearly distinguish scientific information from advertisements. Most nonprofit and government sites contain no advertising, and access to the site and materials offered are usually free.

What Is the Source of the Information and Does It Have Any References?

Has the study been reviewed by recognized scientific experts and published in reputable peer-reviewed scientific journals, like *The New England Journal of Medicine*? Does the information say "some studies show…" or does it state where the study is listed so that you can check the authenticity of the references? For example, can the study be found in the National Library of Medicine's database of literature citations (*www.nlm.nih.gov*)?

How Recent Is the Information?

Check the date when the material was posted or updated. Often, more recent research or other findings will not be reflected in older material. For example, side effects or interactions with other products may have just been discovered, but that information won't appear on the Web site. Ideally, health and medical sites should be updated frequently.

Here are some government and nonprofit sources of health and medical information…

- American Botanical Council
  www.herbalgram.org

- American Cancer Society
  www.cancer.org

- American Heart Association
  www.americanheart.org

- American Medical Association
  www.ama-assn.org

- Centers for Disease Control and Prevention
  www.cdc.gov

- Consumer.gov
  www.consumer.gov

- US Food and Drug Administration
  www.fda.gov

- Healthfinder
  www.healthfinder.gov

- International Food Information Council
  www.ific.org

- National Cancer Institute
  www.cancer.gov

- National Center for Complementary and Alternative Medicine
  http://nccam.nih.gov

- National Institutes of Health
  www.nih.gov

- National Institute of Allergy and Infectious Diseases
  www.niaid.nih.gov

- National Library of Medicine
  www.nlm.nih.gov

- MedWatch, FDA Safety Information and Adverse Event Reporting Program
  www.fda.gov/medwatch/safety.htm

- Mayo Clinic
  www.mayoclinic.com

- Memorial Sloan-Kettering Cancer Center, New York City
  www.mskcc.org

- Nutrition.Gov
  www.nutrition.gov

Here are other Web sites that offer health information, especially about herbs and supplements…

- www.webmd.com

- www.healthcentral.com

- www.mindbodyfocused.com/body/nutritional-supplements.php

- www.backtohealth.net

- www.wholehealthmd.com

- www.healthatoz.com

- www.drmagaziner.com

- www.aarp.org/health/staying_healthy/eating

- www.herbsforhealth.com

- www.reference.com

- www.naturalhealthweb.com

- www.intelihealth.com

- www.berkeleywellness.com

- www.questhealthlibrary.com

- www.supplementinfo.org

- www.drugdigest.org

- www.healthandage.com

- www.healthlinkplus.org

- www.altmedicine.com

- www.amfoundation.org

- www.herbmed.org

- www.mdheal.org

PLEASE NOTE: Addresses, telephone numbers and Web sites listed in this book are accurate at the time of publication but they are subject to frequent change.

Where You Can Buy Supplements: State-By-State Listing

Alabama

Albertville
Mountain Herb Shop
5930 Hwy. 431, Ste. 13
256-878-6300

Andalusia
City Health Mart Drugs
224 S Three Notch St.
334-222-1131

Anniston
Herb Shop
121 E 14th St.
256-237-1550

Athens
Herbs & More
609 US Hwy. 72 W
256-233-0073

Auburn
Dayspring Nature Shoppe
223 Opelika Rd.
334-821-1965

Peachtree Natural Foods #2
1625 E University Dr.
334-821-7749

Bessemer
Health Food Shoppe
550 W Town Plaza
205-424-5293

Birmingham
B & C Nutrition
1615 Montgomery Hwy.
205-979-8307

Golden Temple Health Foods
3309 Lorna Rd., Ste. 7
205-823-7002

Green Door Vitamins & Health
2843 Culver Rd.
205-871-2651

Health Food Source
420 Cahaba Park Circle
205-991-0994

Health Food West
1923 Bessemer Rd.
205-923-0001

Decatur
Gloria's Good Health
1820–L 6th Ave.
256-355-2439

Pill Box Pharmacy
474 Hwy. 67 S
256-353-0100

Florence
Valley Health Foods
117 S Cherry St.
256-764-5340

Gadsden
Seeds of Health
1210 Noccalula Rd.
256-543-8551

Gardendale
Garden Health Foods
1224 Main St.
205-631-8816

Guntersville
Healthy Hints Herb Shop
12761 US Hwy. 431
256-505-0000

Hartselle
Abundant Health
1813 Hwy. 31 SW
256-773-0060

Huntsville
Foods For Life
1407 Memorial Pkwy NW,
  Ste. C
256-533-2050

Pearly Gates Natural Foods
2308 Memorial Pkwy SW
256-534-6233

Ruth's Nutrition
7540 SW Memorial Pkwy.
256-883-4127

Jasper
Enjoy Health Foods
1608 Hwy. 78 W
205-384-4372

Madison
Herb & Life Health Foods
7185 Hwy. 72 W
256-722-9198

Montgomery
Health Wise Foods Inc.
5153 Atlanta Hwy.
334-277-9925

Herb Shop
8151 Vaughn Rd.
334-271-2882

Natural Gourmet
2580 Eastern Blvd.
334-271-6887

Muscle Shoals
Valley Health Foods
1601 Woodward Ave.
256-381-4260

Northport
Robertson's Health Food Center
734 McFarland Blvd.
205-333-0966

Oxford
St. John's Nutrition
832 Snow St.
256-835-9588

Pelham
Healthy Harvey's Natural Foods
3183 Pelham Pkwy.
205-620-3752

Pell City
Stan's Natural Foods
2305 Stemley Bridge Rd.
205-884-1160

Phenix City
Belinda Kay's Health Store
2021 280 By-Pass
334-297-7005

Peachtree Natural Foods #3
1811 Stadium Dr.
334-480-0284

Scottsboro
Herbs For Health
410 Parks Ave., Ste. B
256-259-3821

Scottsboro Herb Shop
902 S Broad St., Ste. B
256-259-5399

Trussville
Honey & Spice Health Foods
218 Main St.
205-655-0307

Alaska

Anchorage
Anna's Health Food
1403 Hyder St.
907-277-2662

Natural Pantry
3801 Old Seward Hwy.
907-770-1444

Roy's Health Foods
501 E Northern Lights Blvd.
907-277-3226

Fairbanks
Sunshine Health Foods
410 Trainor Gate Rd.
907-456-5433

Homer
Smoky Bay Natural Foods
248 W Pioneer Ave.
907-235-7252

Kenai
Peninsula Health & Nutrition
10767 Spur Hwy.
907-283-4145

Ketchikan
Rain Country Nutrition
625 Mission St.
907-225-8910

Kodiak
Cactus Flats Natural Foods
338 Mission Rd.
907-486-4677

Palmer
Ideal Nutrition & Books
642 S Alaska St.
907-745-8487

Sitka
Evergreen Natural Foods
2 Lincoln St., Ste. A1
907-747-6944

Valdez
A Rogues Garden
354 Fairbanks St.
907-835-5880

Wasilla
Healthy Herbs Shoppe
1700 Lucas Rd.
907-376-7444

Arizona

Apache Junction
The Good Apple Natural Market
100 N Plaza Rd.
480-982-2239

Bisbee
Bisbee Food Cooperative
72 Erie St.
520-432-4011

Casa Grande
Monique's Health Shoppe
1237 E Florence Blvd.
520-836-9488

Tri-Valley Health Food
1355 E Florence Blvd., Ste. 131
520-421-3090

Chandler
Naturally To You Nutrition & Wellness
1550 W Hackberry Dr.
480-963-2927

Nature's Health Shoppe
973 W Elliot Rd., Ste. 2
480-821-1986

Douglas
Bee-Health-E
426 E 11th St.
520-364-8224

Flagstaff
Bashas' Health Foods
1000 N Humphreys St., Ste. 112
928-774-2101

Healthy Trails
2775 S Woodlands Village
   Blvd., #2
928-774-7374

*New Frontiers Natural
   Marketplace*
1000 S Milton Rd.
928-774-5747

Fort Mohave
Country Health Market
4410 S Hwy. 95, #A
928-758-4717

Fountain Hills
To Your Health Inc.
17007 E Colony Dr., Ste. 106
480-837-7590

Nature's Finest Health Market
16838 E Parkview Ave.
480-837-4588

Glendale
Arizona Health Foods
4330 W Bell Rd.
602-938-3088

Kingman
Healthy Habits
432 E Beale St.
928-753-3336

Natural Planet
3787 Stockton Hill Rd., Ste. A
928-757-7774

Lake Havasu City
A To Z Health Foods
1963 McCulloch Blvd.
928-453-6200

Havasu Health
2109 McCulloch Blvd. N
928-855-2204

Herbal Emporium
1960 Mesquite Ave., Ste. B
928-854-1511

Herb's Herbs
2026 McCulloch Blvd. N
928-453-8182

Lakeside
Lavida Health Foods
13 W White Mountain Blvd.
928-367-4297

Mesa
Nature's Finest Health Market
1925 E Brown Rd.
480-962-8288

Hi-Health
1229 S Power Rd., #110
480-641-2070

Vitamin World
2050 S Roslyn Pl., Ste. 132
480-986-9690

Nogales
Happy Home Nutrition Center
158 N Grand Ave.
520-287-3765

Payson
Back to Basics Health Food Market
908 N Beeline Hwy.
928-474-8935

Phoenix
Arizona Health Foods
3152 E Camelback Rd.
602-224-0099

Arizona Health Foods
13802 N 32nd St.
602-482-0347

Arnie's Health Foods
5138 E Thomas Rd.
602-840-0540

Arizona Health Foods
4424 N 19th Ave.
602-265-7474

Hi-Health
2005 E Camelback Rd.
602-957-0412

Hi-Health
3121 N 3rd Ave., Ste. 101
602-279-5200

Prescott
Arizona Health Foods
1781 E State Rte. 69, #47
928-777-8401

Arizona Health Foods
180 East Sheldon
928-445-8061

Prescott Natural Foods
330 W Gurley St.
928-778-5875

*New Frontiers Natural
   Marketplace*
1112 W Iron Springs Rd.
928-445-7370

Scottsdale
Arizona Health Foods
14700 N Frank Lloyd Wright
480-661-6300

Arizona Health Foods
7119 E Shea Blvd., Ste. 101
480-443-0053

Nutrition Works
6941 N Hayden Rd., Ste. B1
480-609-8812

Wild Oats Natural Marketplace
8688 E Raintree Dr.
480-368-1279

Sedona
*New Frontier's Natural
   Marketplace*
1420 W Hwy. 89A
928-282-6311

Show Low
Nature's Realm
11 E Deuce Of Clubs
928-532-0359

Health Touch
4431 S White Mountain Rd.
928-537-2012

Tempe
Doc Watson's
1804 E Southern Ave., Ste. 4
480-730-6688

Gentle Strength
9 East Southern #102
480-968-4831

Vitamin World
5000 S Arizona Mills Circle
480-897-3167

Tucson
Aqua-Vita
2801 North Country Club Rd.
520-293-7770

Health Hut
2561 E Fort Lowell Rd.
520-327-4116

Wild Oats Natural Marketplace
3360 E Speedway Blvd.
520-795-9844

Wild Oats Natural Marketplace
7133 N Oracle Rd.
520-297-5394

Toole Avenue Market
350 S Toole Ave.
520-622-3911

Warehouse Vitamins
6421 N Oracle Rd.
520-297-7377

Warehouse Vitamins
485 E Wetmore Rd., #H107
520-293-4392

Warehouse Vitamins
2605 E Speedway Blvd.
520-321-4262

Warehouse Vitamins
7822 E Speedway Blvd.
520-298-8952

Warehouse Vitamins
9121 E Tanque Verde Rd., #115
520-760-1450

Arkansas

Ashdown
People Health Mart
401 N 2nd St.
870-898-2400

Batesville
Heartline Health
2509 Harrison St.
870-793-9400

Blytheville
Main Street Natural Foods
808 E Main St.
870-762-1212

Clarksville
Clarksville Health Food Store
800 W Main St.
479-754-5880

Clinton
One Stop Health Shop
2519 Hwy. 65 S
501-745-4144

Conway
Nature's Pantry & Kitchen Store
704 Locust St.
501-329-1370

Crossett
Harmony Health Food Store
617 W 1st Ave.
870-364-6555

De Queen
Forty Carrots Health Foods
110 N 3rd St.
870-584-3821

El Dorado
Olde Towne Store
113 N Jefferson Ave.
870-862-1060

Fayetteville
Avalon Nutrition & Indian Foods
1388 N College Ave.
479-582-9158

Ozark Natural Foods
1554 N College Ave.
479-521-7558

Fort Smith
Olde Fashioned Foods Market
4600 Towson Ave., Ste. 50
479-649-8200

Gentry
Sleepy Hollow Store
12761 S Hwy. 59
479-736-2320

Harrison
Nature's Wonders
307 N Olive St.
870-741-1973

Almond Tree Natural Foods
126 N Willow St.
870-741-8980

Highland
Steven's Nutrition Center
1628 Hwy. 62-412
870-856-3985

Hope
Little Herb Shoppe
203 S Main St.
870-777-2535

Hot Springs
Good Earth Natural Foods
234 Cornerstone Blvd.
501-520-4551

Old Country Store
455 Broadway
501-624-1172

Natural Way Health Foods
444 W Grand St.
501-623-3038

Jonesboro
Country Natural Health Food
1801 Paragould Plaza Park
870-236-8009

Jonesboro Health Food
1321 Stone St., #A
870-932-5301

Lincoln
*Eden Herbs & Global Health
  Products*
10301 S Jackson Hwy.
479-824-3727

Little Rock
Wild Oats Natural Marketplace
10700 N Rodney Parham Rd.
501-221-2331

Malvern
Earnest's Health Foods
848 N Main St.
501-337-0658

Morrilton
Chris's Health Food Corner
302 North St. Joseph St.
501-354-9930

Mountain Home
Natural Health Foods
699 Baxter Ave. 56
870-425-7789

Nature's Way Health Food
18 E 7th St.
870-425-7677

Bonnie's Nutrition Center
911 E 9th St.
870-425-2702

N. Little Rock
Riley's Herbs & More
3008 Martineau Place
501-753-5194

Pine Bluff
Natural Way Health Foods
2508 S Olive St.
870-534-5335

Sweet Clover Natural Foods
2624 W 28th Ave.
870-536-0107

Prattsville
Mom's Health Foods
Hwy. 270
870-699-4818

Rogers
Cook's Health Mart
412 S 8th St.
479-936-8484

Russellville
Country Cupboard Natural Foods
122 E 4th St.
479-968-6944

Springdale
Mary's Natural Foods
220 Hwy. 71B S
479-751-4224

California

Agoura Hills
Agoura Meadows Health Foods
5629 Kanan Rd.
818-889-0320

Holistic Resource Center
29020 Agoura Rd., Ste. A8
818-597-0966

Alameda
Health Is
1650 Park St.
510-865-1500

Alamo
Natural Temptations
190 Alamo Plaza, Ste. A
925-820-0606

Alhambra
Alhambra Nutrition Center
125 E Main St.
626-284-3261

Alta Loma
J. C. Discount Health Food
7211 Haven Ave., Ste. 853
909-980-6893

Rancho Health Foods
9602 Baseline Rd.
909-989-7000

Altadena
O' Happy Days Natural Food Store
2283 Lake Ave.
626-797-0383

Anaheim
All Nature's Own Nutrition
2713 W Lincoln Ave.
714-821-6811

Naturway Natural Foods
1010 N Euclid St.
714-956-0260

Royal Prestige Nutrition Center
708 N Marengo
626-795-4953

The Vitamin Store
2221 W Ball Rd.
714-635-3160

Vista Drugs
931 S Euclid St.
714-533-1337

Angels Camp
Angel's Health Foods
45 S Main St., Ste. 49
209-736-4236

Apple Valley
BJ's Health Foods
21825 US Hwy. 18
760-240-4121

Aptos
Aptos Natural Foods
7506 Soquel Dr.
831-685-3334

Deluxe Foods of Aptos
783 Rio Del Mar Blvd., Ste. 25
831-688-8211

Arcadia
Foji Acupuncture & Herbs
662 W Duarte Rd.
626-446-3668

V.P. Discount Vitamins
1127 W Huntington Dr.
626-821-1028

Arcata
Moonrise Herbs
826 G St.
707-822-5296

Wildberries Marketplace
747 13th St.
707-822-0095

Arroyo Grande
Grande Foods Market
1154 E Grand Ave.
805-489-1584

Atascadero
Harvest Natural Foods
6985 San Luis Ave.
805-466-3202

Auburn
Auburn Nutrition Center
13112 Lincoln Way
530-885-5095

Country Naturals
346 Elm Ave.
530-823-1615

Sunrise Natural Foods
2160 Grass Valley Hwy.
530-888-8973

Vena's Healthy Things
516 Auburn Ravine Rd.
530-823-7788

Bakersfield
Apple Tree Health Foods
1910 N Chester Ave.
661-393-6287

Cay Health Foods
902 18th St.
661-325-7627

Cone's Health Food Store
1002 Wible Rd., Ste. K
661-832-5669

Nature's Foodwagon
9339 Rosedale Hwy., #1
661-587-9989

Bell Gardens
Sunshine Gardens
5962 Florence Ave.
323-771-9676

Bellflower
B & B Pharmacy & Health Care Center
10244 Rosecrans Ave.
562-866-8363

Benicia
Raley's
892 Southampton Rd.
707-746-1203

Berkeley
Berkeley Bowl Market Place
2020 Oregon St.
510-843-6929

Berkeley Natural
1336 Gilman St.
510-526-2456

El Cerrito Natural Grocery
10367 San Pablo Ave.
510-526-1155

General Nutrition Center
2165 Shattuck Ave.
510-845-4128

Lhasa Karnak Herb
1938 Shattuck Ave.
510-548-0372

Lhasa Karnak Herb Company
2482 Telegraph Ave.
510-548-0380

Vitamin Express
1400 Shattuck Ave.
510-841-1798

Whole Foods Market
3000 Telegraph Ave.
510-649-1333

Beverly Hills
Great Earth
258 N Beverly Dr.
310-278-1180

Whole Foods Market
239 N Crescent Dr.
310-274-3360

Bishop
Holmes Health Haven
192 W Line St.
760-872-5571

Bloomington
Nature's Sunshine
9828 Alder Ave.
909-877-1232

Brea
Great Earth Vitamins
2500 E Imperial Hwy., Ste. 156
714-671-2980

New Horizons Nutrition
912 E Imperial Hwy.
714-990-6766

Brentwood
Health Hut
601 1st St.
925-634-5361

Burbank
Tower Pharmacy
140 N San Fernando Blvd.
818-843-2241

Burlingame
Earthbeam Natural Foods
1399 Broadway
650-347-2058

Mollie Stone's Markets
1477 Chapin Ave.
650-558-9992

Calistoga
Cal Mart
1491 Lincoln Ave.
707-942-6271

Camarillo
Lassens Health Foods
2207 Pickwick Dr.
805-482-3287

Cameron Park
Cameron Park Health Foods
3342 Coach Lane
530-677-8087

Campbell
Rainbow Revelation Health Center
1645 Bascom, Ste. # 9
408-559-9241

Whole Foods Market
1690 S Bascom Ave.
408-371-5000

Canoga Park
Follow Your Heart
21825 Sherman Way
818-348-3240

Vitamin Barn
22335 Sherman Way
818-340-0689

Canyon Country
Bob Cannon's Vitamins
18344 Soledad Canyon Rd.
661-252-6624

Capitola
New Leaf Community Market
1210 41st Ave.
831-479-7987

Vitamin Center
1955 41st Ave., Ste. 215
831-462-4697

Carmel
Cornucopia Community Market
26135 Carmel Rancho Blvd.
831-625-1454

Castro Valley
Health Unlimited
3446 Village Dr.
510-581-0220

Cathedral City
Herb Cellar
33725 Date Palm Dr.
760-324-5495

Cerritos
Great Earth Vitamins
12751 Towne Center Dr., Ste. L
562-809-6300

Chico
Chico Natural Foods
818 Main St.
530-891-1713

Herb Store & Education Center
2201 Pillsbury Rd.
530-345-8600

Chino
Health Plus
13837 Magnolia Ave.
909-627-9393

Nutrition Pros Health Foods
5483 Philadelphia St., Ste. D
909-465-9220

Chula Vista
Great Earth Vitamins
386 East 'H' St.
619-691-0998

Henry's Marketplace
941 Otay Lakes Rd.
619-656-6434

Nature's Storehouse
307 3rd Ave.
619-425-7480

Claremont
Claremont Nutrition Center
843 W Foothill Blvd.
909-621-5163

Cloverdale
Cornucopia Natural Food Store
228 S Cloverdale Blvd.
707-894-3164

Compton
New Earth Health Food Store
523 W Compton Blvd.
310-638-9882

Concord
Harvest House Natural Foods
2395 Monument Blvd., #M
925-676-2305

Vita Plus
785 Oak Grove Rd., Ste. H
925-687-1765

Corona
Al's Best Corona Health Foods
106 E 6th St.
951-737-5101

Cotati
Oliver's Market
546 E Cotati Ave.
707-795-9501

Covina
A 2 Z Vitamins
577 N Azusa Ave.
626-339-9202

Crescent City
Harvest Natural Foods
265 L St.
707-464-1926

Culver City
Elite Health Foods
10738 Jefferson Blvd.
310-559-9739

Cupertino
Cupertino Nutrition
10265 S De Anza Blvd.
408-253-1277

Whole Foods Market
20830 Stevens Creek Blvd.
408-257-7000

Cypress
Great Earth Vitamins
10141 Valley View
714-826-7131

Danville
Vita Mill Nutrition Center
410 Sycamore Valley Rd. W
925-820-3131

Davis
Natural Food Works
624 4th St.
530-756-1862

Desert Hot Springs
Diane's Nutrition Center
12331 Palm Dr.
760-329-2026

Downey
*Aunt Sophie's Organic Health
Foods*
10033 Paramount Blvd.
562-806-2556

Naturway Natural Foods
10309 Lakewood Blvd.
562-869-4918

El Cajon
Great Earth Vitamins
310 Parkway Plaza
619-593-6463

El Cerrito
General Nutrition Center
230 El Cerrito Plaza
510-524-2494

El Segundo
Renee's Nutrition Center
150 S Sepulveda Blvd., Ste. G
310-615-1013

Elk Grove
Raley's & Bel Air
8787 Elk Grove Blvd.
916-685-2282

Bel Air Supermarkets
5100 Laguna Blvd.
916-684-7000

Elk Grove Vitamins
9647 E Stockton Blvd.
916-686-4488

Escondido
Vitamins 4 U
1631 E Valley Pkwy.
760-781-3396

Eureka
Eureka Cooperative
25 4th St.
707-443-1209

Eureka Natural Foods
1626 Broadway St.
707-442-6325

Fair Oaks
Sunshine Natural Foods
8121 Madison Ave., Ste. A5
916-966-8021

Fairfax
*Good Earth Natural & Organic
    Foods*
1966 Sir Francis Drake Blvd.
415-454-0123

Fallbrook
Herbs Etc. Wellspring
1223 S Mission Rd.
760-728-1244

Folsom
Elliott's Natural Foods
641 E Bidwell St.
916-983-9225

Fort Bragg
Down Home Foods
115 S Franklin St.
707-964-4661

Harvest Market
171 Boatyard Dr.
707-964-7000

Freedom
Mission Health Foods
1998 Freedom Blvd.
831-722-3633

Fremont
General Nutrition Center
39055 Fremont Hub
510-792-3000

Fresno
*B Alive Vitamins & Natural
    Foods*
6757 N Cedar Ave.
559-431-0881

Great Earth Vitamins
505 E Shaw Ave.
559-229-7022

Joie's Health Centers
7468 N Fresno St.
559-261-2929

Fullerton
GMP Vitamins and Health Food
1319 S Harbor Blvd.
714-879-5315

*Nature's Sunshine Herbs &
    Vitamins*
1537 E Commonwealth Ave.
714-871-4675

Plaza Herbs & Vitamins
1312 E Chapman Ave.
714-525-4050

Garberville
Chautauqua Natural Foods
436 Church St.
707-923-2452

Garden Grove
Marie's Health Foods
PO Box 2496
714-895-1707

Nature's Way
10072 Chapman Ave.
714-537-6250

Super Health
9580 Garden Grove Blvd.
714-530-1610

Goleta
Isla Vista Food Cooperative
6575 Seville Rd.
805-968-1401

Granada Hills
Granada Discount Health Foods
17540 Chatsworth St.
818-363-2050

Granite Bay
Raley's
6845 Douglas Blvd.
916-791-8015

Grass Valley
Briar Patch Co-Op
131 Joerschke Dr.
530-272-5333

Natural Valley Health Foods
562 Sutton Way
530-273-6525

Greenbrae
Bon Air Health
298 Bon Air Center
415-461-0761

Gualala
Surf Supermarket Inc.
39250 S Hwy. 1
707-884-4184

Hacienda Heights
Great Earth Vitamins
1673 S Azusa Ave.
626-964-0097

GM Health Center
2037 S Hacienda Blvd.
626-961-7220

Half Moon Bay
Healing Moon Health Foods
523 Main St.
650-726-7881

Hayward
Kraski's Nutrition
22491 Foothill Blvd.
510-581-2608

Hemet
Henry's Marketplace
1295 S State St.
951-766-6746

Norton's Nutrition East
2115 E Florida Ave.
951-652-7711

Norton Nutrition
3061 W Florida Ave.
951-658-9445

Huntington Beach
Mother's Market
19770 Beach Blvd.
714-963-6667

Huntington Park
Huntington Park Health Foods
2618 E Florence Ave.
323-587-7517

Imperial Beach
Seacoast Vitamin & Herbs
600 Palm Ave., Ste. 103
619-429-1779

Inglewood
Inglewood Health Foods
524 E Nutwood St.
310-677-1128

Irvine
Nutrimart
8681 Irvine Center Dr.
949-753-1211

Jackson
Gold Trail Natural Foods
625 S State Hwy. 49
209-223-1896

Kentfield
Woodlands Market
735 College Ave.
415-457-8160

La Jolla
Great Earth Vitamins
8843 Villa La Jolla Dr.
858-452-9775

Total Health
5621 La Jolla Blvd.
858-454-1198

Whole Foods Market
8825 Villa La Jolla Dr.
858-642-6700

La Mesa
Grossmont Nutrition
5500 Grossmont Center Dr.,
   Ste. 213
619-465-5225

Henry's Marketplace
4630 Palm Ave.
619-460-7722

K & L Nutrition
5280 Baltimore Dr.
619-465-8102

La Puente
Good & Natural Nutrition
1415 N Hacienda Blvd.
626-917-7006

La Quinta
Lifestyles Nutrition Center
78321 US Hwy. 111
760-564-5569

La Verne
*Nature's Way Health Foods
   Center*
1512 Foothill Blvd.
909-596-1575

Laguna Beach
Wild Oats Natural Marketplace
283 Broadway
949-376-7888

Laguna Niguel
Apple A Day Health Food
30262 Crown Valley Pkwy.
949-495-3250

Farm to Market
30190 Town Center Dr., Ste. G
949-363-0123

*Health Works & Original Juice
   Bistro*
27271 La Paz Rd.
949-831-9777

Lake Forest
Great Earth Vitamins
24412 Rockfield Blvd.
949-770-3079

Nutrition Mart
22421 El Toro Rd.
949-830-0191

Lakewood
Naturway Natural Foods
4037 Hardwick St.
562-531-1155

Lancaster
The Whole Wheatery
44264 10th St. W
661-945-0773

Laytonville
Good Food Store
44850 N Hwy. 101
707-984-6118

Lemon Grove
Henry's Marketplace
3205 Lemon Grove Ave.
619-667-8686

Livermore
Van's Health Foods
2148 1st St.
925-447-2976

Lodi
Sheri's Nutrition Center
6 N School St.
209-368-4800

Loma Linda
*Clark's Nutrition & Natural
   Foods Market*
11235 Mountain View Ave.
909-478-7714

Loma Linda Market
24954 Prospect Ave.
909-558-4565

Long Beach
Beach Health Tree
305 Redondo Ave.
562-434-1155

Circle Nutrition
1910 Ximeno Ave.
562-498-3257

Healthway Foods
535 E Bixby Rd.
562-424-9760

Vitamin City
6247 E Spring St.
562-425-6411

Vitamin Warehouse
5935 E Spring St.
562-420-9728

Los Altos
Peggy's Health Center
151 First St.
650-948-9191

Los Angeles
Apothecary Pharmacy
11670 National Blvd.
310-737-7277

Cuevas Health Food Store
738 S Atlantic Blvd.
323-261-1156

Daybreak Health Foods
1565 Colorado Blvd.
323-258-3881

Farmer's Market Pharmacy
6333 W 3rd St.
323-938-2737

Foods of Nature
1700 S Robertson Blvd.
310-837-8755

Great Earth Vitamins
420 N Larchmont Blvd.
323-460-6331

Great Earth Vitamins
1653 N La Brea Ave.
323-851-9437

Great Earth Vitamins
11640 San Vicente Blvd.,
Ste. 101
310-826-3549

Great Earth Vitamins
10739 W Pico Blvd.
310-475-5785

Great Earth Vitamins
10250 Santa Monica Blvd., #167
310-286-9844

Great Earth Vitamins
8365 Santa Monica Blvd.
310-650-0181

Green Farms Nutrition
4972 West Pico Blvd., #104
323-937-1120

Nature Mart
2080 Hillhurst Ave.
323-660-0052

Nutrition Center
5534 N Figueroa St.
323-254-3260

Rainbow Acres
13208 W Washington Blvd.
310-306-8330

San Angel Health Store
3524 W 3rd St.
213-386-4312

Super Health
333 S Alameda St., Ste. 202
213-625-1905

Svetlana Herbs
7907 Santa Monica Blvd.
323-656-5652

V. P. Discount Health Foods
12740 Culver Blvd.
310-448-2715

V. P. Discount Health & Food Mart
8001 Beverly Blvd.
323-658-6506

Whole Foods Market
11737 San Vicente Blvd.
310-826-4433

Whole Foods Market
11666 National Blvd.
310-996-8840

Los Banos
Trini's Health Foods
1341 E Pacheco Blvd., Ste. G
209-827-1927

Los Gatos
Whole Foods Market
15980 Los Gatos Blvd.
408-358-4434

Lucerne
Lucerne Health Foods
5980 E Hwy. 20
707-274-1963

Malibu
Pacific Coast Greens
22601 Pacific Coast Hwy.
310-456-0353

Manhattan Beach
Bristol Farms Inc.
1570 Rosecrans Ave.
310-643-5229

Great Earth Vitamins
3010 N Sepulveda Blvd.
310-546-3478

Be Well
1590 E Rosecrans Blvd., Ste. D
310-643-9050

Marina del Rey
Rainbow Acres
4756 Admiralty Way
310-823-5373

V. P. Discount Health Food
4375 Glencoe Ave.
310-448-2716

Martinez
Martinez Natural Foods
708 Ferry St.
925-228-4747

Mentone
Discount Health Village
1248 Wabash Ave.
909-389-4634

Modesto
Cornucopia Natural Foods
2625 Coffee Rd., Ste. V
209-575-1650

Great Earth Vitamins
3900 Pelandale Ave.
209-545-2885

Nancy's Apple Tree Health Foods
817 W Roseburg Ave.
209-527-5721

Peppermint Herb Shop
2301 Davis Way
209-581-9773

Rejuvenate
901 N Carpenter Rd., #33
209-577-5503

Secreto's Natural Health
1545 Tully Rd.
209-523-0016

The Carrot
1508 10th St.
209-521-6470

Village Health Foods
1700 McHenry Ave.
209-523-3466

Montebello
Great Earth Vitamins
2115 Montebello Town Centre
323-722-4343

Kincaid's Nutrition Center Inc.
711 Newmark Mall
323-726-1947

Normandy Health Foods
1005 W Beverly Blvd.
323-726-0822

Montecito
Montecito Natural Foods
1014 Coast Village Rd., Ste. B
805-969-1411

Monterey
Whole Foods Market
800 Del Monte Centre
831-333-1600

Monterey Park
Sam's Nutrition Center
116 N Garfield Ave.
626-288-2595

Weidner's Nutrition Center
127 E Garvey Ave.
626-288-4344

Montrose
Discount Vitamin Store
2064 N Verdugo Blvd., Ste. G
818-248-0422

Morro Bay
Sunshine Health Foods
415 Morro Bay Blvd.
805-772-7873

Mount Shasta
Berryvale Grocery
305 S Mount Shasta Blvd.
530-926-1576

Mt. Shasta Herb and Health
108 Chestnut St.
530-926-0633

Napa
Golden Carrot Natural Foods
1621 W Imola Ave.
707-224-3117

Optimum Natural Foods
633 Trancas St.
707-224-1514

Newbury Park
Premier Health Foods
1570 D-2 Newbury Rd.
805-498-2393

Newhall
Bob Cannon's Vitamins
24144 Lyons Ave.
661-259-6069

Vitamin Valley
24424 Walnut St.
661-259-5122

North Hollywood
V. P. Discount Health Food
13023 Victory Blvd.
818-769-6114

North Park
Henry's Marketplace
4175 Park Blvd.
619-291-8287

Northridge
Accent on Health
18559 Devonshire St.
818-360-1516

V. P. Discount Health Food
9130 Reseda Blvd.
818-349-8190

Norwalk
Great Earth Vitamins
11560 E Rosecrans St.
562-864-8252

Novato
Lighthouse Health
1559 S Novato Blvd., Ste. H
415-897-7603

Oasis Natural Foods
2021 Novato Blvd.
415-897-4706

Oakland
Healthy Life Vitamins
6130 Medau Place
510-338-0667

Lakeshore Natural Foods
3321 Lakeshore Ave.
510-452-1079

Natural Health Center
4925 Telegraph Ave.
510-653-6680

Village Market
5885 Broadway Terrace
510-547-3200

Ojai
Rainbow Bridge Natural Food
   Store
211 E Matilija St.
805-646-4017

Olympic Valley
Alice's Mountain Market
1985 Squaw Valley Rd.
530-581-2014

Ontario
Ontario Health Foods
106 W G St.
909-983-0334

Orange
Nature's Way
1804 N Tustin St.
714-283-0171

Oxnard
Lassen's Health Foods
3471 Saviers Rd.
805-486-8266

Pacific Beach
Henry's Marketplace
1260 Garnet Ave.
858-270-8200

Pacific Grove
Grove Nutrition Center
543 Lighthouse Ave.
831-372-6625

Palm Desert
Harvest Health Foods
73-910 Hwy. 111
760-346-3215

Palm Springs
Nature's RX
555 S Sunrise Way, Ste. 301
760-323-9487

Oasis Natural Foods
188 S Indian Canyon Dr.
760-327-7502

Palo Alto
Whole Foods Market
774 Emerson St.
650-326-8676

Panorama City
Great Earth Vitamins
8401 Van Nuys Blvd.
818-891-6627

Pasadena
Whole Foods Market
3751 East Foothill Blvd.
626-351-5994

Wild Oats Natural Marketplace
603 S Lake Ave.
626-792-1778

Paso Robles
Paso Robles Health Foods
1191 Creston Rd., Ste. 113
805-238-3987

The Natural Alternative Nutrition Center
1213 Pine St.
805-237-8290

Petaluma
Whole Foods Market
621 E Washington St.
707-762-9352

Petaluma Market
210 Western Ave.
707-762-8452

Placerville
Placerville Health Foods
1488 Broadway
530-622-7434

Pleasanton
Valley Health Mill
3037 Hopyard Rd., Ste. J
925-462-9354

Pomona
Discount Nutrition Center
3176 N Garey Ave.
909-596-2929

Nature's Gold House
2239 N Garey Ave.
909-593-2679

Quincy
Quincy Natural Foods
269 Main St.
530-283-3528

Rancho Palos Verdes
Health Food Village
29223 S Western Ave.
310-831-5198

Redding
Enterprise Health Foods
1380 Hartnell Ave.
530-222-4404

Orchard Nutrition
221 Locust St.
Cypress Square
530-244-9141

Redondo Beach
Blaine's Nutrition Center
206 Ave. I
310-540-4826

The Vitamin Store
619 N Pacific Coast Hwy.
310-376-8644

Whole Foods Market
405 N Pacific Coast Hwy.
310-376-6931

Redwood City
Apple Health Foods
1011 El Camino Real
650-368-3124

Whole Life Nature's Cupboard Foods
344 Woodside Plaza
650-364-4946

Reedley
Dianne's Health Foods
1140 G St.
559-638-4014

Rialto
The Complete Health Store
214 E Foothill Blvd.
909-875-6321

Smith's Health Foods
2012 N Riverside Ave.
909-350-3550

Richmond
William's Natural Foods
12249 San Pablo Ave.
510-232-1911

Ridgecrest
Mother Earth Market
221 Balsam St.
760-375-9550

Ripon
Nature's RX
131 W Main St.
209-599-5441

Riverside
Great Earth Vitamins
1322 Galleria at Tyler
951-359-5926

Health Max
17024 Van Buren Blvd., #B
951-789-2901

La Sierra Natural Foods
11550 Pierce St.
951-785-5763

Rocklin
Bel Air
2341 Sunset Blvd.
916-632-0180

Roseville
Bel Air
1039 Sunrise Ave.
916-786-6101

Bel Air
4008 Foothills Blvd.
916-783-1173

Sunrise Natural Foods
1950 Douglas Blvd.
916-789-8591

Rowland Heights
Manning United Drugs
1724 Nogales St.
626-810-8211

Sacramento
Raley's and Bel Air
4320 Arden Way
916-972-7028

Bel Air
1301 Florin Rd.
916-421-6766

Bel Air
1540 W El Camino Ave.
916-920-2493

Bel Air
7465 Rush River Dr.
916-399-9112

Bel Air
7901 Walerga Rd.
916-725-6940

Bel Air
6231 Fruitridge Rd.
916-739-8647

Sacramento Natural Foods Co-Op
1900 Alhambra Blvd.
916-455-2667

San Diego
Henry's Marketplace
3358 Governor Dr.
858-457-5006

Henry's Marketplace
3315 Rosecrans St.
619-523-3640

Jimbo's Naturally
12853 El Camino Real
858-793-7755

OB People's Organic Foods Co-Op
4765 Voltaire St.
619-224-1387

Whole Foods Market
711 University Ave.
619-294-2800

San Francisco
Buffalo Whole Food & Grain Co.
598 Castro St.
415-626-7038

Good Life Grocery
448 Cortland Ave.
415-648-3221

Rainbow Grocery
1745 Folsom St.
415-863-0621

Real Food Company
3060 Fillmore St.
415-567-6900

Real Food Company
2140 Polk St.
415-673-7420

Sunshine Health Foods
98 Battery St.
415-788-1382

Thom's Natural Foods
5843 Geary Blvd.
415-387-6367

Vitamin Express
1428 Irving St.
415-564-8160

Whole Foods Market
1765 California St.
415-674-0500

San Leandro
Health Unlimited
182 Pelton Center Way
510-483-3630

San Luis Obispo
Natural Foods Co-Op
745 Francis Ave.
805-544-7928

San Pedro
Artista's Nutrition Center
870 N Western Ave.
310-519-7111

Santa Ana
Tony's Nutrition
3698 S Bristol St.
714-540-7953

Santa Barbara
Lassen's Health Food
5154 Hollister Ave.
805-683-7696

Lazy Acres
302 Meigs Rd.
805-564-4410

Santa Maria
Lassen's Natural Food
1790 S Broadway
805-925-3432

Santa Monica
Co-Opportunity
1525 Broadway
310-451-8902

Wild Oats Market
1425 Montana Ave.
310-576-4707

Santa Rosa
Community Market
1899 Mendocino Ave.
707-546-1806

Whole Foods Market
1181 Yulupa Ave.
707-575-7915

Vitamin Adventure
2188 Santa Rosa Ave.
707-570-0145

Santee
Henry's Marketplace
9751 Mission Gorge Rd.
619-258-4060

Sausalito
Real Food Company
200 Caledonia St.
415-332-9640

Sebastopol
Whole Foods Market
6910 McKinley Ave.
707-829-9801

Sherman Oaks
Healthy Discounts
14427-1/2 Ventura Blvd.
818-995-7685

Simi Valley
Kay's Nutrition & Health Center
5766 E Los Angeles Ave.
805-527-5971

The Vitamin Station
1407 E Los Angeles Ave., Ste. Q
805-583-3628

Stockton
Artesian Health Foods
6349 Pacific Ave.
209-952-8787

Temecula
Sprouts Natural Market
40458 Winchester Rd.
951-296-3444

Thousand Oaks
Lassen's Health Food
2857 E Thousand Oaks Blvd.
805-495-2609

Torrance
Lindberg Nutrition
3804 Sepulveda Blvd.
310-378-9490

Ventura
Lassen's Health Food
4071 E Main St.
805-644-6990

Vista
Henry's Marketplace
705 E Vista Way
760-758-7175

West Los Angeles
V. P. Discount Health Food
11665 Santa Monica Blvd.
310-444-7949

Whittier
Herbies Natural
13306 Whittier Blvd.
866-HERBIES/562-789-1510

Colorado

Arvada
Vitamin Cottage
7745 Wadsworth Blvd.
303-423-0990

Aurora
Vitamin Cottage
15270 E Hampden Ave.
303-680-2344

Avon
Nature's Providers
2121 N Frontage Rd. W
970-949-9404

Boulder
Wild Oats Market
1651 Broadway St.
303-442-0909

Ideal Market
1275 Alpine Ave.
303-443-1354

King Soopers
3600 Table Mesa Dr.
303-499-4004

Leffler's Vitamin Shop
1155 Alpine Ave., Ste. 180
303-444-5000

Wild Oats Market
2584 Baseline Rd.
303-499-7636

Colorado Springs
A-1 Nutrition Center
2905 Galley Rd.
719-574-9935

Mountain Mama
1625 W Uintah St.
719-633-4139

Desert Sage
2631 W Colorado Ave.
719-632-2516

Vitamin Cottage
1780 E Woodmen Rd.
719-536-9606

Cortez
The Abundant Life
201 E Main St.
970-565-4995

Denver
Wild Oats Market
900 E 11th Ave.
303-832-7701

Vitamin Cottage
5231 Leetsdale Dr.
303-399-0164

The Natural Vitamin Store
1685 S Colorado Blvd.
303-756-8338

Wild Oats Market
1111 S Washington St.
303-733-6201

Durango
A Health Forest
1021 Main Ave.
970-385-4659

Fort Collins
Wild Oats Market
200 W Foothills Pkwy.
970-225-1400

Greenwood Village
Vitamin Cottage
9670 E Arapahoe Rd.
303-790-0488

Wild Oats Market
5910 S University Blvd.
303-798-9699

Lakewood
Vitamin Cottage
3333 S Wadsworth Blvd.
303-989-4866

Vitamin Cottage
9030 W Colfax Ave.
303-232-6266

Vitamin Cottage
12612 W Alameda Pkwy.
303-986-5700

Littleton
Vitamin Cottage
11550 W Meadows Dr.
303-948-9944

Pueblo
Ambrosia
112 Colorado Ave.
719-545-2958

Schrock's Health Foods
1515 Moore Ave.
719-564-0940

Connecticut

Danbury
Chamomile Natural Foods
58-60 Newton Rd.
203-792-8952

Fairfield
Mrs. Greens Natural Market
1916 Post Rd.
203-255-4333

Greenwich
Greenwich Healthmart
30 Greenwich Ave.
203-869-9658

Whole Foods Market
90 E Putnam Ave.
203-661-0631

Madison
Madison Health Foods
59 Wall St.
203-245-8607

Milford
Healthy Foods Plus
246 New Haven Ave.
203-882-9011

New Canaan
Healthfare
2 Morse Ct.
203-966-5400

New Haven
Edge of the Woods
379 Whalley Ave.
203-787-1055

Newington
World of Nutrition
200 Market Square
860-666-6863

Stratford
Nature's Way Health Foods
922 Barnum Ave. Cutoff
203-377-3652

Waterbury
Health-Land
741 Wolcott St.
203-755-3327

Woodbury
*New Morning Natural and
    Organic Foods*
738 Main St. S
Middle Quarter Mall
203-263-4868

Delaware

Hockessin
Harvest Market
1216 Old Lancaster Pike
302-234-6779

Newark
Tomorrow's Health
230 E Main St.
302-737-7986

Wilmington
Nature's Way
2400 Kirkwood Hwy., Ste. 201
302-995-6525

Florida

Altamonte Springs
Chamberlin's
1086 Montgomery Rd.
407-774-8866

Economy Health Foods
1035 Academy Dr.
407-869-0000

Aventura/N. Miami Beach
Whole Foods Market
21105 Biscayne Blvd.
305-933-1543

Boca Raton
All American Nutrition
624 Glades Rd.
561-395-9599

Donigan's
2831 N Federal Hwy.
561-395-5521

Health Depot
1662 N Federal Hwy.
561-750-4611

Vitamin World
193 Town Center Rd.
561-394-7203

Brandon
General Nutrition Center
616 Oakfield Dr.
813-689-2195

Clearwater
Value Center
514 Park St.
727-445-1188

Coral Springs
*Tunie's Super Save Nutrition
Center*
8132 Wiles Rd.
954-345-0940

Dade City
Nancy's Natural Foods
14140 8th St.
352-523-0044

Deland
Health Foods for Life
1319 S Woodland Blvd.
386-734-2343

Destin
Feelin' Good Health Foods
300 Harbor Blvd.
850-654-1005

Fernandina Beach
Nassau Health Foods
833 TJ Courson Rd.
904-277-3158

Fort Lauderdale
Whole Foods Market
2000 N Federal Hwy.
954-565-5655

Life Extension Foundation
1100 W Commercial Blvd.
954-766-8433

Wild Oats Market
2501 E Sunrise Blvd.
954-566-9333

Fort Myers
Healthy Habits
11763-7 S Cleveland Ave.
239-278-4442

Mother Earth Natural Foods
13860-G N Cleveland Ave.
239-997-6676

Mother Earth Natural Foods
15271 McGregor Blvd.
239-489-3377

Gainesville
Mother Earth Market
521 NW 13th St.
352-378-5224

Mother Earth Market West
1237 NW 76th Blvd.
352-331-5224

Hallandale
Discount Vitamins & Health Foods
417 W Hallandale Beach Blvd.
954-457-4140

Hilliard
Beaton's Vitamin Shoppe
542103 Hwy. 1, Ste. 4
904-879-4042

Homestead
Betty's Health Foods
692 N Homestead Blvd.
305-248-6767

Jacksonville
Native Sun Natural Foods
10000 San Jose Blvd.
904-260-6950

Regency Health Foods
Regency Square Mall
9501 Arlington Expwy.
904-725-3003

Kissimmee
The Organic Place
1246 S John Young Pkwy.
407-944-9095

Lake Mary
Tom's Naturals
3801 W Lake Mary Blvd.,
Ste. 155
407-321-7512

Largo
Vitamin Outlet
3690 East Bay Dr.
727-536-0120

Maitland
Chamberlin's
430 N Orlando Ave.
407-647-3330

Miami
Apple A Day
1534 Alton Rd.
305-538-4569

Beehive Natural Foods
5750 Bird Rd.
305-666-3360

General Nutrition Center
3423 Maine Hwy.
305-461-1933

Nutrition Mart
10740 W Flagler St., Ste. 6
305-553-0342

North Miami Beach
General Nutrition Center
1851 NE Miami Gardens Dr.
305-932-5140

Naples
Naples Health Hut
2368 Immokalee Rd.
239-596-3000

Sunsplash Market
850 Neapolitan Way
239-434-7221

Sunshine Discount Vitamins
2403 Trade Center Way, Ste. 7
239-598-5393

New Smyrna Beach
Heath's Natural Foods
600 E 3rd Ave.
386-423-5126

Ocala
Mother Earth Market
1917 E Silver Springs Blvd.
352-351-5224

Reesers Nutrition
3243 E Silver Springs Blvd.
352-732-0718

Orange City
Debbie's Health Foods
816 Saxon Blvd.
386-775-7002

Orlando
Chamberlin's
4960 E Colonial Dr.
Herndon Village Shoppes
407-894-8452

Ormond Beach
Love Whole Foods Market
275 Williamson Blvd.
386-677-5236

Palm Beach Gardens
Nutrition World
2568 PGA Blvd.
561-626-4377

West Palm Beach
Nutrition World
1937 N Military Trail
561-684-0777

Sunflower Nutrition Center
2138 Okeechobee Blvd.
561-686-2288

Palm Harbor
Palm Harbor Natural Foods
30555 US Hwy. 19 N
727-786-1231

Super Vitamin Outlet
32510 US Hwy. 19 N
727-786-5994

Pembroke Pines
Nutrition Smart
12594 Pines Blvd., Ste. 101-102
954-437-0035

Plantation
Whole Foods Market
7720 Peters Rd.
954-236-0600

General Nutrition Center
8241 W Sunrise Blvd.
954-476-7196

Pompano Beach
Nutrition Depot
413 N Federal Hwy., Ste. 954
954-786-9323

Port Charlotte
Fegers Health Foods
3058 Tamiami Trail
941-625-5561

Port Orange
Harvest House
4032 S Ridgewood Ave.
386-756-3800

Royal Palm Beach
Nutrition World
516 N State Rd. 7
561-790-4747

Saint Petersburg
John's Foods For Health
601 34th St. N
727-323-5014

Nature's Finest Foods
6651 Central Ave.
727-347-5682

Rollin' Oats Cafe
2842 9th St. N
727-895-4910

Medical Arts Natural Foods
459 4th St. N
727-526-3851

Sarasota
The Granary
1930 Stickney Point Rd.
941-924-4754

The Granary
1279 N Beneva Rd.
941-365-3700

Tallahassee
The Health Food Store
1989 Capital Circle NE
850-671-1452

Honeytree
1660 N Monroe St., Ste. 3
850-681-2000

New Leaf Market
1235 Apalachee Pkwy.
850-942-2557

Tampa
Abby's Health Food
14374 N Dale Mabry
813-265-4951

Nature's Harvest
1021 N MacDill Ave.
813-873-7428

Temple Terrace
Chuck's Natural Foods Outpost
11301 N 56th St.
813-980-2005

Titusville
Sunshine Health Foods
2916 S Washington Ave.
321-269-4848

Georgia

Athens
Earth Fare
1689 S Lumpkin St.
706-227-1717

Phoenix Natural Food Market
296 W Broad St.
706-548-1780

Atlanta
Atlantis Natural Foods
2488 Mount Vernon Rd.
770-393-1297

Nutrition Naturally
2855 N Druid Hills Rd. NE
404-929-8900

Nuts 'N Berries
4274 Peachtree Rd.
404-237-6829

Return To Eden
2335 Cheshire Bridge Rd. NE
404-320-3336

Unity Natural Foods
2955 NE Peachtree Rd.
404-261-8776

Decatur
Rainbow Natural Foods
2118 N Decatur Rd.
404-636-5553

Hinesville
Farmers Natural Foods
754 E.G. Miles Pkwy.
912-368-7803

Marietta
Life Grocery
1453 Roswell Rd.
770-977-9583

Natural Market Place
4719 Lower Roswell Rd.,
    Ste. 160
770-973-4061

Norcross
Good Nutrition
463 Beaver Ruin Rd.
770-409-8844

Roswell
Good Nutrition
10687 Alpharetta Hwy.
770-992-2363

Sunburst Natural Foods Inc.
625 W Crossville Rd.
770-645-0892

Sandy Springs
Health Nut 3
5975 Roswell Rd.
404-256-0892

Savannah
Brighter Day
1102 Bull St.
912-236-4703

St. Mary's
Act Natural Health Foods
6100 Hwy. 40 E
912-882-2563

Suwanee
Best Nutrition II
3245 Peachtree Pkwy.
770-886-4997

Tucker
Mother Nature's Market
3853 E Lawrenceville Hwy.
770-491-0970

Hawaii

Hilo
*Abundant Life Natural Foods &
    Cafe*
292 Kamehameha Ave.
808-935-7411

Honolulu
Vim & Vigor Foods
1450 Alamoana Blvd., #1014
808-955-3600

Kailua Kona
Kona Natural Foods
75-1027 Henry St., Ste. 105
808-329-2296

Kapaa
Papaya's Natural Foods
4-831 Kuhio Hwy., Ste. 330
808-823-0190

Idaho

Boise
Boise Co-Op
888 W Fort St.
208-472-4500

Idaho Falls
D C Natural Foods
159 S Corner St.
208-522-6964

Illinois

Alton
River City Nutrition
1629 Washington Ave.
618-465-7867

Antioch
Polson's Natural Foods
960 Main St.
847-395-0461

Aurora
Fruitful Yield
4334 E Fox Valley Center Dr.,
    Ste. A
630-585-9200

Bellwood
Natural Herbal Products
3207 St. Charles Rd.
708-544-0550

Berwyn
Fruitful Yield
7003 Cermak Rd.
708-788-9103

Bloomingdale
Fruitful Yield
154 S Bloomingdale Rd.,
    Ste. 102
630-894-2553

Bradley
Kankakee Natural Foods
1035 Mulligan Dr., #2
815-933-6236

Carpentersville
Golden Harvest Health Foods
202 Spring Hill Rd.
847-551-3551

Chicago
Maple Street Market
22 W Maple St.
312-397-1501

Kramer's Health Foods
230 S Wabash Ave.
312-922-0077

Parkway Drugs
680 N Lake Shore Dr.
312-943-2224

Sherwyn's Health Foods
645 W Diversey Pkwy.
773-477-1934

JS Vitamins and More
5316 N Milwaukee Rd., Ste. C
773-763-1917

Chicago Heights
Glenbrook Health Foods
120 S Halsted Rd.
708-755-9440

Country Club Hills
Heritage Health Foods
4051 W 183rd St.
708-957-0595

Crystal Lake
Crystal Lake Health Foods
25 E Crystal Lake Ave.
815-459-7942

Danville
Country Store Health Foods
3618 N Vermilion St.
217-446-7279

Downers Grove
Fruitful Yield
2159 75th St.
630-969-7614

South Elgin
Fruitful Yield
360 S Randall Rd.
847-888-0100

Evanston
Whole Foods Market
1640 Chicago Ave.
847-733-1600

Godfrey
Cleta's Nutrition
3004 Godfrey Rd.
618-466-1659

Highland Park
Fruitful Yield
149 Skokie Valley Rd.
847-831-0460

Joliet
For The Good Of It
3135 W Jefferson St.
815-744-7659

Lansing
Sunrise Health Foods
17650 Torrence Ave.
708-474-6166

La Salle
Seeds Of Change Natural Foods
2320 St. Vincents Ave.
815-224-5894

McHenry
Nature's Cornucopia
1717 N Richmond Rd.
815-385-4500

Osco
4222 W Elm St.
815-385-7030

Moline
Heritage Natural Foods
1317 6th Ave.
309-764-1912

Mount Prospect
*Sweetgrass Vitamin & Health
  Market*
1742 W Golf Rd.
847-956-1939

Niles
Natural Food
9359 N Milwaukee Ave.
847-966-5565

Normal
Osco
901 S Cottage Ave.
309-454-6080

Norridge
Plaza Health Foods
4202 N Harlem Ave.
708-453-6825

Oak Forest
Jewel Osco
5616 159th St.
708-614-6700

Orland Park
New Vitality Health Foods
9177 W 151 St.
708-403-0120

Palatine
Whole Foods Market
1331 N Rand Rd.
847-776-8080

River Forest
Whole Foods Market
7245 Lake St.
708-366-1045

Schaumburg
Fruitful Yield
130 W Golf Rd.
847-882-2999

Urbana
Strawberry Fields
306 W Springfield Ave.
217-328-1655

Vandalia
*The Sunshine House Health Food
  Store*
420 W Gallatin St.
618-283-0888

Westmont
Apple Valley Natural Foods
806 E Ogden Ave.
630-789-2270

Wheaton
Whole Foods Market
145 Rice Lake Sq.
630-588-1500

Winfield
Nutrition Network
27W187 Geneva Rd.
630-871-1620

Woodstock
Osco
145 S Eastwood Dr.
815-206-0716

Indiana

Bloomington
Bloomingfoods Market
419 E Kirkwood Ave.
812-336-5300

Bloomingfoods East
3220 E Third St.
812-336-5400

Osco
510 S College Mall Rd.
812-336-0279

Crown Point
Jewel Osco
1276 N Main St.
219-662-0080

Evansville
Adele's Naturally
2704 Lincoln Ave.
812-471-3144

Indianapolis
Georgetown Market
4375 Georgetown Rd.
317-293-9525

Good Earth Natural Food
6350 N Guilford Ave.
317-253-6380

The Good Stuff
222 E Market St.
317-630-9155

Nature's Cupboard
8215 US 31 S
317-888-0557

Nutrition Unlimited
10030 E Washington St.
317-899-3515

CVS
2330 E 46th St.
317-257-9935

Winding Way Farms
5888 E 82nd St.
317-849-3362

Michigan City
Nature's Cupboard
1806 US Hwy. 20 E
219-874-2335

Whiting
Whiting Health Foods
1710 Calumet Ave.
219-659-5848

Iowa

Cedar Rapids
Health Hut
1512 First Ave. NE
319-362-7345

Des Moines
Campbell's Nutrition
4040 University Ave.
515-277-6351

New City Market
4721 University Ave.
515-255-7380

Iowa City
New Pioneer Co-Op
22 S Van Buren St.
319-338-9441

Keokuk
HY Vee Food Stores
525 Blondeau St.
319-524-6790

Waterloo
Osco
2060 Crossroads Blvd.
319-235-6248

Kansas

Lawrence
Community Mercantile Co-op
901 Iowa Ave.
785-843-8544

Lenexa
Emerald Forest
12234 W 95th St.
913-492-6336

Mission
General Nutrition Center
4857 Johnson Dr.
913-384-6605

Wild Oats Natural Market
5101 Johnson Dr.
913-722-4069

Olathe
Nature's Alley
115 N Chester St.
913-764-5155

Wichita
Greenacres Market & Deli
8141 E 21 St.
316-634-1088

Kentucky

Louisville
*Amazing Grace Whole Foods
   & Nutrition*
1133 Bardstown Rd.
502-485-1122

Louisiana

Baton Rouge
*Our Daily Bread Market &
   Bakery*
9414 Florida Blvd.
225-924-9910

Vitality Food Shoppe
750 Oak Villa Blvd.
225-925-5780

Gonzales
Horn of Plenty Health Food
623 E Acension St.
225-644-6080

Lafayette
Sandra's Health Food
111 Rena Dr., Ste. C
337-988-0108

Metairie
Nutrition Fair
4409 Veterans Memorial Blvd.
504-885-5000

Monroe
Fiesta Nutrition Center
2225 Louisville Ave.
318-387-8446

New Orleans
Whole Foods Market
3135 Esplanade Ave.
504-943-1626

Shreveport
Good Life Health Foods
6132 Hearne Ave.
318-635-4753

Slidell
Ruby's Natural Foods
1030 Hwy. 190 W
985-641-1620

Maine

Bangor
Natural Living Center
209 Longview Dr.
207-990-2646

Portland
The Whole Grocer
127 Marginal Way
207-774-7711

Maryland

Annapolis
Whole Foods Market
2504 Solomon's Island Rd.
410-573-1800

Sun & Earth Natural Foods
1933 West St.
410-266-6862

Baltimore
Sunsplash Natural Foods
7006 Reisterstown Rd.
410-486-0979

Whole Foods Market
1330 Smith Ave.
410-532-6700

Bethesda
Fresh Fields Market
5269 River Rd.
301-984-4860

Cabin John
Bethesda Co-Op
6500 Seven Locks Rd.
301-320-2530

Columbia
David's Natural Market
5430 Lynx Lane, Ste. C
410-730-2304

District Heights
L.D. Green Grocer
3430 Donnell Dr.
301-735-2310

Easton
Railway Market
108 Marlboro Rd.
410-822-4852

Frederick
The Common Market
5728 Buckeystown Pike, Ste. 1
301-663-3416

Gaithersburg
Whole Foods Market
316 Kentlands Blvd.
301-258-9500

Laurel
Laurel Health Foods
131 Bowie Rd.
301-498-7191

Rockville
Laurel Health Foods
11711 Parklawn Dr.
301-816-4944

Silver Spring
General Nutrition Center
13733 Connecticut Ave.
301-871-4332

Takoma Park
Takoma Park Co-Op
201 Ethan Allen Ave.
301-891-2667

Towson
The Health Concern
28 W Susquehanna Ave.
410-828-4015

Massachusetts

Andover
Wild Oats
40 Railroad St.
978-749-6664

Boston
Whole Foods Market
15 Westland Ave.
617-375-1010

West Boylston
Nutrition Source
245 W Boylston St.
508-835-2442

Brighton
Whole Foods Market
15 Washington St.
617-738-8187

Cambridge
Whole Foods Market
115 Prospect St.
617-492-0070

Whole Foods Market
186 Alewife Brook Pkwy.
617-491-0040

Cambridge Natural Foods
1670 Mass Ave.
617-492-4452

Harnett's Homeopathy Body Care
47 Brattle St.
617-491-4747

Harvest Co-Op
581 Mass Ave.
617-661-1580

Centerville
Cape Cod Natural Foods
1600 Falmouth Rd.
Bell Tower Mall
508-771-8394

Great Barrington
Locke Stock & Barrel
265 Stockbridge Rd.
413-528-0800

Newton
Whole Foods Market
916 Walnut St.
617-969-1141

Quincy
Good Health Natural Foods
1627 Hancock St.
617-773-4925

Saugus
Wild Oats
357 Broadway
781-233-5341

Worcester
The Living Earth
232 Chandler St.
508-753-1896

Michigan

Allen Park
Health Unlimited
6555 Allen Rd.
313-381-8800

Brighton
Healthy Exposure
134 W Main St.
810-227-0690

The Vitamin Company
421 W Main St.
810-227-5311

East Lansing
East Lansing Co-Op
4960 Northwind Dr.
517-337-1266

Flint
Dale's Natural Foods
4290 Miller Rd.
810-230-8008

Grand Haven
Health Hutt
700 Washington Ave.
616-846-3026

Grand Rapids
Harvest Health Foods
1944 Eastern Ave. SE
616-245-6268

Nutrition Plus
2650 E Beltline Ave. SE
616-940-1453

Nutrition Plus
3560 Alpine Ave. NW
616-785-1010

Grosse Pointe Woods
Healy's Health Hut
19850 Mack Ave.
313-885-5000

Holland
Apple Valley
3013 W Shore Dr., Ste. 70
616-399-8004

Nature's Market
1013 S Washington Ave.
616-394-5250

Jackson
Natural Health Foods
1090 Jackson Crossing
517-787-2279

Kalamazoo
Natural Health Foods
4610 W Main St.
269-342-9459

Sawall Health Foods
2965 Oakland Dr.
Oakwood Plaza
269-343-3619

Lansing
Better Health
6235 W Saginaw Hwy.
517-323-9186

Mt. Pleasant
Green Tree
214 N Franklin St.
989-772-3221

Rochester Hills
Whole Foods Market
1404 Walton Blvd.
248-652-2100

St. Clair Shores
Natural Way
31398 Harper Ave.
586-296-6168

Vitamin Village
23401 Greater Mack Ave.
586-774-6330

Traverse City
Oryana Natural Foods Market
260 E 10th St.
231-947-0191

Troy
Vitamin Village
2971 E Big Beaver Rd.
248-689-6699

Warren
Health Foods International
8399 E 13 Mile Rd.
586-939-8200

Wyoming
Pat's Health Corner
2575 28th St. SW
616-532-4713

Minnesota

Bemidji
Sunrise Natural Foods
802 Paul Bunyan Dr.
218-751-9005

Bloomington
Nutrition Plus
609 W 98th St.
952-881-9790

Chanhassen
Body Mind & Spirit
7814 Market Blvd.
952-975-1819

Minneapolis
Black Cat Natural Foods
2010 E. Hennepin Ave.
612-623-9800

Linden Hills Co-Op
2318 W 43rd St.
612-922-1159

Seward Community Co-Op
2111 E Franklin Ave.
612-338-2465

Tao Natural Foods
2200 Hennepin Ave. S
612-377-4630

Wedge Community Co-Op
2105 Lyndale Ave. S
612-871-3993

Minnetonka
Lakewinds Natural Foods
17515 Minnetonka Blvd.
952-473-0292

Red Wing
Good Life Nutrition
314 Main St.
651-388-8517

St. Paul
Mississippi Market
1810 Randolph Ave.
651-690-0507

Whole Foods Market
30 S Fairview Ave.
651-690-0197

White Bear Lake
Kowalski's
4391 S Lake Ave.
651-429-5913

Mississippi

Hattiesburg
Vitamins Plus
4600 Hardy St., Ste. 12
601-261-3009

Jackson
Rainbow Whole Foods
2807 Old Canton Rd.
601-366-1602

Meridian
Robi's Nutrition
4831 29th Ave.
601-482-8696

Tupelo
Healthy Habits
West Main Shopping Center
101 N Industrial Rd.
662-844-9700

Missouri

Bolivar
New Life Natural Food Store
451 S Springfield Ave., Ste. B
417-326-5701

Camdenton
Vitamin Village
1179 N Hwy. 5
Ryland Center
573-346-7961

Columbia
Clover's Natural Foods
802 Business Loop 70-E
573-449-1650

Florissant
River City Nutrition
8 Grandview Shopping Center
314-837-7290

Grandview
Super Natural Health Food Center
12706 S US Hwy. 71
816-765-1135

Joplin
Suzanne's Natural Foods
3106 S Connecticut Ave.
417-781-0909

Kansas City
Wild Oats Market
4301 Main St.
816-931-1873

Kirkwood
River City Natural Food Market
833 S Kirkwood Rd.
314-822-1406

Ladue
Wild Oats Market
8823 Ladue Rd.
314-721-8004

Lee's Summit
Nature's Market
535 SE Melody Lane
816-525-2625

Poplar Bluff
Bee Hive
900 Ida St.
573-686-3025

Springfield
Spring Valley Herbs & Natural Foods
1738 S Glenstone Ave.
417-882-1033

St. Louis
The Golden Grocer
335 N Euclid Ave.
314-367-0405

Natural Way
12345 Olive Blvd.
314-878-3001

New Harvest Foods
10028 Manchester, Ste. 219
314-966-6767

New World Natural Foods
4053 Union Rd.
314-487-8310

New Dawn Natural Foods
3536 Arsenal St.
314-772-9110

Webster Groves
Natural Way
8110 Big Bend Blvd.
314-961-1880

Montana

Bozeman
Co-Op Community Food
908 W Main
406-587-4039

Missoula
Good Food Store
1600 S 3rd St. W
406-541-3663

Nebraska

Columbus
Mother Nature's Emporium
2707 13th St.
402-564-5666

Lincoln
Open Harvest
1618 South Lincoln St.
402-475-9069

North Platte
Natural Nutrition House
203 W Sixth St.
308-532-9433

Omaha
No Name Nutrition
2032 N 72nd St.
402-393-5812

No Name Nutrition
14469 W Center Rd.
402-333-1300

Nevada

Boulder City
Health Nuts
1635 Nevada Hwy.
702-293-1844

Carson City
Du Bois Health Food Center
201 Hwy. 50 East, Ste. 1
775-882-2844

Elko
Natural Nutrition
1900 E Idaho St., Ste. 106
775-738-8818

Henderson
Better Nutrition
2895 N Green Valley Pkwy., Ste. C
702-435-1111

Las Vegas
Mister GreenGenes
3315 E Russell Rd., #A-3
702-450-2100

The Natural Garden
4512 E Charleston Blvd.
702-453-3380

Rainbow's End Natural Foods
1100 E Sahara Ave.
702-737-7282

Semilla Natural Foods
510 University Ave.
505-425-8139

Siemens Health Foods
1004 E Charleston Blvd.
702-385-4404

Stay Healthy
840 S Rancho Dr., Ste. 14
702-877-2494

Sun Naturals
9901 W Charleston Blvd., Ste. 1
702-966-2525

Winnemucca
Nature's Corner
330 W Winnemucca Blvd.
775-625-4330

New Hampshire

Concord
Granite State Natural Foods
164 N State St.
603-224-9341

Hanover
Hanover Food Co-Op
45 S Park St.
603-643-2667

Keene
VitaSource
599 Main St.
603-357-3639

Manchester
A-Market
125 Loring St.
603-668-2650

New London
14 Carrots Natural Foods
277 Newport Rd.
603-526-2323

Wilton
Bursey's Gourmet Market
438 Gibbons Hwy.
603-654-6572

New Jersey

Bayonne
John's Natural Foods
486 Broadway
201-858-0088

Chester
Health Shoppe
207 Rte. 206 S
908-879-7555

Closter
Closter Health Food Store
90 Closter Plaza
201-767-7541

Englewood
Aylward's II
14 N Van Brunt St.
201-567-1489

Fairview
Natural Selection
357 Fairview Ave.
201-945-7200

Flemington
Basil Bandwagon
276 US Hwy. 202/31
908-788-5737

Forked River
Franklin Vitamins
136 Rte. 9 S
609-971-6737

Hackensack
Aylward's Natural Foods
342 Main St.
201-342-1932

Hamilton Square
Black Forest Acres
1100 Rte. 33
609-586-6187

Linden
Clear Light Natural Foods
306 N Wood Ave.
908-486-9446

Medford
Health Haven II
5 S Main St.
609-953-7744

North Arlington
Roots
493 Ridge Rd.
201-246-0294

North Bergen
Vitamin Shoppe
2101 91st St.
201-758-0404

Northvale
Organica Natural Foods
246 E Livingston St.
201-767-8182

Paramus
General Nutrition Center
Paramus Park Mall 610
201-262-9714

Phillipsburg
General Nutrition Center
1200 Rte. 22 East
908-454-8363

Princeton
Health Foods
1273 Rte. 206
609-279-1636

Whole Earth Center
360 Nassau St.
609-924-7429

Ramsey
Good & Natural
State Rte. 17 N
201-327-1230

Teaneck
Aquarius Health Foods
408 Cedar Lane
201-836-0601

Tenafly
Healthway Natural Foods
35 River Edge Rd.
201-569-4558

West Trenton
Simply Natural
1505 Parkway Ave.
609-406-0818

Washington
Washington Health Foods
5 E Washington Ave.
908-689-5228

New Mexico

Albuquerque
BK's Health Pantry
119 San Pasquale SW
505-243-0370

The Herb Store
107 Carlisle Blvd. SE
505-255-8878

Keller's Farm Stores
2912 Eubank Blvd. NE
505-294-1427

Keller's Farm Stores
6100 Coors Blvd. NW
505-898-6121

La Montanita Food Co-Op
3500 Central Ave. SE
505-265-4631

Moses Kountry Health Food
7115 4th St. NW
505-898-9763

R Downs Nutrition Center
7400 Montgomery NE, #23
505-881-3150

Vitamin Trader
211 Montano Rd. NW
505-344-6060

Wild Oats Market
6300 San Mateo Blvd. NE
505-823-1933

Wild Oats Market
11015 Menaul Blvd. NE
505-275-6660

Clovis
Makin' It Natural
2502 Ashford Dr.
505-763-8282

Las Cruces
Mountain View Market
1300 El Paseo Rd.
505-523-0436

Santa Fe
Tico's Health Food Shop
720 St. Michael's Dr., Ste. E
505-474-0304

Silver City
Silver City Food Co-Op
520 N Bullard St.
505-388-2343

Taos
Cid's Food Market
623 Paseo del Pueblo Norte
505-758-1148

Taos Herb Co.
710 Paseo del Pueblo Sur, Ste. J
505-758-1991

New York

Albany
Dean's Natural Foods
911 Central Ave.
Westgate Shopping Center
518-489-5723

Honest Weight Co-Op
484 Central Ave.
518-482-2667

Ardsley
Liggett Rexall Drug Store
708 Saw Mill River Rd.
914-693-2003

Baldwin
South Shore Health Food Center
2134 Grand Ave.
516-623-4432

Sunburst Biorganics
15 Grand Ave.
516-623-8478

Bayside
Health Nuts
211-35 26th Ave.
718-225-8164

Bronx
Eden Natural Garden
528A Morris Ave.
718-402-0707

Good 'n Natural
2173 White Plains Rd.
718-931-4335

Parkchester Health Food
1663 Metropolitan Ave.
718-931-6699

Brooklyn
Back to the Land
142 7th Ave.
718-768-5654

Boro Park Natural Health Food
5203 13th Ave.
718-851-8809

Downtown Natural Market
51 Willoughby St.
718-834-1215

Everything Natural
1661 Ralph Ave.
718-531-9192

Homeopathy Vitamin Center
1954 Coney Island Ave.
718-336-3714

Natural Vitamins
671 Manhattan Ave.
718-389-2596

Naturally Healthy
594 Grand St.
718-599-7527

Perelandra Natural Food Center
175 Remsen St.
718-855-6068

Zahler's Nutrition Center
4720 New Utrecht Ave.
718-438-5336

Canton
Nature's Storehouse
21 Main St.
315-386-3740

Catskill
Catskill Natural Products
254 W Bridge St.
518-943-2830

Chappaqua
The Healthy Choice Apothecary
6 S Greeley Ave.
914-238-1700

Chestnut Ridge
Hungry Hollow Co-Op
841 Chestnut Ridge Rd.
845-356-3319

Commack
Mung Bean
6522 Jericho Tpke.
631-499-2362

Elmira Heights
Good Earth
2068 College Ave.
607-734-5447

Farmingdale
Total Nutrition
75 Bi County Blvd.
Rte. 109
631-694-7358

Floral Park
Nature's Pantry
324 Jericho Tpke.
718-347-3037

Flushing
Queens Health Emporium
15901 Horace Harding Expwy.
718-358-6500

Forest Hills
Vitality Store
5 Continental Ave.
718-261-7499

Fresh Meadows
*Quantum Leap Natural Foods
  Market*
6560 Fresh Meadows Lane
718-762-3572

Garden City
Food For Thought
154 Seventh St.
516-747-5811

Glen Cove
Rising Tide Natural Foods
42 Forest Ave.
516-676-7895

Great Neck
Health Nuts
45 Northern Blvd.
516-829-8400

Hamburg
Feel-Rite
6000 South Park Ave.
716-649-6694

The Ground Up
4900 Lake Shore Rd.
716-627-7742

Hamilton
Hamilton Whole Foods
28 Broad St.
315-824-2930

Hastings
Food For Thought
7 Spring St.
914-478-3600

Hewlett
House of Nutrition
1743 Peninsula Blvd.
516-374-2099

Hudson
*Kaaterskill Farm Natural
     Storehouse*
173 Healy Blvd.
Corner Plaza
518-822-0790

Huntington
Capitol Health Nutrition Mart
357 New York Ave.
631-271-5577

Islip
*Country Health and Diet
     Foods Inc.*
484 Main St.
631-581-7722

Jackson Heights
Jackson Heights Health Food
8306 37th Ave.
718-429-9511

Jamaica
Vital Health Foods
19614 Linden Blvd.
718-525-0992

Johnson City
Health Best Natural Foods
214 Main St.
607-797-1001

Lake Grove
Mr. Vitamin
3201 Middle Country Rd.
631-467-4404

Levittown
General Nutrition Center
3525 Hempstead Tpke.
516-579-0866

Long Beach
Bob's Natural Foods
104 W Park Ave.
516-889-8955

Lynbrook
Rubie's Health Foods
603 Sunrise Hwy.
Philip's Plaza
516-593-0385

Manhasset
Whole Foods Market
2101 Northern Blvd.
516-869-8900

Massapequa Park
Vitamin's World
5272 Sunrise Hwy.
516-795-6523

Mt. Vernon
Sunbeam Health Foods
10 Gramatan Ave.
914-663-9108

New City
Back to Earth
306 S Main St.
845-634-3511

New York City
A Matter of Health
1478 1st Ave.
212-288-8280

Columbus Natural Foods
725 Columbus Ave.
212-663-0345

Food Liberation
1349 Lexington Ave.
212-348-2286

Health Nuts
835 Second Ave.
212-490-2979

Health Nuts
1208 Second Ave.
212-593-0116

Health Nuts
2611 Broadway
212-678-0054

Hickey Chemists
888 Second Ave.
212-223-6333

Hickey Chemists III
1258 Third Ave.
212-744-5944

House of Health
1014 Lexington Ave.
212-772-8422

Integral Yoga Natural Foods
229 W 13th St.
212-243-2642

Life Thyme
410 6th Ave.
212-420-9099

Lotus Health Foods
1309 Lexington Ave.
212-423-0345

Natural Green Market
162 Third Ave.
212-780-0263

275 Organic Market
275 7th Ave.
212-243-9927

Vitamin Shoppe
740 Broadway
212-995-8716

Vitamin Shoppe
375 6th Ave.
212-929-6553

Vitamin Shoppe
120 W 57th St.
212-664-0048

Vitamin Shoppe
666 Lexington Ave. #8
212-421-0250

Vitamin Shoppe
2086 Broadway
212-580-7620

Vitamin Shoppe
460 7th Ave.
212-736-6137

Vitamin Shoppe
145 Spring St.
212-966-3463

Vitamin Shoppe
1193 Third Ave.
212-288-6053

Westerly Natural Market
913 8th Ave.
212-586-5262

Whole Foods Market
2421 Broadway
212-874-4000

Wholesome Market
93 University Pl.
212-353-3663

Willner Chemists
100 Park Ave.
212-682-2817

Newburgh
General Nutrition Center
1401 Rte. 300
845-566-7425

North Syracuse
Mother Earth
733 South Bay Rd.
315-458-2717

Nyack
Back to Earth
1 S Broadway
845-353-3311

Oceanside
Jandi's Natural Market
3000 Long Beach Rd.
516-536-5535

Peekskill
General Nutrition Center
Main St. Beach Shopping
    Center
914-737-1422

Plainview
Dr. B. Well Naturally
8 Washington Ave.
516-932-9355

Nutrition Warehouse
100 E Jericho Tpke.
516-294-7084

Port Jefferson
General Nutrition Center
1106 Rte. 112
631-331-2859

Richmond Hill
Someday Health Foods
12514 Liberty Ave.
718-848-4928

Wholesome Living
11311 Liberty Ave.
718-843-9430

Riverhead
Green Earth Natural Foods
50 E Main St.
631-369-2233

Rockville Centre
*The Natural Choice Health
    Market*
287 Merrick Rd.
516-766-1703

Rocky Point
Back to Basics
632 Rte. 25A
631-821-0444

Almond Tree Health Food
55 Rte. 25A
631-821-1412

Sag Harbor
Provision's
7 Main St.
631-725-3636

Sayville
Cornucopia
39 N Main St.
631-589-9579

Scarsdale
Mrs. Green's Natural Market
780 White Plains Rd.
914-472-0111

Mrs. Green's Natural Market
365 Central Park Ave.
914-472-9675

Seaford
All Natural Health
3830 Sunrise Hwy.
Seaford Plaza Shopping Center
516-785-5521

West Seneca
Feel-Rite Natural Foods
3521 Seneca St.
716-675-6620

East Setauket
Wild By Nature
198 Main St.
631-246-5500

St. James
St. James Natural Foods
296 Lake Ave.
631-862-6076

Staten Island
Family Health
177 New Dorp Lane
718-351-7004

Taste Buds Natural Foods
1807 Hylan Blvd.
718-351-8693

Troy
*Uncle Sam's Good Natural
    Products*
77 Fourth St.
518-271-7299

Valley Stream
*Valley Stream Health Food
    Center*
135 Rockaway Ave.
516-561-1441

Westbury
Health Nuts
92 Old Country Rd.
516-683-9177

Westhampton Beach
Westhampton Natural Foods
96 Old Riverhead Rd.
631-288-8947

White Plains
Manna Foods
171 Mamaroneck Ave.
914-946-2233

Williston Park
Dave's Health Food & Vitamins
215 Hillside Ave.
516-742-1257

Yonkers
House of Nutrition
600 Tuckahoe Rd.
914-793-7927

North Carolina

Asheville
Earth Fare
66 Westgate Shopping Ct.
828-253-7656

Banner Elk
The Health Connection
2945 Tynecastle Hwy.
828-898-8482

Carrboro
Weaver Street Market
101 E Weaver St.
919-929-0010

Chapel Hill
Whole Foods Market
81 S Elliott Rd.
919-968-1983

Charlotte
Berry Brook Farms
1257 East Blvd.
704-334-6528

Talley's Green Grocery
1408 East Blvd., Ste. C
704-334-9200

Durham
Whole Foods Market
621 Broad St.
919-286-2290

Forest City
Earth Fare
213 Oak St. Ext.
828-245-6578

Goldsboro
Health Habit Natural Foods
606 N Spence Ave.
919-751-0300

Murphy
Whole Store
5635 Hwy. 64 W
828-837-5408

Raleigh
Harmony Farms
5653 Creedmoor Rd.
919-782-0064

Whole Foods Market
3540 Wade Ave.
919-828-5805

Wilmington
Paula's Health Hut
3405 Wrightsville Ave.
910-791-0200

North Dakota

Fargo
Tochi Products
1111 2nd Ave. N
701-232-7700

Grand Forks
Nature's Country Store
1826 S Washington St.
701-772-8086

Nature's Country Store
3001 S Columbia Rd.
701-746-4499

Jamestown
Mill Town Herbs
2400 Hwy. 281 S Buffalo Mall
701-252-2284

Ohio

Ada
Health Chek
117 S Main St.
419-634-0455

Ashland
LaRue's Picture of Health
910 E Main St.
419-289-6400

Bellefontaine
Au Natural
1810 S Main St.
937-592-9311

Cincinnati
Cincinnati Natural Foods
9268 Colerain Ave.
513-385-7000

Clifton Natural Foods
169 W McMillan St.
513-961-6111

Cincinnati Natural Foods
6911 Miami Ave.
513-271-7777

Natural Life Nutrition Shoppes
2946 Wasson Rd.
513-631-0300

Cleveland
M & R Healthy Solutions
703 Franklin Blvd.
440-442-1150

Columbus
HSU & Co.
2007 Morse Rd.
614-262-5856

HSU & Co.
6101 McNaughten Center
614-861-8108

Parsley Patch Nutrition
2602 Hilliard-Rome Rd.
614-529-9552

Lakewood
Nature's Bin
18120 Sloane Ave.
216-521-4600

Maple Heights
Marshall's Health Foods
5168 Warrensville Ctr. Rd.
216-475-0344

Massillon
Oak Park Nutrition Center
63 Market Place Dr.
330-833-4021

Oxford
Oxford Natural Foods
5154 College Corner Pike
513-523-9702

Reynoldsburg
American Nutrition Center
1639 Brice Rd.
614-866-7834

Toledo
Bassett's Health Foods
3550 Executive Pkwy.
419-531-0334

Westerville
Raisin Rack
618 Westerville Rd.
614-882-5886

Oklahoma

Bartlesville
Billie's Health Food Center
313 SE Osage St.
918-336-8609

Norman
*Dodson's Nutritional Food
    Center*
1305 36th Ave NW
405-329-4613

Oklahoma City
Akin's Natural Foods
2924 NW 63rd
405-843-3033

Nutritional Food Center
1024 N Classen Blvd.
405-232-8404

Okmulgee
Nutrition Shoppe
206 W 6th St.
918-756-3433

Shawnee
House of Health
314 W MacArthur St.
405-275-3327

Tulsa
Akin's Natural Foods
31st Harvard St.
918-742-6630

Oregon

Ashland
Ashland Food Cooperative
237 N First St.
541-482-2237

Bend
Nature's General Store
1900 NE Third St.
541-382-6732

Corvallis
*First Alternative Natural Food
    Co-Op*
1007 SE Third St.
541-753-3115

Eugene
Discount Sports & Vitamins
255 E 18th Ave.
541-343-0971

Evergreen Nutrition
1653 Willamette St.
541-485-5100

Capella Market
2489 Willamette St.
541-345-1014

Sundance Natural Food Store
748 E 24th Ave.
541-343-9142

Hood River
Hood River Nutrition
1235 State St.
541-386-3780

Lake Oswego
General Nutrition Center
3 Monroe Pkwy.
503-636-5922

Nature's Path
334 1st St.
503-635-3799

Portland
Food Front Co-Op
2375 NW Thurman St.
503-222-5658

Wild Oats
3016 SE Division St.
503-233-7374

Wild Oats
8024 E Mill Plain Blvd.
503-223-8260

Salem
Salem Health Foods
401 Center St. NE, #160
503-585-6938

Salem Health Foods
1116 Lancaster Dr. NE
503-362-0763

Springfield
Wynant's Family Health
1859 Pioneer Pkwy. E
541-746-4251

The Dalles
Healthy Habits
320 E 2nd St.
541-298-1906

Tigard
General Nutrition Center
9469 SW Washington Square
    Rd., #115
503-684-0600

Pennsylvania

Annville
Annville Natural Food Market
37 W Main St.
717-867-2773

Devon
Whole Foods Market
821 W Lancaster Ave.
610-688-9400

Lansdale
North Penn Health Food Center
1313 N Broad St.
215-855-1044

Malvern
Venus Nutrition Center
81 Lancaster Ave.
610-644-9111

North Wales
Whole Foods Market
1210 Bethlehem Pike
215-646-6300

Oakmont
Today's Market
612 Allegheny River Rd.
412-828-4244

Palmyra
Palmyra Natural Foods
120 E Main St.
717-838-2501

Philadelphia
Essene Natural Food & Cafe
719 S Fourth St.
215-922-1146

Gene's Health World
8617 Germantown Ave.
215-247-3215

Harry's Natural Food Store
1805 Cottman Ave.
215-742-3807

New World Health
25 S 11th St.
215-923-1633

Whole Foods Market
2001 Pennsylvania Ave.
215-557-0015

Pittsburgh
Back to Basics
300 Mt. Lebanon Blvd.
412-343-8156

Trexlertown
Healthy Alternatives
7150 Hamilton Blvd.
610-366-9866

Warminster
General Nutrition Center
824 W St. Rd.
215-674-1577

Waynesboro
Natural Alternatives & Energy
115 Walnut St.
717-765-0792

West Lawn
Puravita
2512 Penn Ave.
610-670-4647

Wynnewood
General Nutrition Center
50 E Wynnewood Rd.
610-649-6334

Whole Foods Market
339 E Lancaster Ave.
610-896-3737

Rhode Island

Coventry
Nature's Corner
192 Pilgram Ave.
401-826-2795

Newport
Harvest Natural Foods
1 Casino Terrace
401-846-8137

Providence
Whole Foods Market
261 Waterman St.
401-272-1690

South Carolina

Charleston
Earth Fare
74 Folly Rd.
843-769-0794

Columbia
Earth Fare
3312 Devine St.
803-799-0048

Greenville
Earth Fare
6 S Lewis Plaza
864-250-1020

Garner's Natural Market
60 E Antrim Dr.
864-242-4856

South Dakota

Hot Springs
Earth Goods
738 Jennings Ave.
605-745-7715

Mitchell
Wayne & Mary's Nutrition Center
1313 W Havens St.
605-996-9868

Tennessee

Chattanooga
Nutrition World
5762 Brainerd Rd.
423-892-4085

Kingsport
Mac's
1425 E Center St.
423-245-2181

Memphis
Wild Oats Market
5022 Poplar Ave.
901-685-2293

Texas

Amarillo
Eat Rite Health Food
2425 I-40 West
806-353-7476

Fountain of Health
3705 Olsen Blvd.
806-355-5162

Arlington
Good Health Place
2503 S Cooper St.
817-265-5261

Austin
Central Market
4001 N Lamar Blvd.
512-206-1000

Fresh Plus
1221 W Lynn St.
512-477-5574

Fresh Plus
408 E 43rd St.
512-459-8922

Sun Harvest
2917 W Anderson Lane
512-451-0669

Sun Harvest
4006 S Lamar Blvd.
512-444-3079

Wheatsville Co-Op
3101 Guadalupe St.
512-478-2667

Whole Foods Market
9607 Research Blvd., Ste. 300
512-345-5003

Whole Foods Market
601 N Lamar Blvd., Ste. 100
512-476-1206

Azle
Nature's Health Store
103 E Main St.
817-444-6233

Beaumont
American Health Foods
3847 Stagg Dr.
409-833-7488

Basic Food Ltd.
229 Dowlen Rd.
409-861-4424

Bedford
Health Hut
623 Harwood Rd.
817-581-7180

Borger
Sara's Health Foods
527 N Main St.
806-273-5191

Corpus Christi
Nutrition Shop
5840 S Staples St.
361-991-2972

Sun Harvest
1440 Airline Rd.
361-993-2850

Dallas
Ann's Health Food Center
2634 S Zang Blvd.
214-942-9483

Fitness Essentials
3878 Oak Lawn Ave.
214-528-5535

Roy's Natural Market
5934 Royal Ln., Ste. 130
214-987-0213

Sundrops Vitamin Superstore
3920 Oaklawn Ave.
214-521-0550

Whole Foods Market
2218 Lower Greenville Ave.
214-824-1744

El Paso
Sun Harvest
6100 N Mesa St.
915-833-3380

Fairfield
The Healthy Image
127 S Mount St.
903-389-2131

Fort Worth
Richardson's Health Food
5051 Granbury Rd.
817-294-1180

Galveston
Peak Nutrition
6187 Central City Blvd.
409-740-6949

Greenville
Sunshine Shoppe Health Foods
2715 Trader's Rd.
903-454-2742

Houston
Fiesta Mart Inc.
1005 Blalock Rd.
713-461-9664

Fiesta Food Mart
3803 Dunlavy St.
713-529-7352

Southwest Health Food
8328 SW Freeway
713-981-7707

Tri-health Inc.
11025 Fuqua at Gulf Freeway
713-947-7373

Whole Foods Market
6401 Woodway Ave.
713-789-4477

Whole Foods Market
2955 Kirby Dr.
713-520-1937

Whole Foods Market
11145 Westheimer Rd.
713-784-7776

Hurst
A Garden of Health
512 W Harwood Rd.
817-577-2733

Longview
Granary Street
913 W Loop 281
903-759-2744

Lubbock
Alternative Food Co.
2611 Boston Ave.
806-747-8740

McAllen
Hector's Health Company
4500 N 10th St.
956-687-5920

Major Health Foods
1001 S 10th St.
956-687-7759

McKinney
Mike's Health Collection
1434 N Central Expwy.
972-562-4039

Mesquite
Family Health Food Store
111 N Town East Blvd., Ste. 1
972-270-4505

Midland
Natural Foods Market
2311 W Wadley Ave.
432-699-4048

Pasadena
Peak Nutrition
324 Southmore Ave.
713-473-9443

Plano
Whole Foods Market
2201 Preston Rd.
972-612-6729

Richardson
Whole Foods Market
60 Dal-Rich Village
972-699-8075

Roanoke
Abundant Life Health Foods
500 N Hwy. 377
817-430-4624

San Antonio
Garden Ville
5121 Crestway, Ste. 511
210-654-7728

Sun Harvest
8101 Callaghan Rd.
210-979-8121

Sun Harvest
2502 Nacogdoches Rd.
210-824-7800

Whole Foods Market
255 E Basse Rd., Ste. 130
210-826-4676

Texas City
The Health Food Store
2326 Palmer Hwy.
409-948-4404

The Woodlands
Pert Ner Perfect Vitamins
440 Sawdust Rd.
281-367-9711

Tomball
Family Farm
27676 B Tomball Pkwy./State
   Hwy. 249
281-351-4372

Wimberley
Hill Country Natural Foods
2325 Ranch Rd.
512-847-3291

Utah

Ogden
Harvest Health Foods
341 27th St.
801-621-1627

Orem
Good Earth
500 S State St.
801-765-1616

Provo
Good Earth
1045 S University Ave.
801-375-7444

Salt Lake City
Wild Oats Market
1131 E Wilmington Ave.
801-359-7913

Wild Oats Market
645 E 400 S
801-355-7401

Sandy
Good Earth
7905 S 700 East
801-562-2209

Vermont

Brattleboro
Brattleboro Food Co-Op
2 Main St.
802-257-0236

Burlington
City Market
82 S Winooski Ave.
802-863-3659

Montpelier
Hunger Mountain Co-Op
623 Stone Cutters Way
802-223-6910

Randolph
Randolph Co-Op
24 Pleasant St.
802-728-9554

South Burlington
Healthy Living
4 Market St.
802-863-2569

White River Junction
Upper Valley Co-Op
193 N Main St.
802-295-5804

Virginia

Abingdon
The Whole Health Center
611 E Main St.
276-628-3170

Alexandria
Cash Grocer Natural Foods
1315 King St.
703-549-2758

Healthway Natural Foods
1610 Belleview Blvd.
703-660-8603

Annandale
Whole Foods Market
6548 Little River Tpke.
703-914-0040

Healthway Natural Foods
4113 John Marr Dr.
703-354-7782

Charlottesville
Whole Foods Market
300 Shoppers World Ct.
434-973-4900

Integral Yoga Natural Foods
923 Preston Ave.
434-293-4111

Rebecca's Natural Foods
1141 Emmet St. N
434-977-1965

Fredericksburg
Healthway Natural Foods
4211 Plank Rd., Ste. B
540-786-4844

Newport News
Health Trail
10848 Warwick Blvd.
757-596-8018

Norfolk
Health Food Center
7639 Granby St.
757-489-4242

Richmond
Ellwood Thompson's
4 N Thompson St.
804-359-7525

Good Foods Grocery
3062 Stony Point Rd.
804-320-6767

Good Foods Grocery
1312 Gaskins Rd.
804-740-3518

Roanoke
Nature's Outlet
3548 Electric Rd.
540-989-5109

Roanoke Natural Foods Co-Op
1319 Grandin Ave.
540-343-5652

Springfield
Healthway Natural Foods
6402 Springfield Plaza
703-569-3533

Sterling
Healthway Natural Foods
46900 Cedar Lake Lane
703-430-4430

Tyson's Corner
Whole Foods Market
7511 Leesburg Pike
703-448-1600

Vienna
Whole Foods Market
143 Maple Ave. E
703-319-2000

Warrenton
Natural Marketplace
5 Diagonal St.
540-349-4111

Yorktown
Advanced Nutrition
209 Village Ave., Ste. A
757-872-8865

Washington

Anacortes
Anacortes Health
1020 7th St.
360-293-8849

Bainbridge Island
Willow's Naturally
169 Winslow Way E
206-842-2759

Bellevue
Evergreen Health Pantry
1645 140th Ave. NE
425-746-4776

Larry's Market
699 120th Ave. NE
206-343-8646

Nature's Pantry
10200 NE 10th St.
425-454-0170

Nature's Pantry
15600 NE 8th
425-957-0090

Bellingham
Community Food Co-Op
1220 N Forest
360-734-8158

Cost Cutter
4131 Meridan
360-734-4110

Centralia
Good Health Nutrition
503 Harrison Ave.
360-736-3830

Edmonds
Pilgrim's Natureway
23632 Hwy. 99, Ste. R
206-774-7777

Everett
Quality Food Centers
4919 Evergreen Way
425-259-3444

Kirkland
Larry's Market
12321 120th Pl. NE
425-820-2300

Puget Consumers Co-Op
10718 NE 68th St.
425-828-4622

*Pilgrim's Natureway Nutrition
    Centers*
12618 120th Ave. NE
425-821-1819

Langley
The Star Store Basics
199 2nd St.
360-221-2425

Mt. Vernon
Skagit Valley Food Co-Op
202 S 1st St.
360-336-9777

Oak Harbor
Pilgrim's Natureway
751 NE Midway Blvd.
360-675-0333

Olympia
Good Life Health Foods
236 N Division St.
360-786-1500

J-Vee's Health Foods
3720 Pacific Ave. SE
360-491-1930

Olympia Food Co-Op
921 Rogers St. NW
360-754-7666

Olympia Food Co-Op
3111 Pacific Ave. SE
360-956-3870

Smart Nutrition
3405 Capitol Blvd.
360-943-8255

Port Angeles
Country Aire Natural Foods
117 E First St.
360-452-7175

Port Orchard
Natural Health
1700 S Kitsap Mall
360-876-1134

Port Townsend
Port Townsend Food Co-Op
414 Kearney St.
360-385-2883

Poulsbo
Poulsbo Central Market
20148 10th Ave. NE
360-779-1881

Redmond
VitaminLife
15940 Redmond Way
425-869-7000

Seattle
Madison Market
1600 E Madison St.
206-329-1545

Ballard Market
1400 NW 56th St.
206-783-7922

Bee Well Vitamin Shoppe
1901 N 45th St.
206-632-7040

The Grainery
13629 First Ave. S
206-244-5015

The Herbalist
2106 NE 65th St.
206-523-2600

Larry's Market
100 Mercer St.
206-213-0778

Larry's Market
10008 Aurora Ave. N
206-527-5333

Mother Nature's Natural
516 1st Ave. N
206-284-4422

Pilgrim's Natureway
1524 3rd Ave.
206-625-9722

Pilgrim's Natureway
401 NE Northgate Way
206-365-7590

Pilgrim's Natureway
4455 California Ave. SW
206-935-4200

Pike Place Natural Foods
1501 Pike Place Market
206-623-2231

Puget Consumers Co-Op
2749 California Ave. SW
206-937-8481

Puget Consumers Co-Op
600 N 34th St.
206-632-6811

Quality Food Centers
1531 NE 145th St.
206-363-5717

Quality Food Centers
2746 NE 45th St.
206-526-5160

Rainbow Natural Remedies
409 15th Ave. E
206-329-8979

Seattle Super Supplements
4336 Roosevelt Way NE
206-633-4428

Zenith Supplies
6300 Roosevelt Way NE
206-525-7997

Silverdale
Helen's Health Foods
10315 Silverdale Way
360-698-1550

Vancouver
Nature's Wild Oats Market
8024 E Mill Plain Blvd.
360-695-8878

Vashon Island
Minglemint
19526 Vashon Hwy. SW
206-463-9672

Wenatchee
Wenatchee Natural Foods
222 N Wenatchee Ave.
509-662-6413

East Wenatchee
General Nutrition Center
511 Valley Mall
509-884-3911

Winslow
Town & Country Market
343 E Winslow Way
206-842-3848

Washington D.C.

Whole Foods Market
4530 40th St. NW
202-237-5800

Naturally Yours
2029 P St. NW
202-429-1718

Wellness Cafe
325 Pennsylvania Ave. SE
202-543-2266

Whole Foods Market
2323 Wisconsin Ave. NW
202-333-5393

Yes! Organic Market
3425 Connecticut Ave. NW
202-363-1559

West Virginia

Elkins
Good Energy Foods
214 3rd St.
304-636-5169

Martinsburg
Healthway Natural Foods
740 Foxcroft Ave.
304-263-7728

Healthy Lifestyle Market
280 Berkeley Plaza
304-263-5244

Morgantown
Sunflowers
1137 Van Voorhis Rd.
304-598-0668

Wisconsin

La Crosse
People's Food Co-Op
315 5th Ave. S
608-784-5798

Madison
Whole Foods Market
3313 University Ave.
608-233-9566

Williamson St. Co-Op
1221 Williamson St.
608-251-6776

Milwaukee
Health Hut
2225 S 108th St.
414-545-8844

Lee's Health Mart
5919 W North Ave.
414-774-3120

Outpost Natural Foods
100 E Capitol Dr.
414-961-2597

Spencer
Plan It Earth
101 W Clark St.
715-659-5436

Wyoming

Jackson
Harvest Natural Foods
130 W Broadway
307-733-5418

PLEASE NOTE: Addresses, telephone numbers and Web sites listed in this book are accurate at the time of publication but they are subject to frequent change.

Where You Can Buy Supplements On-Line

- www.mothernature.com
- www.nutricraze.com
- www.vitamin-connection.com
- www.herbalremedies.com
- www.vitacost.com
- www.drugstore.com
- www.nutritionalsupplements.com
- www.totaldiscountvitamins.com
- www.herbshop.com
- www.gnc.com
- www.theherbsplace.com
- www.vitaminlife.com
- www.soulhealer.com
- www.searchingforherbs.com
- www.ripplecreek.com
- www.iherb.com
- www.evitamins.com
- www.virtuvites.com
- www.health-happiness.com
- www.herbvine.com
- www.springvalleyherbs.com
- www.freedavitamins.com
- www.nutrinadirect.com
- www.vitaminexpress.com
- www.internationalsupplements.com
- www.supplementauthority.com
- www.wellfx.com
- www.medwing.com
- www.allstarhealth.com
- www.advantagenutrition.com
- www.affordablesupplements.com
- www.eclecticherb.com
- www.naturalconnections.com
- www.meganutrition.com
- www.herbsmd.com
- www.vitaganza.com
- www.greatestherbsonearth.com
- www.vitaminshoppe.com
- www.hilife-vitamins.com
- www.vitaminlife.com
- www.vnfnutrition.com
- www.koshervitamins.com
- www.houseofnutrition.com
- www.smartbomb.com
- www.vitaminbargain.com
- www.healthwaynaturalfoods.com
- www.supervaluevitamins.com
- www.vitaminproshop.com
- www.btnature.com
- www.vitaminusa.com
- www.thegoodearth.net
- www.burmansnaturalfoods.com
- www.incrediblenutrition.com
- www.healthyeden.com
- www.tunies.com
- www.onevitaminway.com
- www.alternativesnatural.com
- www.healthydaysonline.com
- www.supervaluenutrition.com
- www.mistergreengenes.com
- www.stayleaner.com
- www.vitaminsandsuch.net
- www.n101.com
- www.discountvitaminshop.com
- www.4naturesfinest.com
- www.birrs.net/katsherbs
- www.health-marketplace.com
- www.vitamins-and-health-info.com
- www.allnatural.net
- www.findsupplements.com
- www.lifeplusvitamins.com
- www.nowfoods.com
- www.vitamin-resource.com
- www.thebetterhealthstore.com
- www.nutrimart.com
- www.vitasaver.com
- www.naturallydirect.net
- www.naturemade.com
- www.cybervitamins.com
- www.herbalhut.com
- www.a1supplements.com
- www.ediblenature.com
- www.bestofnutrition.com
- www.valuenutritioncenter.com
- www.toolsforwellness.com
- www.discount-vitamins-herbs.net

- www.health-heart.org/vitamins.htm
- www.americannutrition.com
- www.naturalways.com
- www.enkueros.net
- www.epic4health.com
- www.wholefoodsmarket.ca
- www.watertogo.com
- www.wonderlabs.com
- www.bestpricevitamins.com
- www.puritan.com
- www.justintimevitamins.com
- www.wholehealthproducts.com
- www.smartbodyz.com
- www.vitamintrader.com
- www.shopnatural.com
- www.healthyroads.com
- www.nutricentre.com
- www.4nutritionalsupplements.com
- www.worldimage.com
- www.truefoodsmarket.com
- www.youngagain.org
- www.naturesrs.com
- www.wholesale-vitamins-herbals.com
- www.nutritiongeeks.com
- www.netheal.com
- www.wellnesstrader.com
- www.health-n-energy.com
- www.vitaminlab.com
- www.kalahealth.com
- www.vitamindiscountwarehouse.com
- www.thevitaminbin.com
- www.1001herbs.com
- www.healthworks2000.com
- www.flaxseedpro.com
- www.goldenflax.com
- www.vitaminworld.com
- www.seacoastvitamins.com
- www.doctorstrust.com
- www.egetbetter.com
- www.vigorousliving.com

PLEASE NOTE: Addresses, telephone numbers and Web sites listed in this book are accurate at the time of publication but they are subject to frequent change.

GLOSSARY

acetic acid—CH₃COOH; a sour, colorless liquid found in vinegar.

acetyl—CH₃CO; a two-carbon acetic acid molecule from which a hydroxyl group (OH) has been removed.

acetyl-coenzyme A (acetyl-COA)—a condensation product of acetic acid and coenzyme A. It is an intermediate in the transfer of two-carbon molecules in the metabolism of sugars and fatty acids.

acetylation—the formation of an acetyl derivative.

acetylcholine—a chemical formed by choline and an acetyl group. It is a neurotransmitter in the nervous system used to transmit nerve impulses. Acetylcholine slows down heart rate, dilates blood vessels, and increases activity of the gastrointestinal system. In the brain, acetylcholine is involved with learning and memory.

acetylcholinesterase—the enzyme that breaks down acetylcholine into choline and acetate or acetic acid. It is located in the synaptic cleft.

ACTH (adrenocorticotrophic hormone)—a hormone secreted by the pituitary gland. It stimulates the adrenal gland to make steroids, particularly cortisol. ACTH is released in response to stress, leading to high cortisol levels.

ADD (attention deficit disorder)—a common neurological condition in children characterized by learning difficulties and poor attention.

ADHD (attention deficit hyperactivity disorder)—similar to ADD; children with ADHD additionally suffer with poor impulse control and hyperactive behavior.

affective disorders—psychological conditions involving mood, such as depression and bipolar disorder.

age-related cognitive decline (ARCD)—the gradual loss of mental abilities with age.

agonist—a drug or compound capable of attaching to a receptor and initiating a reaction. Compare with antagonist.

alkaloid—any of hundreds of compounds found in plants with a nitrogen atom connected to two-carbon atoms, and often formed in a ring structure. Many commonly known chemicals and drugs are alkaloids, including nicotine, cocaine, quinine, morphine, and ephedrine.

Alzheimer's disease—A progressive brain disease leading to memory loss, interference with thinking abilities, and other losses of mental powers. Brain cells show degenerative damage. Neurons that use the neurotransmitter acetylcholine are most affected.

amino acid—a molecule that contains nitrogen and serves as a unit of structure for proteins.

amyloid—any of a group of proteins that deposit in the brain and cause amyloidosis. Amyloidosis is often associated with Alzheimer's disease.

analgesic—a drug that reduces or takes away pain.

androgen—a hormone that encourages the development of male sexual characteristics. Some of the androgens made by the adrenal glands are DHEA, androstenedione, and testosterone.

antagonist—a drug or compound that interferes with the action of, or counteracts the action of, another drug.

antioxidant—a substance that combines with damaging molecules, neutralizes them, and thus prevents the deterioration of DNA, RNA, lipids, and proteins. Vitamins C, E, and beta-carotene are the best-known antioxidants, but more and more are being discovered each year.

ARCD—see Age-related cognitive decline.

atherosclerosis—a condition in which the arteries in the heart and other parts of the body accumulate plaque and become narrow, decreasing the flow of blood and increasing the risk for a clot; it's also known as "hardening of the arteries."

atom—the ultimate, indivisible, and smallest particle of an element. For instance, hydrogen and oxygen are atoms. When two hydrogen atoms and one oxygen atom get together, they form a molecule of water.

ATP (adenosine triphosphate)—the primary energy currency of a cell, derived from the metabolism of glucose, amino acids, and fatty acids.

ayurveda—a traditional system of medicine practiced in India since the first century A.D. Ayurvedic practitioners combine herbs, oils, and other natural systems in treating diseases. Many herbs used in Ayurvedic medicine are now gaining popularity in Western countries.

benzodiazepine—a class of medicines such as Valium, Dalmane, and Xanax that act on GABA receptors to induce relaxation and sleep. Too much, used too often, can lead to memory loss. There are also receptors in the brain for benzodiazepines.

blood-brain barrier—the filtering system that prevents some of the substances in the regular circulatory system to easily get into the brain. Most of the nutrient supplements discussed in this book have the ability to cross this barrier.

capillaries—very small, hairline-thin vessels supplying blood to tissues.

cardiolipin—one of the components of a cell membrane.

catecholamines—neurotransmitters such as dopamine, norepinephrine, and epinephrine.

catecholaminergic system—neurons that use catecholamines.

cell—the smallest organized unit of living structure in the body. There are trillions of cells in humans. The brain alone has close to one trillion.

cell membrane—a thin layer consisting mostly of fatty acids that surrounds each cell.

central nervous system—the brain and the nerves in the spinal cord. The peripheral nervous system refers to the nerves in the body outside of the central nervous system.

cerebrum—the upper, main part of the brain, consisting of left and right sides. It controls voluntary thought and movements.

cerebral cortex—the outer part of the cerebrum.

cholesterol—the most abundant steroid in animal tissues. It is present in some of the animal foods we eat. Our liver can also make some if there's not enough in our diet. Cholesterol is used to make steroid hormones.

cholinergic system—brain cells that use the neurotransmitter acetylcholine.

coenzyme—a substance that is necessary or enhances the activity of an enzyme. Several vitamins act as coenzymes.

cognition—mental activities such as thinking, memory, perception, judgment, and learning.

cognitive—involving cognition.

control—in any study, whenever a group of animals or humans are given a certain medicine, they are compared to a second group of animals or humans who are in similar circumstances regarding everything except the medicine. This second group is known as the control. This way, researchers can find out the role of the medicine independent of any other factors.

cortisol—same as hydrocortisone, a sterol (related to a steroid) secreted by the human adrenal glands. It is often released in high amounts during stress. High doses lead to interference with the proper functioning of the immune system.

coumadin—a drug that has blood-thinning abilities, often prescribed for patients who clot easily.

crossover—in a research study, the placebo and medicine groups are switched (crossed over) to determine a more accurate effect of the medicine. The group that initially got the medicine now gets the placebo, and the group that initially got the placebo now gets the medicine.

cytokines—hormonelike small proteins secreted by the immune system.

cytoplasm—the fluid gel substance inside a cell, enclosed by the cell membrane. It does not include the nucleus.

dementia—the loss of intellectual function caused by a variety of disorders. Alzheimer's disease is a type of dementia.

dendrite—the treelike branching arms of a neuron.

diosgenin—a saponin found in the roots of plants such as the yam. In the laboratory, parts of diosgenin can be cleaved in order to make certain steroids. Our body is not known to have the proper enzymes to convert diosgenin into pregnenolone, progesterone, or DHEA. Therefore, ingesting wild-yam extracts will not lead to DHEA production.

dopamine—a neurotransmitter made from tyrosine and L-dopa.

dopaminergic—brain cells that use dopamine as their neurotransmitter.

double-blind—a research study where neither the researchers nor the volunteers know who's getting the medicine and who's getting the placebo until the code is broken at the end of the study.

epinephrine—a hormone made by the medulla (center) of the adrenal gland, and also made in the brain and other parts of the nervous system. It is a potent stimulator of heart rate, tightens some blood vessels while relaxing others, and relaxes the bronchi (tubes) in the lungs. In the brain it is considered a neurotransmitter that leads to alertness and vigilance. Epinephrine is made from nor-epinephrine.

estrogen—a hormone made by the ovaries, adrenal glands, and also in various cells of the body. Estrogen promotes female characteristics. The most common estrogens are estrone, estradiol, and estriol. Premarin, the product name of conjugated estrogens, is actually derived from the urine of horses.

excitotoxin—toxins that bind to certain receptors such as glutamate receptors in neurons, and cause injury or death to these neurons.

fat—a greasy material found in animal tissues and made from glycerol attached to three fatty acids.

fatty acid—a long-chain molecule made of carbon atoms and capped at the end with a carboxyl group (COOH).

GABA—gamma-aminobutyric acid, a brain chemical that causes sedation. Medicines such as Valium act on receptors for GABA to induce relaxation. GABA also refers to the receptors themselves.

glucocorticoid—any steroid-like compound capable of significantly influencing some aspects of metabolism, such as the promotion of glycogen deposition in the liver, and having anti-inflammatory effects. Cortisol is the most potent of the naturally occurring glucocorticoids, but some synthetic derivatives, such as prednisone, are more potent.

glucose—a sugar found in foods, and the product of the digestion of starches. It is the primary compound metabolized for energy in the brain.

glutamate—an amino acid found in proteins that also acts as a neurotransmitter in the brain.

glycerol—a three-carbon substance that forms the backbone of fatty acids in fats.

gonad—a testicle or ovary.

HDL—see Lipoprotein.

hippocampus—a complex, convoluted structure located in the brain involved in many functions including memory.

homocysteine—an intermediary compound in the metabolism of the amino acid methionine. High levels in the blood can cause atherosclerosis. Recently it has been suspected that high amounts of homocysteine can also be toxic to neurons. B vitamins, particularly folic acid, B-12, and B-6, can lower homocysteine levels.

hormone—a chemical messenger produced by a gland or organ that influences a number of metabolic actions in nearby or distant cells.

hydrogenation—the process of adding hydrogen to unsaturated fatty acids in order to make them harder. Many processed foods are hydrogenated, making them potentially unhealthy.

hypothalamus—a small area of the brain above and behind the roof of the mouth. The hypothalamus is prominently involved with the functions of the autonomic nervous system (the independent nervous system outside of voluntary control) and the hormonal system. It also plays a role in mood and motivation.

immune globulins—a group of proteins found in blood. Immune globlins (or immuno-globulins) fight off infections by attaching to and killing bacteria and viruses. The best known is gamma globulin.

immunomodulatory—a substance that has an influence on the immune system.

in vitro—a Latin term, meaning a study performed in a laboratory and not involving animals or humans.

in vivo—a Latin term, meaning a study performed on animals or humans.

inositol—an essential nutrient made from glucose that forms part of phosphatidyl-inositol, one of the phospholipids in the cell membrane. Inositol is widely available in foods and can be made in the human body when needed.

insulin—a hormone made by the pancreas that helps regulate blood-sugar levels.

interferon—a small protein produced by white blood cells to fight some forms of cancer and infections, especially viral infections.

interleukin—similar to interferon; a small protein produced by white blood cells to fight infections and some forms of cancer. There are many types of interleukins, numbered 1, 2, 3...up to 10 or more. Some interleukins have beneficial effects; others are harmful.

LDL—see Lipoprotein.

libido—sex drive.

lipid—a fat-soluble substance.

lipofuscin—"wear-and-tear" brown pigment granules consisting of lipid-containing residues of metabolism. These granules can be found in liver, brain, and heart muscle, and are a sign of aging.

lipoproteins—compounds that contain lipids and proteins. Almost all of the lipids in blood, including cholesterol, are transported as lipoprotein complexes. There are a number of these lipoproteins in blood. The two best known by the public are HDL (high-density lipoproteins, the "good" cholesterol) and LDL (low-density lipoproteins, the "bad" cholesterol).

lymphocyte—a type of white blood cell that fights infections. Two major types are B lymphocytes and T lymphocytes.

lymphokine—a substance released by lymphocytes to help with immune function. Interferon is a type of lymphokine.

macrophage—a large cell of the immune system that has the ability to be phagocytic, that is, engulf and kill germs. This cell is also thought to be involved in plaque formation in arteries.

macular degeneration—the macula is the small area in the retina of the eye, 3 to 5 millimeters in size, that provides the sharpest and clearest vision. The macula can degenerate with the aging process, perhaps due to oxidation. The fatty acid DHA is present in large amounts in the retina.

metabolism—the continuous chemical and physical processes in the body involving the creation and breakdown of molecules; for instance, glucose can be metabolized to release its energy as ATP.

methyl—a molecule made of carbon and three hydrogen atoms. A methyl donor is any substance that can donate a methyl group to another molecule.

mitochondria—the chemical factories of cells, where energy is made. Thousands of mitochondria are present in each cell.

molecule—the smallest possible combination of atoms that retains the chemical properties of the substance. For instance, a molecule of water consists of three atoms— two are hydrogen and one is oxygen.

monoamine oxidase—the enzyme that breaks down dopamine, norepinephrine, and epinephrine in synapses. Two types are present, types A and B. Certain drugs can inhibit the action of MAOs; these drugs are called MAO inhibitors.

multiple sclerosis—a chronic disease in which there is loss of myelin (the covering of a nerve) in the central nervous system; it is characterized by speech defects and loss of muscular coordination.

natural killer cell—a type of white blood cell that can destroy certain cancer cells and germs.

nerve-growth factor—a type of compound in the brain involved in stimulating the growth of nerve cells.

neural—any structure composed of nerve cells.

neuron—a cell in the brain. There are billions of neurons in the brain that communicate with each other, using neurotransmitters, through connections called synapses.

neurotransmitter—a biochemical substance, such as norepinephrine, serotonin, dopamine, acetylcholine, and endorphin, that relays messages from one neuron to another.

norepinephrine—a hormone made by the brain and the adrenal gland. It is similar in some ways to epinephrine, but weaker.

NSAID (non-steroidal anti-inflammatory drug)—a group of drugs, such as aspirin and ibuprofen, that reduce inflammation by acting on prostaglandins and other substances.

omega—the twenty-fourth and final letter of the Greek alphabet. In naming fatty acids, omega signifies the last carbon on the chain.

omega-3—fatty acids whose first double bond is three carbons away from the end.

omega-6—fatty acids whose first double bond is six carbons away from the end.

organelle—a small structure in the cell. Mitochondria are a type of organelle.

oxidant—a substance that causes oxidation.

oxidation—the process by which a compound reacts with oxygen and loses a hydrogen or electron.

PDV (percent daily value)—a nutritional guideline on the appropriate doses of different vitamins and minerals required for good health. The values are similar to, but generally toward the upper range of, the RDA.

peptide—a compound made from two or more amino acids. Very long chains of amino acids are called proteins.

perinatal—occurring before, during, or after birth.

peroxidation—the process by which fatty acids get oxidized.

phospholipids—fatty acids combined with the mineral phosphorus and other molecules that make up the lining of a cell membrane.

placebo—a dummy pill that contains no active ingredient.

placebo-controlled—a study where a group of volunteers gets a medicine and another group, called the control, gets a placebo.

platelet—a small, round, or oval cell found in the blood, which is involved in blood-clotting.

postpartum—the period after childbirth.

precursor—a substance that precedes and is the source of another substance; for instance, 5-HTP is the precursor to serotonin.

pro-oxidant—a substance that causes oxidation and damage to cells and surrounding molecules. Some antioxidants in very high doses can turn into pro-oxidants.

prostaglandin—one of a number of substances derived from fatty acids and involved in a number of important functions in tissues and cells.

randomized—a study where the volunteers are assigned to receive a medicine or a placebo without bias.

RDA (recommended daily allowance)—a nutritional guideline proposed by the government on the appropriate doses of different vitamins and minerals required for good health. Some scientists think that ingesting more than the RDA for certain nutrients may provide additional health benefits. PDV, or percent daily value, is a number similar to the RDA.

receptor—a special arrangement on a cell that recognizes a molecule and interacts with it. This allows the molecule to either enter the cell or to stimulate it in a specific way. Neurotransmitters, such as serotonin, have receptors that they interact with.

remethylation—replacing a methyl group on a substance.

retina—the back of the eye where light falls and visual input is perceived and later transmitted to the brain for interpretation. The retina contains a large amount of the fatty acid DHA.

reuptake—when a neurotransmitter is released into the synaptic cleft, it is either broken down by enzymes or returns back to the neuron that released it in the first place; the latter process is called a reuptake.

saponin—compounds of plant origin found commonly in herbs such as ginseng, cat's claw, and licorice root, and some vegetables such as yams.

serotonergic—nerves that use serotonin for communication.

serotonin—a brain chemical (neurotransmitter) that relays messages between brain cells (neurons). It is one of the primary mood-regulating neurotransmitters. It is derived from the amino acid tryptophan. Serotonin can also be converted to melatonin.

steroid—a large family of chemical substances that includes hormones and drugs that have a chemical structure comprised of a few rings attached to each other. Most steroids contain twenty-seven or more carbon atoms.

sterol—a steroid of twenty-seven or more carbon atoms with one OH (alcohol) group.

substantia nigra—a large, dark-colored cell mass in the middle of the brain involved in controlling movement. Damage to the SN leads to the movement disorder known as Parkinson's disease.

synapse—a connection between two neurons.

synaptic cleft—the small gap at a synapse, between neurons, where neurotransmitters are released.

testosterone—a hormone made by the testicles and adrenal glands, and also in various cells of the body, that promotes masculine traits.

thromboxane—a group of compounds biochemically related to the prostaglandins and initially made from fatty acids. Different fatty acids lead to different thromboxanes, and each type of thromboxane has a different action. For instance, thromboxane B-2 can induce clot formation.

trans-fatty acids—fatty acids that have been altered by food processing and take on abnormal shapes not normally useful to the body.

triglyceride—a type of fat that circulates in the bloodstream. A glycerol molecule forms the backbone to which one, two, or three fatty acids attach. High blood triglyceride levels can lead to atherosclerosis (blockage of arteries).

tripeptide—a substance made from three amino acids.

BIBLIOGRAPHY

Baskys, A., and G. Remington. *Brain Mechanisms and Psychotropic Drugs*. CRC Press: Boca Raton, Florida, 1996.

Cass, H., and P. Holford. *Natural Highs*. Avery: New York, 2003.

Cooper, J. R., Bloom, F. E., and R. H. Roth. *The Biochemical Basis of Neuropharmacology*, 8th edition. Oxford University Press: New York, 2003.

Dean, W., Morgenthaler, J., and S. Fowkes. *Smart Drugs II: The Next Generation*. Smart Publications: Petaluma, California, 1993.

Frankel, P., and F. Madsen. *Stop Homocysteine Through the Methylation Process*. TRC Publications: Thousand Oaks, California, 1998.

Lombard, J., and C. Germano. *The Brain Wellness Plan*. Kensington Books: New York, 2000.

Marks, D. B., Marks, A.D., and C. M. Smith. *Basic Medical Biochemistry: A Clinical Approach*. Lippincott Williams & Wilkins: Baltimore, Maryland, 1996.

McCully, K. S. *The Homocysteine Revolution*. Contemporary Books/McGraw–Hill: New York, 1999.

Sahelian, R., and D. Tuttle. *Creatine: Nature's Muscle Builder*. Avery: New York, 1998.

Ibid. *DHEA: A Practical Guide*. Avery: New York, 1996.

Ibid. *5-HTP: Nature's Serotonin Solution*. Avery: New York, 1998.

Ibid. *Kava: The Miracle Antianxiety Herb*. St. Martin's Press: New York, 1998.

Schmidt, M. *Brain-Building Nutrition: The Healing Power of Fats & Oils*. Frog, Ltd.: Berkeley, California, 2001.

Siegel, G. J., Agranoff, B. W., and M. E. Uhler, eds. *Basic Neurochemistry: Molecular, Cellular, and Medical Aspects*, 6th edition. Lippincott Williams & Wilkins: Baltimore, Maryland, 1998.

Shils, M. E., Olson, J. A., M. Shike, and A. C. Ross, eds. *Modern Nutrition in Health and Disease*, 9th edition. Lippincott Williams & Wilkins: Baltimore, Maryland, 1998.

Simopoulos, A. P., and J. Robinson. *The Omega Diet*. Quill: New York, 1999.

Stedman's Medical Dictionary, 27th edition. Lippincott Williams & Wilkins: Baltimore, Maryland, 2000.

Tyler, V. E., and S. Foster. *Tyler's Honest Herbal*. Haworth Press: Binghamton, New York, 1999.

REFERENCES

Aloia, R., and W. Mlekusch, 1988. "Techniques of quantitative analysis of organ and membrane phospholipids and cholesterol." In *Methods of Studying Membrane Fluidity*. Alan R. Liss, Inc: New York.

Alvarez X. A., et al., 1997. "Citicoline improves memory performance in elderly subjects." *Methods Find. Exp. Clin. Pharmacol.* 19(3):201–10.

Babb, S. M., et al., 1996. "Differential effect of CDP-choline on brain cytosolic choline levels in younger and older subjects as measured by proton magnetic resonance spectroscopy." *Psychopharmacology* 127(2):88–94.

Balestreri, R., et al., 1987. "A double-blind placebo-controlled evaluation of the safety and efficacy of vinpocetine in the treatment of patients with chronic vascular senile cerebral dysfunction." *J. Am. Geriatr. Soc.* 35(5):425–30.

Barak, A. J., et al., 1996. "Betaine, ethanol, and the liver: a review." *Alcohol* 13(4):395–8.

Barkworth, M. F., et al., 1985. "An early phase I study to determine the tolerance, safety and pharmacokinetics of idebenone following multiple oral doses." *Arzneimittelforschung* 35(11):1704–7.

Bell, K. M., et al., 1994. "S-adenosylmethionine blood levels in major depression: changes with drug treatment." *Acta. Neurol. Scand.* Suppl; 154:15–8.

Bella, R., et al., 1990. "Effect of acetyl-L-carnitine on geriatric patients suffering from dysthymic disorders." *Int. J. Clin. Pharmacol. Res.* 10(6):355–60.

Benton, D., Griffiths, R., and J. Haller, 1997. "Thiamine supplementation on mood and cognitive functioning." *Psychopharmacology (Berl).* 129(1):66–71.

Benton, D., Haller, J., and J. Fordy, 1995. "Vitamin supplementation for one year improves mood." *Neuropsychobiology* 32(2):98–105.

Benton, D., and P. Y. Parker, 1998. "Breakfast, blood glucose, and cognition." *Am. J. Clin. Nutr.* 67(4):772S–778S.

Bergamasco, B., et al., 1994. "Idebenone, a new drug in the treatment of cognitive impairment in patients with dementia of the Alzheimer type." *Funct. Neurol.* 9(3):161–8.

Bertoni-Freddari, C., et al., 1991. "Neurobiology of the aging brain: morphological alterations at synaptic regions." *Arch. Geron. Ger.* 12: 253–60.

Bhattacharya, S. K., Satyan, K. S., and S. Ghosal, 1997. "Antioxidant activity of glycowithanolides from Withania somnifera." *Indian J. Exp. Biol.* 35(3):236–9.

Birdsall, T. C., 1998. "Therapeutic applications of taurine." *Altern. Med. Rev.* 3(2):128–36.

Birkmayer, G. D., et al., 1991. "The coenzyme nicotinamide adenine dinucleotide (NADH) as biological antidepressive agent: experience with 205 patients." *New Trends Clin. Neuropharm.* 5:75–86.

Birkmayer, J. G. D., et al., 1993. "NADH—a new therapeutic approach to Parkinson's disease, comparison of oral and parenteral application." *Acta Neurol. Scand.* 87(Suppl 146):32–35.

Birkmayer, J. G. D., et al., 1996. "The new therapeutic approach for improving dementia of the Alzheimer type." *Ann. Clin. Lab. Sci.* 26:1–9.

Black, J., et al., 1991. "Usual versus successful aging: some notes on experiential factors." *Neurobiol. Aging* 12:325–28.

Blanchard, J., et al., 1997. "Pharmacokinetic perspectives on megadoses of ascorbic acid." *Am. J. Clin. Nutr.* 66(5):1165–71.

Blokland, A., et al., 1999. "Cognition-enhancing properties of subchronic phosphatidylserine (PS) treatment in middle-aged rats: comparison of bovine cortex PS with egg PS and soybean PS." *Nutrition* 15(10):778–83.

Bottiglieri, T., Hyland, K., and E. H. Reynolds, 1994. "The clinical potential of S-adenosylmethionine in brain mapping, cerebrovascular hemodynamics, and immune factors." *Ann. N.Y. Acad. Sci.* 17;777:399–403.

Bressa, G. M., 1994. "S-adenosyl-methionine (SAMe) as antidepressant: meta-analysis of clinical studies." *Acta. Neurol. Scand. Suppl.* 154:7–14.

Bruhwyler, J., et al., 1998. "Facilitatory effects of chronically administered citicoline on learning and memory processes in the dog." *Prog. Neuropsychopharmacol. Biol. Psychiatry* 22(1):115–28.

Busse, E., et al., 1992. "Influence of alpha-lipoic acid on intracellular glutathione in vitro and in vivo." *Arzneimitterlforschung* 42:829–31.

Byung, K., et al., 1998. "Melatonin protects nigral dopaminergic neurons from 1-methyl-4-phenylpyridinium (MPP) neurotoxicity in rats." *Neuroscience Letters* 245:61–64.

Cacabelos, R., et al., 1996. "Therapeutic effects of CDP-choline in Alzheimer's disease. Cognition, brain mapping, cerebrovascular hemodynamics, and immune factors." *Ann. N.Y. Acad. Sci.* 17;777:399–403.

Caffarra, P., et al., 1980. "The effect of Deanol on amnesic disorders. A preliminary trial (author's transl)." *Ateneo Parmense* [*Acta Biomed.*] 51(4):383–9.

Campbell, F., et al., 1998. "Placental membrane fatty acid-binding protein preferentially binds arachidonic and docosahexanoic acids." *Life Sciences* 63:235–40.

Cardoso, S. M., et al., 1998. "The protective effect of vitamin E, idebenone and reduced glutathione on free radical mediated injury in rat brain synaptosomes." *Biochem. Biophys. Res. Commun.* 29;246(3):703–10.

Carta, A., et al., 1993. "Acetyl-L-carnitine and Alzheimer's disease: pharmacological considerations beyond the cholinergic sphere." *Ann. N.Y. Acad. Sci.* 4;695:324–6.

Caso Marasco, A., et al., 1996. "Double-blind study of a multivitamin complex supplemented with ginseng extract." *Drugs Exp. Clin. Res.* 22(6):323–9.

Cenacchi, T., et al., 1993. "Cognitive decline in the elderly: a double-blind, placebo-controlled multicenter study on efficacy of phosphatidylserine administration." *Aging: Clinical and Experimental Research* (Italy) 5:123–33.

Cestaro, B., 1994. "Effects of arginine, S-adenosylmethionine and polyamines on nerve regeneration." *Acta. Neurol. Scand.* Suppl; 154:32–41.

Charlton, C. G., 1997. "Depletion of nigrostriatal and forebrain tyrosine hydroxylase by S-adenosylmethionine: a model that may explain the occurrence of depression in Parkinson's disease." *Life Sciences* 61;5:495–502.

Cheng, D. H., Ren, H., and X. C. Tang, 1996. "Huperzine A, a novel promising acetylcholinesterase inhibitor." *Neuroreport.* 20;8(1):97–101.

Cheng, D. H., and X. C. Tang, 1998. "Comparative studies of huperzine A, E2020, and tacrine on behavior and cholinesterase activities." *Pharmacol. Biochem. Behav.* 60(2):377–86.

Chung, H., et al., 1999. "Ginkgo biloba extract increases ocular blood flow velocity." *J. Ocul. Pharmacol. Ther.* 15(3):233–40.

Cipolli, C., and G. Chiari, 1990. "Effects of L-acetylcarnitine on mental deterioration in the aged: initial results." *Clin. Ter. Mar.* 31;132(6 Suppl):479–510.

Crook, et al., 1991. "Effects of phosphatidylserine in age-associated memory impairment." *Neurology* 41:644–49.

Crook, T., et al., 1992. "Effects of phosphatidylserine in Alzheimer's disease." *Psychopharmacology Bulletin* 28:61–66.

D'Angelo, L., et al., 1986. "A double-blind, placebo-controlled clinical study on the effect of a standardized ginseng extract on psychomotor performance in healthy volunteers." *J. Ethnopharmacol.* 16(1):15–22.

Davis, M. A., et al., 1993. "Differential effect of cyanohydroxybutene on glutathione synthesis in liver and pancreas of male rats." *Toxicol. Appl. Pharmacol.* 123:257–64.

Davis, S., et al., 1996. "Androgens and the postmenopausal woman." *J. Clin. Endocrinol. Metab.* 81:2759–63.

De Deyn, P. P., et al., 1998. "Superoxide dismutase activity in cerebro-spinal fluid of patients with dementia and some other neurological disorders." *Alzheimer Dis. Assoc. Disord.* 12(1):26–32.

Dhuley, J. N., 1998. "Effect of ashwagandha on lipid peroxidation in stress-induced animals." *J. Ethnopharmacol.* 60(2):173–8.

Dini, A., et al., 1994. "Chemical composition of *Lepidium meyenii*." *Food Chemistry* 49:347–49.

Drevon, C. A., 1992, "Marine oils and their effects." *Nutrition Reviews* 50(4):38–45.

Elsakka, M., et al., 1990. "New data referring to chemistry of *Withania somnifera* species." *Rev. Med. Chir. Soc. Med. Nat. Lasi.* 94(2):385–7.

Engel, R. R., et al., 1992. "Double-blind crossover study of phosphatidylserine versus placebo in patients with early dementia of the Alzheimer type." *Eur. Neuropsychopharmacol.* 2(2):149–55.

Fariello, R. G., Ferraro, T. N., and G. T. Golden, 1988. "Systemic acetyl-L-carnitine elevates nigral levels of glutathione and GABA." *Life Sci.* 43:289–92.

Ferris, S. H., et al., 1977. "Semile dementia: treatment with deanol." *J. Am. Geriatr. Soc.* 25(6):241–4.

Fisman, M., et al., 1981. "Double-blind trial of 2-dimethylaminoethanol in Alzheimer's disease." *Am. J. Psychiatry* 138(7):970–2.

Flood, J., Morley, J., and E. Roberts, 1995. "Pregnenolone sulfate enhances post-training memory processes when injected in very low doses into limbic system structures: the amygdala is by far the most sensitive." *Proc. Natl. Acad. Sci.* 7;92:10806–10.

Forsyth, L. M., et al., 1998. "The use of NADH as a new therapeutic approach in chronic fatigue syndrome." Presented at the 1998 annual meeting of the American College of Allergy, Asthma and Immunology.

Gerster, H., 1998. "Can adults adequately convert alpha-linolenic acid (18:3n-3) to eicosapentaenoic acid (20:5n-3) and docosahexaenoic acid (22:6n-3)?" *Int. J. Vitam. Nutr. Res.* 68(3):159–73.

Gillin, J. C., et al., 1981. "Effects of lecithin on memory and plasma choline levels: a study in normal volunteers." In *Cholinergic mechanisms: phylogenetic aspects, central and peripheral synapses and clinical significance*; Pepeu, G., and Ladinsky, H., eds; New York: Plenum Press, 937–45.

Gillis, J. C., Benefield, P., and D. McTavish, 1994. "Idebenone. A review of its pharmacodynamic and pharmacokinetic properties, and therapeutic use in age-related cognitive disorders." *Drugs Aging* 5(2):133–52.

Gispin, W., 1993. "Neuronal plasticity and function." *Clin. Neuropharm.* 16S:5–11.

Grioli, S., 1990. "Pyroglutamic acid improves the age-associated memory impairment." *Fundam. Clin. Pharmaco.* 4(2):169–73.

Hamazaki, T., et al., 1996. "The effect of docosahexanoic acid on aggression in young adults: a placebo-controlled double-blind study." *J. Clin. Invest.* 97;4:1129–1134.

Ibid., 1998. "Docosahexaenoic acid does not affect aggression of normal volunteers under nonstressful conditions. A randomized, placebo-controlled, double-blind study." *Lipids* 33(7):663–7.

Hansen, J. B., et al., 1998. "Effects of highly purified eicosapentanoic acid and docosahexaenoic acid on fatty acid absorption, incorporation into serum phospholipids and postprandial triglyceridemia." *Lipids* 33(2):131–8.

Hibbeln, J. R., 1998. "Fish consumption and major depression [letter]." *Lancet* Apr 18;351(9110):1213.

Hindmarch I., et al., 1991. "Efficacy and tolerance of vinpocetine in ambulant patients suffering from mild-to-moderate organic psychosyndromes." *Int. Clin. Psychopharmacol* 6(1):31–43.

Holford, N. H., and K. Peace, 1994. "The effect of tacrine and lecithin in Alzheimer's disease. A population pharmacodynamic analysis of five clinical trials." *Eur. J. Clin. Pharmacol.* 47(1):17–23.

Jin, Z., et al., 1997. "Anti-aging effects of codonopsis and astragalus combination." *International J. Oriental Med.* 22:57–63.

Joseph, J. A., et al., 1998. "Long-term dietary strawberry, spinach, or vitamin E supplementation retards the onset of age-related neuronal signal-transduction and cognitive behavioral deficits." *J. Neurosci.* 18(19):8047–55.

Jumpsen, J. A., et al., 1997. "During neuronal and glial cell development diet n-6 to n-3 fatty acid ratio alters the fatty acid composition of phosphatidylinositol and phosphatidylserine." *Biochimica et Biophysica Acta.* 1347:40–50.

Kalaria, R. N., and S. Harik, 1992. "Carnitine acetyltransferase activity in the human brain and its microvessels is decreased in Alzheimer's disease." *Ann. Neurol.* 32(4):583–6.

Kelly, G. S. 1997. "Clinical applications of N-acetylcysteine." *Altern. Med. Rev.* 3(2):114–27.

Ibid., 1997. "Pantethine: a review of its biochemistry and therapeutic applications." *Altern. Med. Rev.* 5:365–77. (Excellent review article.)

Kiss, B., and E. Karpati, 1996. "Mechanism of action of vinpocetine." *Acta. Pharm. Hung.* 66(5):213–24.

Klein, J., et al., 1998. "Regulation of free choline in rat brain: dietary and pharmacological manipulations." *Neurochem. Int.* 32(5–6):479–85.

Labrie, F., et al., 1997. "Effect of 12-month dehydroepiandrosterone replacement therapy on bone, vagina, and endometrium in postmenopausal women." *J. Clin. Endocrinol. Metab.* 82:3498–3505.

Ladd, S. L., et al., 1993. "Effect of phosphatidylcholine on explicit memory." *Clinical Neuropharmacology* 16;6:540–9.

Landbo, C., and T. Almdal, 1998. ["Interaction between warfarin and coenzyme Q10."] *Ugeskr Laeger* 25;160(22):3226–7.

Laugharne, J. D., Mellor, J. E., and M. Peet, 1996. "Fatty acids and schizophrenia." *Lipids* 31 Suppl:S163–5.

Le Bars, P. L., et al., 1997. "A placebo-controlled, double-blind randomized trial of an extract of ginkgo biloba for dementia." *JAMA* 278:1327–32.

Linde, K, et al., 1996. "St. John's wort for depression—an overview and meta-analysis of randomized clinical trials." *British Medical Journal* 313:253–8.

Little, A., et al., 1985. "A double-blind, placebo-controlled trial of high-dose lecithin in Alzheimer's disease." *Journal of Neurology, Neurosurgery & Psychiatry* 48(8):736–42.

Loehrer, F. M., et al., 1997. "Influence of oral S-adenosylmethionine on plasma 5-methyltetrahydrofolate, S-adenosylhomocysteine, homocysteine and methionine in healthy humans." *Pharmacol. Exp. Ther.* 282(2):845–50.

Loehrer, F. M., et al., 1996. "Effect of methionine loading on 5-methyltetrahydrofolate, S-adenosyl-methionine and S-adenosylhomocysteine in plasma of healthy humans." *Clin. Sci.* (Colch) 91(1):79–86.

Maccari, F., et al., 1990. "Levels of carnitines in brain and other tissues of rats of different ages: effect of acetyl-L-carnitine administration." *Experimental Gerontology* 25:127–34.

Marcus, D. L., et al., 1998. "Increased peroxidation and reduced antioxidant enzyme activity in Alzheimer's disease." *Exp. Neurol.* 150(1):40–4.

Marsh, G. R., and M. Linnoila, 1979. "The effects of deanol on cognitive performance and electrophysiology in elderly humans." *Psychopharmacology* (Berl) 66(1):99–104.

McCaddon, A., and C. L. Kelly, 1994. "Familial Alzheimer's disease and vitamin B-12 deficiency." *Age Ageing* 23(4):334–7.

McEwen, B. S., et al., 1997. "Ovarian steroids and the brain: implications for cognition and aging." *Neurology* 48(5 Suppl 7):S8–15.

Mehta, A. K., et al., 1991. "Pharmacological effects of *Withania somnifera* root extract on GABA receptor complex." *Indian J. Med. Res.* 94:312–5.

Mohs, R. C., et al., 1980. "Choline chloride effects on memory in the elderly." *Neurobiol. Aging* 1:21–5.

Morcos, N. C., 1997. "Modulation of lipid profile by fish oil and garlic combination." *J. Natl. Med. Assoc.* 89(10):673–8.

Mordente, A., et al., 1998. "Antioxidant properties of 2,3-dimethoxy-5-methyl-6-(10-hydroxydecyl)-1,4-benzoquinone (idebenone)." *Chem. Res. Toxicol.* 11(1):54–63.

Morris, M. C., et al., 1998. "Vitamin E and vitamin C supplement use and risk of incident Alzheimer disease." *Alzheimer. Dis. Assoc. Disord.* 12(3):121–6.

Orvisky, E., et al., 1997. "High-molecular-weight hyaluronan—a valuable tool in testing the antioxidative activity of amphiphilic drugs stobadine and vinpocetine." *J. Pharm. Biomed. Anal.* 16(3):419–24.

Ortega, R. M., et al., 1997. "Dietary intake and cognitive function in a group of elderly people." *Am. J. Clin. Nutr.* 66(4):803–9.

Packer, L., Roy, S., and C. K. Sen, 1997. "Alpha-lipoic acid: a metabolic antioxidant and potential redox modulator of transcription." *Advances in Pharmacology* 38:79–101.

Pappolla, M., et al., 1998. "Inhibition of Alzheimer beta-fibrillogenesis by melatonin." *J. Biol. Chem.* Mar. 27;273(13):7185–8.

Parnetti, L., 1995. "Clinical pharmacokinetics of drugs for Alzheimer's disease." *Clin. Pharmacokinet.* 29(2):110–29.

Parnetti, L., Bottiglieri, T., and D. Lowenthal, 1997. "Role of homocysteine in age-related vascular and non-vascular diseases." *Aging* (Milano) 9(4):241–57.

Passeri, M., et al., 1990. "Acetyl-L-carnitine in the treatment of mildly demented elderly patients." *Int. J. Clin. Pharmacol. Res.* 10(1–2):75–9.

Pearce, R. K., et al., 1997. "Alterations in the distribution of glutathione in the substantia nigra in Parkinson's disease." *J. Neural Transm.* 104(6-7):661–77.

Peet, M., et al., 1998. "Depletion of omega-3 fatty acid levels in red blood cell membranes of depressive patients." *Biol. Psychiatry* 1;43(5):315–9.

Perkins, A. et al., 1999. "Association of antioxidants with memory in a multiethnic elderly sample using the third national health and nutrition examination survey." *Am. J. Epid.* 150:37–44.

Pettegrew, J., et al., 1995. "Clinical and neurochemical effects of acetyl-L-carnitine in Alzheimer's disease." *Neurobiology of Aging* 16;1:1–4.

Piovesan, P., et al., 1994. "Acetyl-L-carnitine treatment increases choline acetyltransferase activity and NGF levels in the CNS of adult rats following total fimbria-fornix transection." *Brain Research* 633:77–82.

Pisano, P., et al., 1996. "Plasma concentrations and pharmacokinetics of idebenone and its metabolites following single and repeated doses in young patients with mitochondrial encephalomyopathy." *Eur. J. Clin. Pharmacol.* 51(2):167–9.

Porciatti V., et al., 1998. "Cytidine-5'-diphosphocholine improves visual acuity, contrast sensitivity and visually-evoked potentials of amblyopic subjects." *Curr. Eye. Res.* 17(2):141–8.

Prasad, M. R., et al., 1991. "Regional membrane phospholipid alterations in Alzheimer's disease." *Neurochemical Research* 23(1):81–88.

Purmova, J., and L. Opletal, 1995. "Phytotherapeutic aspects of diseases of the cardiovascular system. Saponins and possibilities of their use in prevention and therapy." *Ceska. Slov. Farm.* 44(5):246–51.

Qian, B. C., et al., 1995. "Pharmacokinetics of tablet huperzine A in six volunteers." *Chung Kuo Yao Li Hsueh Pao* 16(5):396–8.

Rai, G., et al., 1990. "Double-blind, placebo-controlled study of acetyl-L-carnitine in patients with Alzheimer's dementia." *Curr. Med. Res. Opin.* 11(10):638–47.

Refsum, H., et al., 1998. "Homocysteine and cardiovascular disease." *Annu. Rev. Med.* 49:31–62.

Riggs, K. M., et al., 1996. "Relations of vitamin B12, vitamin B6, folate, and homocysteine to cognitive performance in the normative aging." *Am. J. Clin. Nutr.* 63(3):306–14.

Sahelian, R., and S. Borken, 1998. "DHEA and cardiac arrhythmia." *Ann. Int. Med.* Oct 1; volume 129;7:588.

Rupprecht, R., and F. Holsboer, 1999. "Neuroactive steroids: mechanisms of action and neuropsychopharmacological perspectives." *Trends Neurosci.* 22(9):410–6.

Salmaggi, P., et al., 1993. "Double-blind, placebo-controlled study of S-adenosyl-L-methionine in depressed postmenopausal women." *Psychother. Psychosom.* 59(1):34–40.

Sano, M., et al., 1997. "A controlled trial of selegiline, alpha-tocopherol, or both as treatment for Alzheimer's disease." *N. Engl. J. Med.* 336:1216–22.

Schliebs, R., 1997. "Systemic administration of defined extracts from Withania *somnifera* (Indian ginseng) and Shilajit differentially affects cholinergic but not glutamatergic and GABAergic markers in rat brain." *Neurochem. Int.* 30(2):181–90.

Schneider, L. S., and M. Farlow, 1997. "Combined tacrine and estrogen replacement therapy in patients with Alzheimer's disease." *Ann. N.Y. Acad. Sci.* 26;826:317–22.

Schoenen, J., et al., 1998. "Effectiveness of high-dose riboflavin in migraine prophylaxis. A randomized controlled trial." *Neurology* 50(2):466–70.

Secades, J. J., and G. Frontera, 1995. "CDP-choline: pharmacological and clinical review." *Methods Find Exp. Clin. Pharmacol.* 17 Suppl B:2–54.

Seitz, G., et al., 1998. "Ascorbic acid stimulates DOPA synthesis and tyrosine hydroxylase gene expression in the human neuroblastoma cell line SK-N-SH." *Neuroscience Letters* 244:33–36.

Sergio, W., 1988. "Use of DMAE (2-dimethylaminoethanol) in the induction of lucid dreams." *Med. Hypotheses* 26(4):255–7.

Shigenaga, M. K., et al., 1994. "Oxidative damage and mitochondrial decay in aging." *Proc. Natl. Acad. Sci.* 8;91(23):10771–8.

Shults, C. W., et al., 1998. "Absorption, tolerability, and effects on mitochondrial activity of oral coenzyme Q10 in parkinsonian patients." *Neurology* 50(3):793–5.

Shults, C. W., et al., 1997. "Coenzyme Q10 levels correlate with the activities of complexes I and II/III in mitochondria from Parkinsonian and nonParkinsonian subjects." *Ann. Neurol.* 42(2):261–4.

Singh, H. K., and B. N. Dhawan, 1982. "Effect of *Bacopa monniera Linn.* (brahmi) extract on avoidance responses in rat." *J. Ethnopharmacol.* 5(2):205–14.

Sitaran, N., Weingartner, H., and J. C. Gillin, 1978. "Human serial learning: enhancement with arecholine and choline and impairment with scopolamine." *Science* 201:274–6.

Skaper, S. D., et al., 1998. "Melatonin prevents the delayed death of hippocampal neurons induced by enhanced excitatory neurotransmission and the nitridergic pathway." *FASEB J.* 12(9):725–31.

Skolnick, A. A., 1997. "Old Chinese herbal medicine used for fever yields possible new Alzheimer disease therapy [news]." *JAMA* 12;277(10):776.

Soderberg, M., et al., 1991. "Fatty acid composition of brain phospholipids in aging and in Alzheimer's disease." *Lipids* 26:421–5.

Sorgatz, H., 1987. "Effects of lecithin on memory and learning." In *Lecithin: technological, biological, and therapeutic aspects.* Hanin, I., Ansell, G. G., eds.; Proceedings of the fourth international colloquium on lecithin. New York: Plenum Press: 147–53.

Sotaniemi, E. A., et al., 1995. "Ginseng therapy in non-insulin-dependent diabetic patients." *Diabetes Care* 18(10):1373–5.

Spagnoli, A., et al., 1991. "Long-term acetyl-L-carnitine treatment in Alzheimer's disease." *Neurology* 41(11):1726–32.

Spallholz, J. E., 1997. "Free radical generation by selenium compounds and their pro-oxidant toxicity." *Biomed. Environ. Sci.* 10(2–3):260–70.

Sprong, R. C., et al., 1998. "Low-dose N-acetylcysteine protects rats against endotoxin-mediated oxidative stress, but high-dose increases mortality." *Am. J. Respir. Crit. Care Med.* 157(4 Pt 1):1283–93.

Stoll, S., et al., 1993. "The potent free radical scavenger alpha-lipoic acid improves memory in aged mice. Putative relationship to NMDA receptor deficits." *Pharmacol. Behav.* 46:799–805.

Stoll, A. L., et al., 1996. "Choline in the treatment of rapid-cycling bipolar disorder; clinical and neurochemical findings in lithium-treated patients." *Biol. Psychiatry* 40(5):382–8.

Strijks, E., Kremer, H. P., and M. W. Horstink, 1997. "CoQ10 therapy in patients with idiopathic Parkinson's disease." *Mol. Aspects Med.* 18 Suppl:S237–40.

Subhan, Z., 1985. "Psychopharmacological effects of vinpocetine in normal healthy volunteers." *Eur. J. Clin. Pharmacol.* 28(5):567–71.

Suzuki, H., et al., 1998. "Effect of the long-term feeding of dietary lipids on the learning ability, fatty acid composition of brain stem phospholipids and synaptic membrane fluidity in adult mice: a comparison of sardine oil diet with palm oil diet." *Mechanisms of Ageing and Development* 101:119–28.

Suzuki, K., 1981. "Chemistry and metabolism of brain lipids." In *Basic Neurochemistry,* 3rd edition; Seigel, G.J., et al., eds., Little, Brown: Boston, 355–70.

Teri, L., McCurry, S., and R. Logsdon, 1997. "Memory, thinking, and aging. What we know about what we know." *West. J. Med.* 167:269–75.

Thal, L. J., et al., 1989. "The safety and lack of efficacy of vinpocetine in Alzheimer's disease." *J. Am. Geriatr. Soc.* 37(6):515–20.

Thal, L. J., et al., 1996. "A 1-year multicenter placebo-controlled study of acetyl-L-carnitine in patients with Alzheimer's disease." *Neurology* 47:705–11.

Tripathi, Y. B., et al., 1996. *"Bacopa monniera Linn* as an antioxidant: mechanism of action." *Indian J. Exp. Biol.* 34(6):523–6.

Tweedy, J. R., and C. A. Garcia, 1982. "Lecithin treatment of cognitively impaired Parkinson's patients." *Eur. J. Clin. Invest.* 12(1):87–90.

Uchida, K., 1998. "Induction of apoptosis by phosphatidylserine." *J. Biochem.* (Tokyo) 123(6):1073–8.

Urban, T., et al., 1997. "Neutrophil function and glutathione-peroxidase activity in healthy individuals after treatment with N-acetyl-L-cysteine." *Biomed. Pharmacother.* 51:388–90.

Villanueva, L., et al., 1991. "Depressive effects of mu and delta opioid receptor agonists on activities of dorsal horn neurons are enhanced by dibencozide." *J. Pharmacol. Exp. Ther.* 257(3):1198–202.

Volz, H. P., and M. Kieser, 1997. "Kava-kava extract WS 1490 versus placebo in anxiety disorders—a randomized placebo-controlled 25-week outpatient trial." *Pharmacopsychiatry* 30:1–5.

Vrecko, K., et al., 1997. "NADH stimulates endogenous dopamine biosynthesis by enhancing the recycling of tetrahydro-biopterin in rat pheochromocytoma cells." *Biochimica et Biophysica Acta* 1361:59–65.

Wakabayashi, C., et al., 1998. "An intestinal bacterial metabolite of ginseng protopanaxadi-ol saponins has the ability to induce apoptosis in tumor cells." *Biochem. Biophys. Res. Comm.* 246:725–30.

Westermarck, T., 1997. "Evaluation of the possible role of coenzyme Q10 and vitamin E in juvenile neuronal ceroid-lipofuscinosis (JNCL)." *Mol. Aspects Med.* 18 Suppl:S259–62.

Weyer, G., et al., 1997. "A controlled study of 2 doses of idebenone in the treatment of Alzheimer's disease." *Neuropsychobiology* 36(2):73–82.

Wesnes, K. A., et al., 1997. "The cognitive, subjective, and physical effects of a ginkgo biloba/panax ginseng combination in healthy volunteers with neurasthenic complaints." *Psychopharmacol. Bull.* (4):677–83.

Wiebke, A., et al., 1999. "Dehydroepiandro-sterone replacement in women with adrenal insufficiency." *N. Engl. J. Med.* 341:1013–20.

Wilkinson, T. J., et al., 1997. "The response to treatment of subclinical thiamine deficiency in the elderly." *Am. J. Clin. Nutr.* 66(4):925–8.

Williams, C. L., et al., 1998. "Hypertrophy of basal forebrain neurons and enhanced visu-ospatial memory in perinatally choline-sup-plemented rats." *Brain Res.* 1;794(2):225–38.

Wood, J. L., and R. G. Allison, 1982. "Effects of consumption of choline and lecithin on neurological and cardiovascular systems." *Fed. Proc.* 41(14):3015–21.

Woodside, J. V., et al., 1998. "Effect of B-group vitamins and antioxidant vitamins on hyper-homocysteinemia: a double-blind, random-ized, factorial-design, controlled trial." *Am. J. Clin. Nutr.* 67(5):858–66.

Wurtman, R. J., 1992. "Choline metabolism as a basis for the selective vulnerability of cholinergic neurons." *Trends in Neurosci.* 15:117–22.

Xu, S. S., et al., 1995. "Efficacy of oral huper-zine-A on memory, cognition, and behavior in Alzheimer's disease." *Chung Kuo Yao Li Hsueh Pao* 16(5):391–5.

Yaffe, K., et al., 1998. "Estrogen therapy in postmenopausal women: effects on cognitive function and dementia." *JAMA* 279:688–95.

Yamada, K., et al., 1997. "Orally active NGF synthesis stimulators: potential therapeutic agents in Alzheimer's disease." *Behav. Brain Res.* 83(1–2):117–22.

Yehuda, S., et al., 1998. "Modulation of learn-ing and neuronal membrane composition in the rat by essential fatty acid prepara-tion: time-course analysis." *Neurochem. Res.* 23(5):627–34.

Yen, S. S., Morales, A. J., and O. Khorram, 1995. "Replacement of DHEA in aging men and women." *Ann. N.Y. Acad. Sci.* 774:128–42.

Zeisel, S. H., 1997. "Choline: essential for brain development and function." *Adv. Pediatr.* 44:263–95.

Zeisel, S. H., and J. K. Blusztajn, 1994. "Choline and human nutrition." *Annu. Rev. Nutr.* 14:269–96.

Zeisel, S. H., et al., 1991. "Choline, an essential nutrient for humans." *FASEB J.* 5:2093–98.

Zeisel, S. H., et al., 1980. "Normal plasma choline responses to ingested lecithin." *Neurology* 30(11):1226–29.

Zhang, R. W., et al., 1991. "Drug evaluation of huperzine A in the treatment of senile memory disorders." *Chung Kuo Yao Li Hsueh Pao* 12(3):250–2.

Zhao, X. Z., et al., 1990. "Antisenility effect of ginseng-rhizome saponin." *Chung Hsi I Chieh Ho Tsa Chih* 10(10):586–9, 579.

Zumoff, B., et al., 1996. "Twenty-four-hour mean plasma testosterone concentration declines with age in normal premenopausal women." *J. Clin. Endocrinol. Metab.* 80:1429–30.

INDEX

241